Praise for *Romanticism and Revo*

'*Romanticism and Revolution* offers a representative anthology of immediate British reactions to the epoch-making events taking place in late eighteenth-century France. Reflections on the Revolution meant debate over the Rights of Man – and Woman – as well as on the nature of Government, patriotism, social and political justice. This careful selection of passages from the most important texts allows modern readers to see the intense contemporary debate unfold, to consider the arguments and to trace the dialogues between different writers. Key players in the great Revolutionary Debate come alive for a modern readership through these memorable passages of highly distinctive prose and are set in context by the other extracts as well as through judicious editorial introductions and notes. Anyone keen to develop a real understanding of the political climate of the early 1790s will find this volume indispensable.'

Fiona Stafford, Somerville College, University of Oxford

'An indispensable volume – in every way a worthy successor to Marilyn Butler's *Burke, Paine, Godwin and the Revolution Controversy*. In *Romanticism and Revolution*, Mee and Fallon provide intelligent, representative, wide-ranging selections from Price, Burke, Wollstonecraft, Paine, and Godwin for a new generation of students and scholars. Due not least to the generosity of their selections, Mee and Fallon revitalize our understanding of – to name but a few contexts – Price's politics of Rational Dissent, Burke's affective rhetoric of the sentiments, both Wollstonecraft's attack on Burkean theatricality and her arguments for female education, Paine's levelling of political language, and Godwin's ideals of political utility and disinterestedness. As Mee and Fallon note, the Revolution controversy was a political battle fought with literary weapons: *Romanticism and Revolution* illuminates this vital affiliation throughout, emphasizing as it does the indissoluble links between the rhetoric of political argument and the politics of literary forms and strategies. *Romanticism and Revolution* forcefully reminds us of the centrality of the Revolution controversy both for the writers of the 1790s, writing as they were under the pressure of events at home and abroad, and for critics of Romanticism ever since, trying to make sense of the incontestable though often unwieldy connections between Romanticism and Revolution. It is essential reading for anyone interested in the heady mix of politics and literature that continues to constitute Romanticism.'

Charles W. Mahoney, University of Connecticut

'This anthology is perfectly pitched to help students understand the ideas and debates that underpin literary Romanticism. The introduction is excellent and the headnotes and footnotes make the texts themselves far more accessible. This is a hugely useful text for any Romantic Period module.'

Sharon Ruston, University of Salford

'Jon Mee and David Fallon's *Romanticism and Revolution: A Reader* is destined to become the first choice for those seeking to analyze the most important context for the emergence of English Romanticism. This work – given the care of its preparation, the concision of its informative introductions, and the greater depth of its entries – will delight students and teachers frustrated by past anthologies and should supplant past anthologies in classrooms at every level of instruction.'

Mark Lussier, Arizona State University

Also Available:

Romanticism: An Anthology (third edition) edited by Duncan Wu
Romantic Poetry: An Annotated Anthology edited by Michael O'Neill
and Charles Mahoney
The Romantic Poets: A Guide to Criticism edited by Uttara Natarajan
Race and the Enlightenment: A Reader edited by Emmanuel Chukwudi Eze

Romanticism and Revolution

A READER

Edited by
Jon Mee and David Fallon

A John Wiley & Sons, Ltd., Publication

Blackwell Publishing was acquired by John Wiley & Sons in February 2007. Blackwell's publishing program
has been merged with Wiley's global Scientific, Technical, and Medical business to form Wiley-Blackwell.

Registered Office
John Wiley & Sons Ltd, The Atrium, Southern Gate, Chichester, West Sussex, PO19 8SQ,
United Kingdom

Editorial Offices
350 Main Street, Malden, MA 02148-5020, USA
9600 Garsington Road, Oxford, OX4 2DQ, UK
The Atrium, Southern Gate, Chichester, West Sussex, PO19 8SQ, UK

For details of our global editorial offices, for customer services, and for information about how to
apply for permission to reuse the copyright material in this book please see our website at
www.wiley.com/wiley-blackwell.

Library of Congress Cataloging-in-Publication Data

Romanticism and revolution : a reader / edited by Jon Mee and David Fallon.
    p.   cm.
Includes bibliographical references and index.
ISBN 978-1-4443-3043-4 (hardcover : alk. paper) – ISBN 978-1-4443-3044-1 (pbk. : alk. paper)
  1. English literature–18th century.   2. Romanticism–Great Britain.   3. France–History–Revolution,
1789–1799–Literature and the revolution.   I. Mee, Jon.   II. Fallon, David James, 1977–
  PR1139.R663 2011
  820.8'0145–dc22

                                                2010038181

A catalogue record for this book is available from the British Library.

Set in 11/13pt DanteMT by Spi Publisher Services, Pondicherry, India
Printed in Malaysia by Ho Printing (M) Sdn Bhd

1   2011

Contents

Preface and Acknowledgements

'Everything rung, and was connected, with the Revolution in France; which for above 20 years, was, or was made, the all in all. Everything, not this or that thing, but literally everything, was soaked in this one event'.[1] So Henry Cockburn recalled the French Revolution's enormous cultural impact throughout Britain. The deluge of pamphlets from the press upon the fall of the *ancien régime* in France was to have a crucial and lasting effect upon British culture, especially among the writers commonly identified with British Romanticism.

'The revolution controversy', as it has become known, is now widely taught in the early weeks of courses on Romantic literature in the United Kingdom, the United States, and other parts of the English-speaking world. In this regard, Marilyn Butler's *Burke, Paine, Godwin and the Revolution Controversy* (1984) was a groundbreaking collection, familiarizing literary students and scholars alike with the idea that the prose of the 1790s not only played a vital part in the formation of Romanticism, but also had important literary qualities of its own. Our anthology offers substantial extracts from the key contributions to the 'debate' on the French Revolution, so readers and students can engage closely with these texts. The chronological arrangement and use of the earliest editions will allow readers to experience the debate as it unfolded and to explore how the different writers responded to each other's arguments and rhetoric. The selections have been chosen mindful of scholarly debate since Butler first published her anthology, but also in order to display the striking rhetorical ingenuity of their authors and the complex inter-relationships between their texts. Finally, the passages, headnotes, and annotations are designed to fuel thinking about these relationships, their broader cultural contexts, and their influence on the literature of the Romantic period in general.

---

[1] Lord Henry Cockburn, *Memorials of his Time*, 2 vols (Edinburgh, 1856), I, 79.

The editors would like to dedicate the volume to Marilyn Butler, in acknowledgement of her defining influence on thinking about the relationship between Romanticism and the politics of the 1790s, and also for the great encouragement she has always given new workers in the field. They would also like to thank Emma Bennett at Blackwell for commissioning the anthology, the University of Warwick and St Anne's College, Oxford, for institutional support, and Jane Huyg and Felicia Gottmann for their help and patience.

A Note on the Texts

Our texts are taken from the first editions, with the exception of Wollstonecraft's *A Vindication of the Rights of Men*, where the second edition emended by Wollstonecraft has been preferred. Footnotes in curly brackets are the author's own original annotation; all other footnotes are ours. Non-standard spellings have been retained, but obvious errors in the original texts have been silently corrected. The peculiarities of the writers' grammar and punctuation also remain; later editions regularize some of these idiosyncrasies, but in the earliest editions these features give the texts a striking rhetorical immediacy. References to texts in the footnotes are to first editions and the place of publication for texts in English is London, unless otherwise stated.

Introduction

Writing to Byron on 6 September 1816, Percy Shelley referred to 'the master theme of the epoch in which we live – the French Revolution'.[1] British literature and culture of the Romantic period are steeped in the discourse generated by the Revolution. This anthology focuses on the first wave of writing in the Revolution controversy, up to and including Godwin's *Enquiry concerning Political Justice* (1793). These texts were crucial to the development and democratization of political debate, not only in terms of their arguments as such, but also in that they released into the culture of politics more generally a series of metaphors and phrases – like Burke's image of revolutionary Don Quixotes (p. 22 below), which would be turned so memorably against him (see front cover and pp. 75, 98). Such tropes were endlessly revisited, argued over, and recast in subsequent texts, opening up political discourse to a much wider audience. Even Godwin's book, despite its elevated manner and price, was widely debated in radical meetings, and its principles were disseminated at popular lectures by radical leaders such as John Thelwall.[2] Paradoxically, radicals themselves recognized the importance of Burke's attack on the Revolution in stimulating public debate. A wave of popular conservatism could even be said to have had the unintended consequence of transforming the political culture which it meant to preserve from innovation.[3]

All the texts represented here bear the mark of the powerful jolt given to European political consciousness by the French Revolution of 1789 – not just the iconic event of the fall of the Bastille, but also the rush of developments that increasingly radicalized

---

[1] *The Letters of Percy Bysshe Shelley*, ed. by Frederick L. Jones, 2 vols (Oxford: Clarendon Press, 1964), I, 504.
[2] *The Politics of English Jacobinism: Writings of John Thelwall*, ed. by Gregory Claeys (University Park, PA: Pennsylvania State University Press, 1995), pp. xxvii–xxx.
[3] See Kevin Gilmartin, *Writing against Revolution: Literary Conservatism in Britain, 1790–1832* (Cambridge: Cambridge University Press, 2007).

Romanticism and Revolution: A Reader.
Edited by Jon Mee and David Fallon.   © 2011 Blackwell Publishing Ltd.

the Revolution, taking France from the constitutional monarchy installed in 1789 to the declaration of a 'Republic' in late 1792, which was followed swiftly by the execution of Louis XVI and by the subsequent war with Britain in early 1793. Initially, the fall of the absolute monarchy and of the established Catholic Church in France were greeted in Britain with a wave of enthusiasm. Many regarded France as realizing a spirit of progress and enlightenment, which was perceived to have characterized the modernizing impulse of the eighteenth century. Nowhere was this idea more powerfully expressed than in the sermon which the dissenting minister Richard Price gave in November 1789. Price was coming to the end of a career as one of the leading voices of radical nonconformism, that is, of those Protestant groups outside the Church of England. Because they would not conform to the Anglican Church's Thirty-Nine Articles, Dissenters had been excluded from various aspects of public life by the Test and Corporation Acts passed after the Restoration (the return of the monarchy) in 1660. Although it has often been pointed out that the penalties and exclusions against Dissenters were not always enforced, men like Price and his close associate Joseph Priestley had been at the forefront of calls for reform for three decades. They were particularly active and visible presences in the expanding print culture of the later eighteenth century, representing the leading edge of the English Enlightenment and enlarging their concern for freedom of conscience in matters of religion into a validation of freedom of enquiry in all quarters. In more literary terms, theirs was an intellectual group that also boasted among its leading lights poets such as Anna Laetitia Barbauld and Helen Maria Williams, both of whom, to their own cost, were to be important supporters of the French Revolution and of reform in Britain. Dissenters had campaigned hard throughout the 1780s for the repeal of the Test and Corporation Acts. Motions for repeal were put before Parliament and defeated in 1787, 1788, and 1790. By the time of the last vote, events in France had raised the political temperature sufficiently to ensure the motion came with the largest margin of defeat among the three.

To associate dissent in religion with political revolution was a long-standing reflex of the establishment of Church and State in Britain, going back to the seventeenth century and to the English Civil War. It was an association confirmed for many by the fiery rhetoric of Price's sermon, with its vision of world liberty as the fulfilment of God's plan for mankind. *A Discourse on the Love of Our Country* also directly addresses an issue that was to become central to the Revolution controversy and to its relationship with Romanticism thereafter. How far were ideas of benevolence defined by local relationships of family, home, and hearth, and how far could they transcend local attachments and sustain a politics that looked to the welfare of all mankind? Like many eighteenth-century philosophers, Price does not represent universal benevolence and love of one's locality as mutually exclusive, rather he sees sympathy naturally progressing from the one to the other.[4]

---

[4]   See Evan Radcliffe, 'Writing, Moral Philosophy, and Universal Benevolence in the Eighteenth Century', *Journal of the History of Ideas*, 54 (1993), 221–40.

In 1794, being at the time very much influenced by Rational Dissent, the poet Samuel Taylor Coleridge also represented 'Philanthropy' as 'a thing of *Concretion* – Some home-born Feeling is the *center* of the Ball, that, rolling on thro' Life collects and assimilates every congenial Affection'.[5] Local attachments teach individuals benevolence, which, properly cultivated, should develop into a concern for humanity as a whole. For Price, emphatically, to be trapped in self-interest and in national pride perverted the natural development of humanity. Burke and subsequent loyalists attacked such ideas of universal philanthropy as 'French' thinking that threatened to dissolve natural attachments. The *Anti-Jacobin* mocked ideas of the 'Universal Man' as absurd: 'No narrow bigot *he*; – *his* reason'd view / Thy interests, England, ranks with thine, Peru!'[6]

For all the fervour of his sermon's language, Price was not calling for the overthrow of the English system of government in favour of a republic, but for a return to the key principles of the Glorious Revolution of 1688 as he saw them, with their guarantee of the Protestant succession and with what was taken to be their protection of the rights of the subject. Like many others, he believed that recent decades had witnessed a growing manipulation of Parliament through the influence of the Crown and of the aristocracy, a process which culminated in the loss of the American colonies. British liberties had become corrupted and needed to be restored. Like many sermons of the period, Price's was quickly printed and sold by sympathetic booksellers such as Joseph Johnson, a major figure in the networks of dissenting intellectuals. For Edmund Burke, the sermon provided a key target for his *Reflections on the Revolution in France* (1790) (see pp. 21–50 below). Many contemporaries expected Burke to support the French reformers. He had championed the American colonists in the 1770s and campaigned for economic reforms in Britain in the 1780s. These associations had earned him the respect of Thomas Paine, who was even – briefly – his guest and corresponded with him amicably about the early events of the Revolution. Burke's antipathy for the Revolution was only clearly signalled in a speech on the army estimates, delivered in Parliament in February 1790. In response to praise of the Revolution from his former ally Charles James Fox, leader of the Whig opposition, and to a suggestion from the Prime Minister, William Pitt the Younger, that military expenditure could be reduced, Burke exploded:

> The French had shewn themselves the ablest architects of ruin that had hitherto existed in the world. In that very short space of time they had completely pulled down to the ground, their monarchy; their church; their nobility; their law; their revenue; their army; their navy; their commerce; their arts; and their manufactures.[7]

---

[5]   To Robert Southey, 13 July 1794, *The Letters of Samuel Taylor Coleridge*, 6 vols, ed. by E. L. Griggs (Oxford: Oxford University Press, 1956–71), I, 86.

[6]   'The New Morality', *The Anti-Jacobin; or, Weekly Examiner*, 36, 9 July 1799.

[7]   'Substance of the Speech on the Army Estimates, 1790', in *The Works of the Right Honourable Edmund Burke*, 7 vols (London: Thomas McLean, 1828), V, 6.

This summary of his speech bristles with the distinctive rhetorical energy of *Reflections on the Revolution in France* (1790), its breathless and additive catalogues conveying the sheer extent to which the Revolution was bringing unprecedented disruption to France. Burke's speech made it clear that he regarded what had happened not just as a local affair, of concern primarily to the French people, but as a fundamental change in the nature of politics in Europe, from which Britain had everything to fear.

Reflections gave forcible expression to this position, indeed with such intensity that even many of Burke's friends thought he had given way to mania. Burke made it plain that he regarded what had happened not just as the death knell of a political system, but potentially as the end of an entire form of civilization. He made a powerful argument for 'precedent' as a force shaping political institutions. Given the uncertainties of human knowledge and reason, what had worked in the past was the best indicator of how human beings should proceed into the future. For Burke, political theories were little better than visionary delusion, unless they were tested by 'experience' (see below, p. 31), and his argument placed a great deal of weight on what the eighteenth century called 'morals and manners'. 'Experience', for Burke, was grounded in what, today, we might call 'culture' – that is, the everyday feelings and attachments that make up the individual's perceptions of the world and are embodied in and expressed by communities and nations. By abolishing aristocratic titles, feudal privileges, and the state-backed power of the Catholic Church, Burke argued, a finely meshed organic entity, evolved over centuries, was being sacrificed to political theory – a theory untried by experience and with no basis in the realities of human nature. Burke attacks Price and the English supporters of the French Revolution as visionary enthusiasts whose assertion of the freedom of conscience and of other abstract rights paid no heed to the historical development of political culture. The Revolution Society, which celebrated 1688, was misunderstanding a very pragmatic British solution to a political crisis and taking it to advocate the dubious principle that the people had the right to cashier their rulers.

The famous set piece on the Queen of France (see pp. 36–39 below) was absolutely crucial to Burke's argument; and yet the choice was a gamble. Marie Antoinette did not have the reputation of a vessel of virtue in either France or Britain, largely because of a flurry of scurrilous libels published in the years leading up to the Revolution, but Burke makes her the centrepiece of his vision of French society as a finely woven tapestry of associations and allegiances that could not be reduced to a mere political 'system'.[8] The queen was the apex of the family of the nation – a focal point of natural affections, which grew naturally from the feelings held by people for their own families. Burke upheld the same principles in his view of British society. For Burke, 1688 was only a slight deviation, aimed at correcting the slow evolution of a political order centred on the feelings of the

---

[8]   For the ramifications of this way of thinking for British Romanticism, see David Simpson, *Romanticism, Nationalism, and the Revolt against Theory* (Chicago and London: University of Chicago Press, 1993).

people for their country. Universal rights, he claimed, made no sense in a world where one's allegiances were defined by a complex tissue of habit and experience, formed in particular circumstances. Such rights ignored 'real social affections' – as they actually existed in any particular society – in the name of dubious theory and of an overblown faith in the perfectibility of man.[9] Those who cannot feel these associations are monstrous and would tear away 'the decent drapery' that makes life bearable, reducing human beings to 'their naked shivering nature' (see p. 37 below). Burke's idea of a 'second nature', a distinctively national character born out of the habits and history of an entire culture – traits that are prior to rational reflection or individual choice – was to be crucial to the developing ideas of Romanticism over the next decades, as well as to conservative thinking ever since. Wordsworth's increasing emphasis on local manners and customs in his poetry of the 1790s may represent his gravitation towards such thinking. Alternatively, it might be an attempt to show that such ideas could have a democratic inflection, registering the customary experiences of the people. Certainly, working out the implications of Burke's ideas became a tortuous and complex process for Wordsworth and his contemporaries.[10]

Many of the more immediate answers to Burke attacked his attitude towards the events of 1688–9, arguing that he was deliberately downplaying the radical nature of the renegotiation of the compact between the monarchy and the people. James Mackintosh's *Vindiciae Gallicae* (1791) even argued that the settlement of 1689 could be understood as a model for events in France. What distinguished Mary Wollstonecraft's very rapid response to Burke was that she recognized the importance of his argument about manners and morals.[11] For Wollstonecraft, Burke's 'second nature' had mistaken the mere theatrical show of affection for the real power of sentiment applied to its proper objects. Like 'the man of feeling' whose travails had been narrated in a generation or more of eighteenth-century novels, Burke had mistaken the indulgence of his own over-refined passions for what she represents as the more obvious objects of pity (such as the sufferings of the French people at large). Wollstonecraft suggests that there is no equivalence between 'the pangs you felt for insulted nobility, the anguish that rent your heart when the gorgeous robes were torn off the idol human weakness had set up' and 'the long-drawn sigh of melancholy reflection' of the ubiquitous poor (p. 69 below). The mistaken belief, as she saw it, that this sensibility was the fount of feminized virtue was to be crucial to her *Vindication of the Rights of Woman* (1792).

---

[9] The phrase 'real social affections' comes from Samuel Parr's attack on William Godwin's ideas in his *A Spital Sermon, Preached at Christ Church, upon Easter Tuesday* (London: J. Mawman, 1801), p. 404. Godwin was shocked by Parr's attack, as Parr had been a personal friend and a supporter of moderate reform in Britain.

[10] For the former argument, see James Chandler, *Wordsworth's Second Nature: A Study of the Poetry and the Politics* (Chicago: Chicago University Press, 1984). For an alternative position, see Nicholas Roe, *Wordsworth and Coleridge: The Radical Years* (Oxford: Clarendon Press, 1988).

[11] For a reading of Wollstonecraft's text in these terms, see David Bromwich, 'Wollstonecraft as a Critic of Burke', *Political Theory*, 23 (1995), 617–34.

The portrayal of Burke as an over-refined sensualist also featured in Thomas Paine's initial response to the *Reflections*. Indeed, it provided the target for one of the most memorably punchy passages in Part I of *Rights of Man* (1791):

> Nature has been kinder to Mr. Burke than he is to her. He is not affected by the reality of distress touching his heart, but by the showy resemblance of it striking his imagination. He pities the plumage, but forgets the dying bird. Accustomed to kiss the aristocratical hand that hath purloined him from himself, he degenerates into a composition of art, and the genuine soul of nature forsakes him. His hero or his heroine must be a tragedy-victim expiring in show, and not the real prisoner of misery, sliding into death in the silence of a dungeon. (P. 76 below)

This passage exemplifies how Paine subverts Burke's own metaphors, memorably turning inside out the 'stuffed birds in a museum, with chaff and rags and paltry, blurred shreds of paper about the rights of man' (p. 41 below). Often misread as an exercise in 'plain style', Paine's lively writing deliberately addressed a popular audience, but in a way that owed more to satirical journalism – including his own writing in America in defence of the colonists – than to any notion of a scientific objectivity.[12] Much of Part I of *Rights of Man* is taken up with questioning Burke's narrative of the Revolution. It contains some blazing set pieces, like the one just quoted, designed to be remembered and debated in political clubs. Although he often appeals to the 'facts' (see pp. 74–75 below) of history against Burke's artificial 'paintings' (p. 74 below), Paine's method continually draws attention to political language as a form of representation. Phrases like 'as it is called' resonate throughout his book, pointing out the conventional nature of political language and encouraging his readers to think differently if they so wish. It was an approach that bore fruit in a series of radical dictionaries offering facetious commentaries on the vocabulary of politics. Among them, Charles Pigott's *Political Dictionary* (1795) defined 'Revolution' with scant respect for the institutions of the English constitution:

> The Revolution of 1688, no good and wise man can applaud. It was the despicable patch-work of a few addle-pated, whig noblemen. The People soon found they had only made an exchange of Tyrants; in fact, it was out of the frying-pan into the fire.[13]

Paine's contribution to the Revolution controversy challenged the norms of political debate, which had usually been conducted with deference towards the 1689 settlement. Like many other radicals, Paine ironically praised Burke for bringing the British political order into representation and thereby making possible this kind of reimagining of it. The 'constitution' ought to be before the country 'in a visible form' (p. 82 below), to make everything available for discussion.

---

[12]   See Bruce Woodcock, 'Writing the Revolution: Aspects of Thomas Paine's Prose', *Prose Studies*, 15 (1992), 171–86 and Jane Hodson, *Language and Revolution in Burke, Wollstonecraft, Paine, and Godwin* (Aldershot: Ashgate, 2007), pp. 115–48.

[13]   Charles Pigott, *A Political Dictionary, Explaining the True Meaning of Words* (London: D. I. Eaton, 1795), p. 117.

What is often missed about Part I of *Rights of Man* is the moderation of its account of the French monarchy. At this stage, early on in 1791, Paine seems to have hoped that Louis XVI would live up to his expected role as father of the Revolution. Like many other political theorists, Paine was probably also sceptical about the possibility that a populous and sophisticated European country would be able to introduce a republic after the manner of the United States. Paine travelled to France after publishing Part I of *Rights of Man* and found himself in a rapidly developing political situation. He quickly became involved in the republican groupings associated with Nicolas de Condorcet and Jacques Pierre Brissot. In June 1791, the king abandoned the Revolution and was caught in Varennes, fleeing in disguise, after which Paine issued a republican manifesto that was widely distributed around Paris. He then returned to Britain in hopes of imparting the same spirit, and began writing Part II of *Rights of Man*.

Meanwhile other participants in the Revolution controversy in Britain were being further radicalized by events unfolding in France. The question of women's roles in the new society had been hotly debated in France, but the constitution of 1791 relegated women (among others) to the status of 'passive citizens'. Wollstonecraft addressed her new books to one of the architects of the Revolution: Charles Maurice de Talleyrand, former Bishop of Autun. Like many theorists of education, especially those influenced by Jean-Jacques Rousseau, Talleyrand acknowledged the importance of female education, but consigned it to the role of preparing women for domestic rather than public duties.[14] The classical republican language of politics, often used by those thinking out the new direction of France, associated 'manly' virtues with patriot activism and tended to identify aristocracy with a feminized sensibility, as did Paine and Wollstonecraft in their attacks on Burke. *A Vindication of the Rights of Woman* to some extent accepts this polarity, but subverts it by insisting that the 'manly virtues, or, more properly speaking, the attainment of those talents and virtues, the exercise of which ennobles the human character' (see p. 93 below), are equally available to women as to men.

Wollstonecraft does continue to identify women with an important domestic role, but now motherhood is defined in terms of the patriotic task of raising 'active' citizens of both sexes. Whereas the idea of women as family-focussed was frequently used to argue that, by nature, they could have no interest in public affairs, Wollstonecraft turned the tables by suggesting that the task needed not the soft manners of an indulged sensibility (qualities she associated with the aristocracy), but the rational virtues of a practical nature. Her opening address makes it clear how far this was an argument that had developed out of her response to Burke on the question of the relations between the affections and virtue:

> Manners and morals are so nearly allied that they have often been confounded; but, though the former should only be the natural reflection of the latter, yet when various

---

[14] See the discussion of the French context in Barbara Taylor, *Mary Wollstonecraft and the Feminist Imagination* (Cambridge: Cambridge University Press, 2003), pp. 208–10.

causes have produced factitious and corrupt manners, which are very early caught, morality becomes an empty name.[15]

Whereas women were often educated to be yielding and submissive in their manners, creatures of sensibility sometimes wielding dubious power though their weakness, Wollstonecraft argued that women's education should be directed at their rational natures, a quality she represents as transcending the gendered body. In this regard, her ideas kept something of Rational Dissent's perspective on female education, with its emphasis on the sexless soul before its God. Generally speaking, in fact, her book was well received in early reviews, as an intervention in debates on female education, but the suggestion that women should exercise political rights was not given much attention in the radical movement.[16] It was only when details of Wollstonecraft's personal life came to light in William Godwin's posthumous memoir that the idea of her as an 'unsex'd female' became really widespread. Vicious attacks by satirists such as T. J. Mathias and Richard Polwhele, who coined the phrase, fixed her in the public imagination as a dangerous and unstable woman.[17] Even women novelists who were not obviously hostile to Wollstonecraft's ideas on education began to create characters based on what was taken to be her combination of sexual promiscuity allied to a transgressive investment in 'manly' virtues. Belinda Botherim in Elizabeth Hamilton's *Memoirs of Modern Philosophers* (1800) and Harriet Freke in Maria Edgeworth's *Belinda* (1801) are both recognizably modelled after Wollstonecraft.

At the end of 1792, Wollstonecraft travelled to France, leaving behind a Britain taken to the edge of panic over the effect of Part II of *Rights of Man* and by the government's response to it. Finally published in March 1792, the second part of Paine's pamphlet had much less to say about Burke or France than its first part. Now its attention was directed much more forcefully at the sacred cows of British politics – the idea of an ancient constitution, the Magna Carta, and the vaunted settlement of 1689. Paine insisted that the British people had the right to act for themselves. They could form a convention after the American example and decide what form of government they wished to live under. The United States is confidently brought forward in Part II of *Rights of Man* as the model of a representative republic, proof that such a system could be sustained in a populous commercial nation. Paine's pamphlet replays the traditional radical idea of monarchy as a wasteful system of war, which drains the wealth of society's useful members

---

[15]   Mary Wollstonecraft, *A Vindication of the Rights of Woman* (London: J. Johnson, 1792), p. vi. (Not included in the present selection.)

[16]   This point ought not to be exaggerated. Radical politics was not intrinsically opposed to women's rights on account of its republican investment in the 'manly' virtues, as is sometimes implied. See the discussion in Taylor, *Mary Wollstonecraft*, pp. 177–8 and nn. 8 and 11.

[17]   See T. J. Mathias, *Pursuits of Literature*, 6th edn (T. Beckett, 1798), p. 194 and Richard Polwhele, *The Unsex'd Females* (London: Cadell and Davies, 1798), lines 14–20, 24–5.

through taxation, but Paine then takes the bold step of proposing a redistributive system that would fund benefits in some regards analogous to those of a modern welfare state.[18] As a rejoinder to Burke's attacks on the 'theoretical' nature of French radicalism, Paine's title page promised a treatise '*Combining Principle and Practice*'. By the end of May 1792 the government had issued a summons against Paine for seditious libel. The information drawn up against him focussed on those passages where he showed most disrespect for the institutions of the British state, but the government made no haste in bringing him to trial. They seemed to prefer to harass printers, publishers, and sellers of the text, and to create the impression that there was a conspiracy afoot to overthrow the state by violence. Only in December, after Paine had left the country to take up a seat in the new French Convention, did the trial begin. Explaining why he had not prosecuted Part I, the Attorney General insisted that Part II had entered a different world, being designed quite specifically to stir up trouble among those radicalized by the French Revolution. Its language, he claimed, was clearly oriented to 'that part of the public whose minds cannot be supposed to be conversant with subjects of this sort'.[19] Even many of those who were sympathetic to his political aims found Paine's style too irreverent and too bold.[20]

Among those who watched the trial was William Godwin. He was in the final stages of completing his masterpiece *Enquiry concerning Political Justice*, finally published in January 1793. Godwin was disgusted at the way the court, and even Paine's defence attorney, Thomas Erskine, seemed more concerned with questions of precedence and tradition than with rational truth. Although he admired and corresponded with Paine, Godwin self-consciously framed his own text as a sober search for 'political truth'. Godwin cast his analytical eye at all the venerable institutions of British politics and evaluated them according to a principle of utility. Affections nurtured by habit and tradition seemed to count for little under this searchlight of truth. In what became the most famous passage in the book, Godwin argues that one ought to be willing to sacrifice 'my wife, my mother or my benefactor' (p. 156 below) in the properly disinterested search for political justice. More generally, Godwin's assertion of the freedom of the intellect had a visionary aspect, whereby he could imagine the mind transcending the constraints of the body, and even death (p. 183 below). His idea of human perfectibility was met with a thrill by young men and women who saw it as pushing aside stale convention. Mary Hays wrote to him enthusiastically, to see if she could borrow the book she had heard so much about. Young men like Wordsworth,

[18] Gareth Stedman Jones, *An End to Poverty? An Historical Debate* (London: Profile, 2004).

[19] See *The Trial of Thomas Paine* (1792) in *Trials for Treason and Sedition, 1792–1794*, 8 vols, ed. John Barrell and Jon Mee (London: Pickering and Chatto, 2006–7), I, 51.

[20] In Charlotte Smith's novel *Desmond*, 3 vols (London: G. G. J. and G. Robinson, 1792), Erasmus Bethel sends the eponymous protagonist a copy of *Rights of Man*, which 'now engrosses all the conversation of this country' and has 'much sound sense in it, however bluntly delivered' (II, ix, 92). Desmond agrees, being 'forcibly struck with truths' which are 'bluntly, sometimes coarsely delivered' (II, x, 115–16).

with more disposable income, devoured it. According to the account given in *The Prelude* (1805), Godwin's ideas

> [...] promised to abstract the hopes of man
> Out of his feelings, to be fixed thenceforth
> For ever in a purer element. (Book X. 807–10)

Thanks in no small part to Wordsworth's account, disillusionment with the French Revolution and a Godwinian faith in the perfectibility of human reason has become a founding narrative of Romantic studies. In fact plenty of radicals, even among Godwin's admirers, were already sceptical of his method, even if they adored its boldness. Hays, for instance, constantly insisted in their correspondence, that human benevolence must always be centred on the affections. Later on, William Hazlitt insisted that *Political Justice* ought to be viewed as a brave experiment designed to see how far such thinking could go, a perspective that Godwin's own revisions and reservations suggest is right.[21] To reduce the Revolution controversy to an opposition between radical utilitarianism and a more affective emphasis on morals and manners is to buy into a narrative that Burke was trying to fix in the minds of his readers from very early on. To accept it would be to ignore, for instance, the subtlety of Wollstonecraft's thinking about morals and manners, or Paine's insistence that not utility but the wishes of the people ought to decide political arrangements. Nevertheless, Burke's polarizing narrative became a powerful part of the myth of the Revolution controversy.

The Revolution controversy was a battle fought with literary weapons. One of its most striking features is the close association between political argument and the rhetoric and forms through which it is communicated. Similarly, there are numerous points of convergence, where contributors wrestle for possession of key items of vocabulary. Burke, Wollstonecraft, and Paine all invest their texts with features derived from the popular epistolary novels and poetry of the eighteenth century, although with markedly different effects. For Burke, the epistolary form embodies those affective connections which guarantee civilization, as well as reinforcing the sincerity of his sentiments, and brings into his practice his opposition to abstraction and theory, allowing him 'the freedom [...] to throw out my thoughts, and express my feelings, just as they arise in my mind, with very little attention to formal method' (p. 23 below). Wollstonecraft and Paine paradoxically make much both of Burke's lack of form and of his insincere artifice; for the latter, Burke's text is 'all miscellany' (p. 85 below), and yet 'degenerates into a composition of art' where 'the genuine soul of nature forsakes him' (p. 76 below). Through the epistolary medium, both sides lay claim to sincerity – that Romantic shibboleth, which for Burke anchors human relations in tradition and experience, while for radicals it necessitates independent, reasoned judgement and candid discussion without delicate deference.

---

[21]   William Hazlitt, *The Spirit of the Age*, 2 vols (London: H. Colburn, 1825), I, 30–1.

Likewise, tracing connections between the debate and the literary culture of the time allows us to reconsider familiar aspects of Romanticism that may seem to have nothing to do with politics. Take, for example, 'nature', which Burke claimed to be preserving, but which Paine accused him of abandoning. The poetry of Wordsworth, Coleridge, and other contemporaries who immersed themselves in the controversy describes nature not simply as phenomena of 'rocks, and stones, and trees', but as a concept which both sides in the debate claimed to be the ground of widely divergent social and political principles. Burke's *Reflections* spins an eclectic web of literary allusions, historical references, contemporary correspondence, and emotive dramatizations. Ranging back and forth between past and present, it embodies the complex tissue of historical and cultural continuity he sought to defend. Paine shadows Burke's back-and-forth movements, but with a critical mindset ready to explode myths and to look for progressive change rather than for Burkean continuity. The challenges to Burke occur even on the level of typography; Wollstonecraft ironically mocks the artifice behind Burke's representations by peppering her text with exclamations and with the well-worn sentimental device whereby the expression of excessive feeling breaks the text into fragments (see p. 69 below). Godwin's systematic, thorough, and discursive opus, with its movement from abstract principles to real-life applications, indicates its author's philosophical ambition, his investment in utilitarian thought, and the enlightenment tradition and conversations out of which the text evolved.

The historian Alfred Cobban described 'the debate on the French Revolution' as 'perhaps the last real discussion of the fundamentals of politics in this country'.[22] The application of the word 'debate' in this context has often been questioned, not least because it seems to imply a disinterested exchange of ideas on a level playing field. The texts assembled in *Romanticism and Revolution* were not written as cool interventions in political theory. They were written under great pressure from contemporary events, most spectacularly in France, but also from developments in Britain, and from the need to respond to the flood of newspaper accounts, pamphlets, and other interventions that poured from the presses in response to the French Revolution. As Cobban's remark shows, the controversy initiated by these texts was foundational for modern British politics. Many of the issues remain contentious today, notably questions of human rights, taxation, welfare provision, central versus local government, and national versus global citizenship. *Romanticism and Revolution* encourages modern readers to look at these texts again for themselves, to involve themselves in the debate, and to draw their own conclusions.

---

[22] Alfred Cobban, *The Debate on the French Revolution 1789–1800*, 2nd edn (London: Adam and Charles Black, 1960), p. 31.

1

Richard Price

A Discourse on the Love of Our Country

(London: T. Cadell, 1789)

The dissenting minister Richard Price (1723–91) was born into the family of a strictly Calvinist clergyman in Glamorgan, Wales. Sent to London for his education, he moved towards anti-trinitarian and libertarian Christianity and became a central figure in the national culture and campaigns of nonconformists. From 1758 to 1783 he was pastor for the Presbyterian chapel at Stoke Newington, a post he held until 1783; he also preached at the Gravel-Pit Meeting Place in Hackney between 1770 and 1791.

From 1771, Price became acquainted with William Petty, Second Earl of Shelburne, and was involved in the Whig intellectual group gathered around his Bowood estate in Wiltshire – where, through Price's influence, the scientist and Unitarian Joseph Priestley became the librarian. Price was also a member of the Club of Honest Whigs, a freethinking society whose members included Priestley, Andrew Kippis, and Benjamin Franklin. Price's numerous other acquaintances and correspondents included the American politicians John Adams, Thomas Jefferson, and George Washington, and radicals and writers such as John Horne Tooke, Thomas Paine, James Boswell, Samuel Rogers, and Mary Wollstonecraft.

Price's career ranged from publishing mathematical papers, undertaking important actuarial work, and advising on the national debt, to membership of the Royal Society. His investment in the value of the independent individual conscience led him to advocate political liberty, notably the repeal of the Test and Corporation Acts, which proscribed dissenters from Oxford and Cambridge universities and from government posts. He was especially prominent in his support for the American patriots, writing a number of pamphlets in their cause, despite the unpopularity that this risked. His *Observations on the Nature of Civil Liberty* (1776) and *Additional Observations* (1777) were

Romanticism and Revolution: A Reader.
Edited by Jon Mee and David Fallon.   © 2011 Blackwell Publishing Ltd.

particularly influential. Believing that liberty was a natural and inalienable right, Price advocated the right of any community to govern itself, although he did not support universal male suffrage, preferring a franchise limited by educational and intellectual capacity.

In 1780, his *Essay on the Population of England* erroneously asserted that the English and Welsh population was declining, in contrast to America's thriving people, a phenomenon reflecting what he saw as the manifestation of relative degrees of liberty. The conclusion of *A Discourse* is partly motivated by his belief that the French Revolution would revitalize a populace previously enervated by tyranny.

The Revolution controversy began in earnest with Price's address to the Society for Commemorating the Revolution in Great Britain at their meeting in Old Jewry on 4 November 1789, the anniversary of William of Orange's landing at Torbay. This sermon was published as *A Discourse on the Love of Our Country*. Price links the English 'Glorious Revolution' of 1688 with American independence and with the revolution in France, in a vision of the progress of universal enlightenment and liberty. This optimistic expectation of human renovation and release from the shackles of superstition and tyranny was voiced in many Romantic texts – notably Blake's 'A Song of Liberty', in *The Marriage of Heaven and Hell* (c.1790–3), Coleridge's 'Religious Musings' (1795–6), and Wordsworth's retrospect of the French Revolution in Book IX of *The Prelude* (1805). The selections illustrate Price's speculative fervour, his faith in reason and human perfectibility, his prophetic and millenarian rhetoric, and his pacific and internationalist vision of Christianity. These were qualities which infuriated Burke and helped to set the agenda for his attack on the French Revolution and on its English supporters.

[What has the love of their country hitherto been among mankind?]

PSALM cxxii. 2d, and following verses.

Our feet shall stand within thy gates, O Jerusalem, whither the tribes go up; the tribes of the Lord unto the testimony of Israel. To give thanks to the name of the Lord, for there sit the thrones of judgment; the throne of the House of David. Pray for the peace of JERUSALEM. They shall prosper that love thee. Peace be within thy walls, and prosperity within thy palaces. For my brethren and companions sake I will now say peace be within thee. Because of the House of the Lord our God, I will seek thy good.

In these words the Psalmist expresses, in strong and beautiful language, his love of his country, and the reasons on which he founded it; and my present design is, to take occasion from them to explain the duty we owe to our country, and the nature, foundation, and proper expressions of that love to it which we ought to cultivate.

I reckon this a subject particularly suitable to the services of this day, and to the Anniversary of our deliverance at the Revolution from the dangers of popery and arbitrary power; and should I, on such an occasion, be led to touch more on political subjects than would at any other time be proper in the pulpit, you will, I doubt not, excuse me.[1]

The love of our country has in all times been a subject of warm commendations; and it is certainly a noble passion; but, like all other passions, it requires regulation and direction. There are mistakes and prejudices by which, in this instance, we are in particular danger of being misled. – I will briefly mention some of these to you and observe,

First, That by our country is meant, in this case, not the soil or the spot of earth on which we happen to have been born; not the forests and fields, but that community of which we are members; or that body of companions and friends and kindred who are associated with us under the same constitution of government, protected by the same laws, and bound together by the same civil polity.

Secondly, It is proper to observe, that even in this sense of our country, that love of it which is our duty, does not imply any conviction of the superior value of it to other countries, or any particular preference of its laws and constitution of government. Were this implied, the love of their country would be the duty of only a very small part of mankind; for there are few countries that enjoy the advantage of laws and governments which deserve to be preferred. To found, therefore, this duty on such a preference, would be to found it on error and delusion. It is, however, a common delusion. There is the same partiality in countries, to themselves, that there is in individuals. All our attachments should be accompanied, as far as possible, with right opinions. – We are too apt to confine wisdom and virtue within the circle of our own acquaintance and party. Our friends, our country, and, in short, every thing related to us, we are disposed to overvalue. A wise man will guard himself against this delusion. He will study to think of all things as they are, and not suffer any partial affections to blind his understanding. In other families there may be as much worth as in our own. In other circles of friends there may be as much wisdom; and in other countries as much of all that deserves esteem; but, notwithstanding this, our obligation to love our own families, friends, and country, and to seek, in the first place, their good, will remain the same.

Thirdly, It is proper I should desire you particularly to distinguish between the love of our country and that spirit of rivalship and ambition which has been common among nations. – What has the love of their country hitherto been among mankind? What has it been but a love of domination; a desire of conquest, and a

---

thirst for grandeur and glory, by extending territory and enslaving surrounding countries? What has it been but a blind and narrow principle, producing in every country a contempt of other countries, and forming men into combinations and factions against their common rights and liberties? This is the principle that has been too often cried up as a virtue of the first rank: a principle of the same kind with that which governs clans of *Indians* or tribes of *Arabs*, and leads them to plunder and massacre. As most of the evils which have taken place in private life, and among individuals, have been occasioned by the desire of private interest overcoming the public affections; so most of the evils which have taken place among bodies of men have been occasioned by the desire of their own interest overcoming the principle of universal benevolence: and leading them to attack one another's territories, to encroach on one another's rights, and to endeavour to build their own advancement on the degradation of all within the reach of their power. – What was the love of their country among the *Jews*, but a wretched partiality to themselves, and a proud contempt of all other nations? What was the love of their country among the old *Romans*? We have heard much of it; but I cannot hesitate in saying that, however great it appeared in some of its exertions, it was in general no better than a principle holding together a band of robbers in their attempts to crush all liberty but their own. What is now the love of his country in a *Spaniard*, a *Turk*, or a *Russian*? Can it be considered as any thing better than a passion for slavery, or a blind attachment to a spot where he enjoys no rights, and is disposed of as if he was a beast?

Let us learn by such reflexions to correct and purify this passion, and to make it a just and rational principle of action.

It is very remarkable that the founder of our religion has not once mentioned this duty, or given us any recommendation of it; and this has, by unbelievers, been made an objection to Christianity. What I have said will entirely remove this objection. Certain it is, that, by inculcating on men an attachment to their country, Christianity would, at the time it was propagated, have done unspeakably more harm than good. Among the *Jews* it would have been an excitement to war and insurrections; for they were then in eager expectation of becoming soon (as the favourite people of Heaven) the lords and conquerors of the earth, under the triumphant reign of the *Messiah*. Among the *Romans*, likewise, this principle had, as I have just observed, exceeded its just bounds, and rendered them enemies to the peace and happiness of mankind. By inculcating it, therefore, Christianity would have confirmed both Jews and Gentiles in one of the most pernicious faults. Our Lord and his Apostles have done better. They have recommended that UNIVERSAL BENEVOLENCE which is an unspeakably nobler principle than any partial affections. They have laid such stress on loving all men, even our enemies, and made an ardent and extensive charity so essential a part of virtue, that the religion they have preached may, by way of distinction from all other religions, be called the Religion of Benevolence. Nothing can be more friendly to the general rights of mankind; and were it duly regarded and practised, every man would consider every other man as his brother, and all the animosity that now takes place among contending nations would be abolished. If you want any proof of this, think of our Saviour's parable of the good Samaritan.[2] The *Jews* and *Samaritans* were two rival nations that entertained a hatred of one another the most inveterate. The design of this parable was to shew to a *Jew*, that even a *Samaritan*, and consequently all men of all nations and religions, were included in the precept, THOU SHALL LOVE THY NEIGHBOUR AS THYSELF.[3]

[A narrower interest must give way to a more extensive interest]

Our regards, according to the order of nature, begin with ourselves; and every man is charged primarily with the care of himself. Next come our families, and benefactors, and friends; and after them our country. We can do little for the interest of mankind at large. To this interest, however, all other interests are subordinate. The noblest principle in our nature is the regard to general justice, and that good-will which embraces all the world. – I have already observed this; but it cannot be too often repeated. Though our immediate attention must be employed in promoting our own interest and that of our nearest connexions; yet we must remember, that a narrower interest must give way to a more extensive interest. In pursuing particularly the interest of our country, we ought to carry our views beyond it. We should love it ardently, but not exclusively. We ought to seek its good, by all the means that our different circumstances and abilities will allow; but at the same time we ought to consider ourselves as citizens of the world, and take care to maintain a just regard to the rights of other countries.

[Every degree of illumination … hastens the overthrow of priestcraft and tyranny]

Ignorance is the parent of bigotry, intolerance, persecution and slavery. Inform and instruct mankind; and these evils will be excluded. – Happy is the person who, himself raised above vulgar errors, is conscious of having aimed at giving mankind this instruction. Happy is the Scholar or Philosopher who at the close of life can reflect that he has made this use of his learning and abilities: but happier far must he be, if at the same time he has reason to believe he has been successful, and

---

[2]   Luke 10: 25–37.
[3]   Leviticus 19: 18 and Matthew 22: 39.

actually contributed, by his instructions, to disseminate among his fellow-creatures just notions of themselves, of their rights, of religion, and the nature and end of civil government. Such were *Milton, Locke, Sidney, Hoadly,* &c. in this country; such were *Montesquieu, Marmontel, Turgot,* &c. in France.[4] They sowed a seed which has since taken root and is now growing up to a glorious harvest. To the information they conveyed by their writings we owe those revolutions in which every friend to mankind is now exulting. – What an encouragement is this to us all in our endeavours to enlighten the world? Every degree of illumination which we can communicate must do the greatest good. It helps to prepare the minds of men for the recovery of their rights, and hastens the overthrow of priestcraft and tyranny. – In short, we may, in this instance, learn our duty from the conduct of the oppressors of the world. They know that light is hostile to them, and therefore they labour to keep men in the dark. With this intention they have appointed licensers of the press; and, in Popish countries, prohibited the reading of the Bible. Remove the darkness in which they envelope the world, and their usurpations will be exposed, their power will be subverted, and the world emancipated.

[The principles of the Revolution]

[…] Let us, in particular, take care not to forget the principles of the Revolution. This Society has, very properly, in its Reports, held out these principles, as an instruction to the public. I will only take notice of the three following:

First; The right to liberty of conscience in religious matters.
Secondly; The right to resist power when abused. And,
Thirdly; The right to chuse our own governors; to cashier then for misconduct; and to frame a government for ourselves.

On these three principles, and more especially the last, was the Revolution founded. Were it not true that liberty of conscience is a sacred right; that power abused justifies resistance; and that civil authority is a delegation from the people – Were not, I say, all this true; the Revolution would not have been an ASSERTION, but an INVASION of rights; not a REVOLUTION, but a REBELLION. Cherish in your

---

[4] Whig heroes of the English republican tradition: John Milton (1608–74), political writer and author of the great English epic *Paradise Lost*; John Locke (1632–1704), whose *Two Treatises on Government* (1689) outlined a contractual theory of government based on popular consent; Algernon Sidney (1623–83), Commonwealth political writer and diplomat, executed in 1683 for treason; Benjamin Hoadly (1676–1761), Anglican priest, writer of the contractual *Original and Institution of Civil Government* (1709). The French writers named here represent the Enlightenment: Charles-Louis de Secondat, Baron de Montesquieu (1689–1755), theorist of government; Jean-François Marmontel (1723–99), historian; Anne-Robert-Jacques Turgot, Baron de Laune (1727–81), economic reformer. In the fourth edition (1790), 'Marmontel' was replaced with 'Fenelon' (see note 14 to Godwin's *Political Justice*, p. 155 below).

breasts this conviction, and act under its influence; detesting the odious doctrines of passive obedience, non-resistance, and the divine right of kings – doctrines which, had they been acted upon in this country, could have left us at this time wretched slaves – doctrines which imply, that God made mankind to be oppressed and plundered; and which are no less a blasphemy against him, than an insult on common sense.

[Be encouraged, all ye friends of freedom and writers in its defence!]

What an eventful period is this! I am thankful that I have lived to it; and I could almost say, *Lord, now lettest thou thy servant depart in peace, for mine eyes have seen thy salvation.*[5] I have lived to see a diffusion of knowledge, which has undermined superstition and error – I have lived to see the rights of men better understood than ever; and nations panting for liberty, which seemed to have lost the idea of it. – I have lived to see THIRTY MILLIONS of people, indignant and resolute, spurning at slavery, and demanding liberty with an irresistible voice; their king led in triumph, and an arbitrary monarch surrendering himself to his subjects. – After sharing in the benefits of one Revolution, I have been spared to be a witness to two other Revolutions, both glorious.[6] – And now, methinks, I see the ardor for liberty catching and spreading; a general amendment beginning in human affairs; the dominion of kings changed for the dominion of laws, and the dominion of priests giving way to the dominion of reason and conscience.

Be encouraged, all ye friends of freedom and writers in its defence! The times are auspicious. Your labours have not been in vain. Behold kingdoms, admonished by you, starting from sleep, breaking their fetters, and claiming justice from their oppressors![7] Behold, the light you have struck out, after setting AMERICA free, reflected to FRANCE, and there kindled into a blaze that lays despotism in ashes, and warms and illuminates EUROPE!

Tremble all ye oppressors of the world! Take warning all ye supporters of slavish governments, and slavish hierarchies! Call no more (absurdly and wickedly) REFORMATION, innovation. You cannot now hold the world in darkness. Struggle no longer against increasing light and liberality. Restore to mankind their rights; and consent to the correction of abuses, before they and you are destroyed together.

---

[5]   Luke 2: 29–30.

[6]   Price refers here to the American and French Revolutions.

[7]   See Milton's *Areopagitica* (1644): 'Methinks I see in my mind a noble and puissant Nation rousing herself like a strong man after sleep, and shaking her invincible locks'. *The Riverside Milton*, ed. by Roy Flanagan (Boston: Houghton Mifflin, 1998), p. 1020.

2

Edmund Burke

Reflections on the Revolution in France, and on the Proceedings in Certain Societies in London relative to That Event

(London: J. Dodsley, 1790)

Born in Dublin to a Protestant attorney and his Catholic wife, Edmund Burke (1729 / 30–97) was educated as a lawyer at Trinity College, Dublin and then at London's Middle Temple. He made his first major impact with his treatise on aesthetics *A Philosophical Enquiry into the Origin of our Ideas of the Sublime and Beautiful* (1757, revised 1759). For Burke, the Sublime is an aesthetic category in which representations of power, immensity, and obscurity stimulate in the observer fear for the self, with an admixture of 'delight' produced by aesthetic distance. By contrast, the Beautiful is produced by diminutive, weak, soft, finite, and (as Wollstonecraft would note) feminine objects, generating pleasure and the social passions. Burke uses these categories in *Reflections*, and his opponents were quick to make reference to his *Enquiry* in their attacks on Burke's artifice and on his emotive style.

In 1759 Burke became private secretary to William Gerard Hamilton, MP, and began a distinguished political career, forging a reputation as a great parliamentary orator. During the 1760s he also became a fixture in London's literary circles, including Samuel Johnson's Literary Club. In 1764 Burke resigned his position under Hamilton and became private secretary to the new prime minister, the Whig Lord Rockingham. This ministry lasted just one year, but Burke's relationship with Rockingham endured. Burke was a liberal Whig, supporting limitations to the power of the Crown and the people's right to petition the government, but also resisting more radical reforms. With growing tensions developing between America and the United Kingdom, the Rockingham Whigs sought to defend American liberty and

Romanticism and Revolution: A Reader.
Edited by Jon Mee and David Fallon.   © 2011 Blackwell Publishing Ltd.

British trading interests. Burke was elected MP for Bristol in 1774 and he made two major speeches on 'Taxation' and 'Conciliation' over the next year, which supported the American patriots and identified him as a defender of constitutional liberties. Burke opposed the human costs of the war against America and led the Rockingham Whigs' secession from Parliament in protest.

The late 1770s and 1780s saw Burke campaigning for financial reform and supporting measures for Catholic relief from civil proscriptions. His Irish background and family connections made him vulnerable to accusations of closet Catholicism. In the Gordon Riots of 1780, when London mobs stirred up by Lord George Gordon attacked Catholic churches and houses, Burke brandished his sword to defend his house. Unsubtle hints at Burke's Catholic sympathies recur in radical responses to the *Reflections*. In 1782 the Rockinghams returned to power, with Burke as Paymaster-General of the army, although his non-aristocratic origins denied him a cabinet post. In July 1782, this ministry was cut short by Rockingham's death. Burke now followed Charles James Fox's leadership, and returned to the same office in the coalition between the Foxite Whigs and their former enemy, Lord North. George III used his influence to undermine the ministry and welcomed William Pitt the younger as prime minister; Burke, like many Whigs, felt that this event gravely undermined British constitutional principles. Burke spent much of the 1780s and early 1790s working for the impeachment of the Governor General of Bengal, Warren Hastings; but, like other Whigs, his reputation was damaged by his support for the Prince of Wales to be made Regent during the king's illness of 1788–9.

Burke's initial responses to the French Revolution seem to have been mixed, but notably less enthusiastic than his friend Fox's opinion that it was 'the greatest event ... that ever happened in the world, & how much the best'. Many allies from the American crisis expected Burke's support for the belated French adoption of British freedoms; by September 1789 he had decided that France was on course for anarchy. He publicly attacked the Revolution in parliamentary debates from early in 1790, which led to a dramatic and emotional split from Fox. Burke had already composed a manuscript of the *Reflections*, conceived of as a letter to Charles-Jean-François Depont, a young Frenchman who had requested his opinions on the revolution. The printed text retains this epistolary form. *Reflections* was published in November 1790, priced at 3 shillings. It was immediately successful and controversial, generating numerous responses, caricatures, and parodies. Quickly translated, it gained Burke an international audience. As the revolution in France became increasingly radical, Burke came to be seen as a prophet who had correctly discerned its course. He promoted and supported the government's prosecution of war against France and accepted a pension in recognition of his work in 1794.

Burke's writings, especially the *Reflections*, had an enormous impact on writers of the Romantic period. Even Hazlitt and Coleridge could agree that 'the speaking of him with contempt might be made the test of a vulgar, democratical mind', as the former recalled in 'My First Acquaintance with Poets'. Burke proved an important influence on Coleridge, especially on his investment in organic metaphors and on his later social thought. Most explicitly, Wordsworth praised 'the Genius of Burke' in *The Prelude* (1850), but his influence is a deep (if ambiguous) presence in all of his poetry of the 1790s. Burke's *Reflections* directly inspired numerous conservative writers, including George Canning, Hannah More, and Walter Scott, whose romances and novels are invested in Burkean chivalry. Burke's famous passage on the subject was still current enough for Byron to invoke it in the preface to his second edition of *Childe Harold's Pilgrimage*, Cantos I and II (1812).

[All the nakedness and solitude of metaphysical abstraction]

I flatter myself that I love a manly, moral, regulated liberty as well as any gentleman of that society,[1] be he who he will; and perhaps I have given as good proofs of my attachment to that cause, in the whole course of my public conduct. I think I envy liberty as little as they do, to any other nation. But I cannot stand forward, and give praise or blame to any thing which relates to human actions, and human concerns, on a simple view of the object, as it stands stripped of every relation, in all the nakedness and solitude of metaphysical abstraction. Circumstances (which with some gentlemen pass for nothing) give in reality to every political principle its distinguishing colour, and discriminating effect. The circumstances are what render every civil and political scheme beneficial or noxious to mankind. Abstractedly speaking, government, as well as liberty, is good; yet could I, in common sense, ten years ago, have felicitated France on her enjoyment of a government (for she then had a government) without inquiry what the nature of that government was, or how it was administered? Can I now congratulate the same nation upon its freedom? Is it because liberty in the abstract may be classed amongst the blessings of mankind, that I am seriously to felicitate a madman, who has escaped from the protecting restraint and wholesome darkness of his cell, on his restoration to the enjoyment of light and liberty? Am I to congratulate a highwayman and murderer, who has broke prison, upon the recovery of his

---

[1] The Society for Commemorating the Revolution in Great Britain.

natural rights? This would be to act over again the scene of the criminals condemned to the gallies, and their heroic deliverer, the metaphysic Knight of the
Sorrowful Countenance.[2]

When I see the spirit of liberty in action, I see a strong principle at work; and
this, for a while, is all I can possibly know of it. The wild *gas*, the fixed air, is plainly
broke loose: but we ought to suspend our judgment until the first effervescence is
a little subsided, till the liquor is cleared, and until we see something deeper than
the agitation of a troubled and frothy surface. I must be tolerably sure, before
I venture publicly to congratulate men upon a blessing, that they have really
received one. Flattery corrupts both the receiver and the giver; and adulation is
not of more service to the people than to kings. I should therefore suspend my
congratulations on the new liberty of France, until I was informed how it had
been combined with government; with public force; with the discipline and obedience of armies; with the collection of an effective and well-distributed revenue;
with morality and religion; with the solidity of property; with peace and
order; with civil and social manners. All these (in their way) are good things too;
and, without them, liberty is not a benefit whilst it lasts, and is not likely to continue long. The effect of liberty to individuals is, that they may do what they
please: We ought to see what it will please them to do, before we risque congratulations, which may be soon turned into complaints. Prudence would dictate this
in the case of separate insulated, private men; but liberty, when men act in bodies,
is *power*. Considerate people before they declare themselves will observe the use
which is made of *power*; and particularly of so trying a thing as *new* power, in *new*
persons, of whose principles, tempers, and dispositions, they have little or no
experience, and in situations where those who appear the most stirring in the
scene may possibly not be the real movers.

All these considerations however were below the transcendental dignity of the
Revolution Society. Whilst I continued in the country, from whence I had the
honour of writing to you, I had but an imperfect idea of their transactions. On my
coming to town, I sent for an account of their proceedings, which had been published by their authority, containing a sermon of Dr. Price, with the Duke de
Rochefoucault's and the Archbishop of Aix's letter, and several other documents
annexed.[3] The whole of that publication, with the manifest design of connecting
the affairs of France with those of England, by drawing us into an imitation of the
conduct of the National Assembly, gave me a considerable degree of uneasiness.

---

[2]   Sancho Panza's nickname for the eponymous protagonist in *Don Quixote* (1605–15), by Miguel de Cervantes
Saavedra (I.xix). Quixote's mind is distorted by his credulous reading of chivalric romances; Burke's critics readily
identified him with this character (see p. 75).
[3]   Louis-Alexandre, duc de La Rochefoucauld d'Enville (1743–92), liberal aristocrat, member of States General
and Constituent Assembly, assassinated in 1792. Jean de Dieu-Raymond de Cucé de Boisgelin (1732–1804),
Archbishop of Aix, President of the National Assembly in 1789. The Revolution Society published Price's sermon
in 1790, with appendices consisting of communications between the Society and members of the National
Assembly in Paris.

The effect of that conduct upon the power, credit, prosperity, and tranquillity of France, became every day more evident. The form of constitution to be settled, for its future polity, became more clear. We are now in a condition to discern, with tolerable exactness, the true nature of the object held up to our imitation. If the prudence of reserve and decorum dictates silence in some circumstances, in others prudence of a higher order may justify us in speaking our thoughts. The beginnings of confusion with us in England are at present feeble enough; but with you, we have seen an infancy still more feeble, growing by moments into a strength to heap mountains upon mountains, and to wage war with Heaven itself.[4] Whenever our neighbour's house is on fire, it cannot be amiss for the engines to play a little on our own. Better to be despised for too anxious apprehensions, than ruined by too confident a security.

Sollicitous chiefly for the peace of my own country, but by no means unconcerned for your's, I wish to communicate more largely, what was at first intended only for your private satisfaction. I shall still keep your affairs in my eye, and continue to address myself to you. Indulging myself in the freedom of epistolary intercourse, I beg leave to throw out my thoughts, and express my feelings, just as they arise in my mind, with very little attention to formal method. I set out with the proceedings of the Revolution Society; but I shall not confine myself to them. Is it possible I should? It looks to me as if I were in a great crisis, not of the affairs of France alone, but of all Europe, perhaps of more than Europe. All circumstances taken together, the French revolution is the most astonishing that has hitherto happened in the world. The most wonderful things are brought about in many instances by means the most absurd and ridiculous; in the most ridiculous modes; and, apparently, by the most contemptible instruments. Every thing seems out of nature in this strange chaos of levity and ferocity, and of all sorts of crimes jumbled together with all sorts of follies. In viewing this monstrous tragic–comic scene, the most opposite passions necessarily succeed, and sometimes mix with each other in the mind; alternate contempt and indignation; alternate laughter and tears; alternate scorn and horror.

[The public declaration of a man much connected with literary caballers]

For my part, I looked on that sermon[5] as the public declaration of a man much connected with literary caballers, and intriguing philosophers; with political theologians, and theological politicians, both at home and abroad. I know they set him

---

[4] Virgil, *Georgics* I.276–83, and Ovid, *Metamorphoses* I.151–62, 185.
[5] Richard Price's to the Revolution Society.

up as a sort of oracle; because, with the best intentions in the world, he naturally *philippizes*, and chaunts his prophetic song in exact unison with their designs.[6]

That sermon is in a strain which I believe has not been heard in this kingdom, in any of the pulpits which are tolerated or encouraged in it, since the year 1648, when a predecessor of Dr. Price, the Reverend Hugh Peters,[7] made the vault of the king's own chapel at St. James's ring with the honour and privilege of the saints, who, with the 'high praises of God in their mouths, and a *two*-edged sword in their hands, were to execute judgment on the heathen, and punishments upon the *people*; to bind their *kings* with chains, and their *nobles* with fetters of iron'.[8] Few harangues from the pulpit, except in the days of your league in France or in the days of our Solemn League and Covenant in England,[9] have ever breathed less of the spirit of moderation than this lecture in the Old Jewry. Supposing, however, that something like moderation were visible in this political sermon; yet politics and the pulpit are terms that have little agreement. No sound ought to be heard in the church but the healing voice of Christian charity.[10] The cause of civil liberty and civil government gains as little as that of religion by this confusion of duties. Those who quit their proper character, to assume what does not belong to them, are, for the greater part, ignorant both of the character they leave, and of the character they assume. Wholly unacquainted with the world in which they are so fond of meddling, and inexperienced in all its affairs, on which they pronounce with so much confidence, they have nothing of politics but the passions they excite. Surely the church is a place where one day's truce ought to be allowed to the dissensions and animosities of mankind.

[The two principles of conservation and correction]

A state without the means of some change is without the means of its conservation. Without such means it might even risque the loss of that part of the constitution which it wished the most religiously to preserve. The two principles of conservation and correction operated strongly at the two critical periods of the

---

[6]   Price was part of Shelburne's Bowood circle, which had links with French figures, including Mirabeau. Joseph Priestley, another member, is probably alluded to as a 'political theologian'. To *'philippize'* (originally, to write in the style of Demosthenes' diatribes against Philip of Macedon) means in this context to speak or write falsely in favour of another under the guise of divine inspiration.

[7]   Hugh Peter (1598–1660), Independent minister and leading Parliamentarian in the English Civil War, who preached to encourage the army, supported the regicide, and gave a notorious sermon on Isaiah 14: 19–20 the day before Charles I's execution. He was himself executed in the Restoration.

[8]   {Psalm cxlix.}

[9]   The Catholic League was formed in 1576, during the French Wars of Religion, to drive Protestants out of the country. The Solemn League and Covenant was an agreement made in 1643 between Scottish Covenanters and the English Parliament to support militarily the reformed Protestantism and to oppose Catholicism.

[10]   See Price, p. 14 above.

Restoration and Revolution, when England found itself without a king. At both those periods the nation had lost the bond of union in their ancient edifice; they did not, however, dissolve the whole fabric. On the contrary, in both cases they regenerated the deficient part of the old constitution through the parts which were not impaired. They kept these old parts exactly as they were, that the part recovered might be suited to them. They acted by the ancient organized states in the shape of their old organization, and not by the organic *moleculæ* of a disbanded people. At no time, perhaps, did the sovereign legislature manifest a more tender regard to that fundamental principle of British constitutional policy, than at the time of the Revolution, when it deviated from the direct line of hereditary succession. The crown was carried somewhat out of the line in which it had before moved; but the new line was derived from the same stock. It was still a line of hereditary descent; still an hereditary descent in the same blood, though an hereditary descent qualified with protestantism. When the legislature altered the direction, but kept the principle, they shewed that they held it inviolable.

[The very idea of the fabrication of a new government, is enough to fill us with disgust and horror]

The ceremony of cashiering kings, of which these gentlemen talk so much at their ease, can rarely, if ever, be performed without force. It then becomes a case of war, and not of constitution. Laws are commanded to hold their tongues amongst arms; and tribunals fall to the ground with the peace they are no longer able to uphold. The Revolution of 1688 was obtained by a just war, in the only case in which any war, and much more a civil war, can be just. '*Justa bella quibus necessaria.*'[11] The question of dethroning, or, if these gentlemen like the phrase better, 'cashiering', kings, will always be, as it has always been, an extraordinary question of state, and wholly out of the law; a question (like all other questions of state) of dispositions, and of means, and of probable consequences, rather than of positive rights. As it was not made for common abuses, so it is not to be agitated by common minds. The speculative line of demarcation, where obedience ought to end, and resistance must begin, is faint, obscure, and not easily definable. It is not a single act, or a single event, which determines it. Governments must be abused and deranged indeed, before it can be thought of; and the prospect of the future must be as bad as the experience of the past. When things are in that lamentable condition, the nature of the disease is to indicate the remedy to those whom nature has qualified to administer in extremities this critical, ambiguous, bitter potion to a distempered state. Times and occasions, and provocations, will teach their own lessons. The wise will determine from the gravity of the case; the irritable, from

---

[11] Livy, *From the Foundation of Rome* (c. 27–25 BC), IX.i: 'Wars are just to those for whom they are necessary.'

sensibility to oppression; the high-minded, from disdain and indignation at abusive power in unworthy hands; the brave and bold from the love of honourable danger in a generous cause: but, with or without right, a revolution will be the very last resource of the thinking and the good.

The third head of right, asserted by the pulpit of the Old Jewry, namely, the 'right to form a government for ourselves', has, at least, as little countenance from anything done at the Revolution, either in precedent or principle, as the two first of their claims. The Revolution was made to preserve our *antient* indisputable laws and liberties, and that *antient* constitution of government which is our only security for law and liberty. If you are desirous of knowing the spirit of our constitution, and the policy which predominated in that great period which has secured it to this hour, pray look for both in our histories, in our records, in our acts of parliament, and journals of parliament, and not in the sermons of the Old Jewry, and the after-dinner toasts of the Revolution Society. – In the former you will find other ideas and another language. Such a claim is as ill-suited to our temper and wishes as it is unsupported by any appearance of authority. The very idea of the fabrication of a new government, is enough to fill us with disgust and horror. We wished at the period of the Revolution, and do now wish, to derive all we possess as *an inheritance from our forefathers*. Upon that body and stock of inheritance we have taken care not to inoculate any cyon[12] alien to the nature of the original plant. All the reformations we have hitherto made, have proceeded upon the principle of reverence to antiquity; and I hope, nay, I am persuaded, that all those which possibly may be made hereafter, will be carefully formed upon analogical precedent, authority, and example.

[Our liberties, as an *entailed inheritance* derived to us from our forefathers]

You will observe, that from Magna Charta to the Declaration of Right,[13] it has been the uniform policy of our constitution, to claim and assert our liberties, as an *entailed inheritance* derived to us from our forefathers, and to be transmitted to our posterity; as an estate specially belonging to the people of this kingdom, without any reference whatever to any other more general or prior right. By this means our constitution preserves an unity in so great a diversity of its parts. We have an inheritable crown; an inheritable peerage; and an house of commons and a people inheriting privileges, franchises, and liberties, from a long line of ancestors.

---

12   Variant spelling of 'scion', which denotes a graft of a plant.
13   Magna Carta: a legal charter of 1215, in which King John accepted the rights of freemen and the limitation of his sovereignty by law. The 1688 Declaration of Right invited William III and Mary II to be joint sovereigns of England.

This policy appears to me to be the result of profound reflection; or rather the happy effect of following nature, which is wisdom without reflection, and above it. A spirit of innovation is generally the result of a selfish temper and confined views. People will not look forward to posterity, who never look backward to their ancestors. Besides, the people of England well know, that the idea of inheritance furnishes a sure principle of conservation, and a sure principle of transmission; without at all excluding a principle of improvement. It leaves acquisition free; but it secures what it acquires. Whatever advantages are obtained by a state proceeding on these maxims, are locked fast as in a sort of family settlement, grasped as in a kind of mortmain forever.[14] By a constitutional policy, working after the pattern of nature, we receive, we hold, we transmit our government and our privileges, in the same manner in which we enjoy and transmit our property and our lives. The institutions of policy, the goods of fortune, the gifts of Providence, are handed down, to us and from us, in the same course and order. Our political system is placed in a just correspondence and symmetry with the order of the world, and with the mode of existence decreed to a permanent body composed of transitory parts; wherein, by the disposition of a stupendous wisdom, moulding together the great mysterious incorporation of the human race, the whole, at one time, is never old, or middle-aged, or young, but in a condition of unchangeable constancy, moves on through the varied tenour of perpetual decay, fall, renovation, and progression. Thus, by preserving the method of nature in the conduct of the state, in what we improve we are never wholly new; in what we retain we are never wholly obsolete. By adhering in this manner and on those principles to our forefathers, we are guided not by the superstition of antiquarians, but by the spirit of philosophic analogy. In this choice of inheritance we have given to our frame of polity the image of a relation in blood; binding up the constitution of our country with our dearest domestic ties; adopting our fundamental laws into the bosom of our family affections; keeping inseparable, and cherishing with the warmth of all their combined and mutually reflected charities, our state, our hearths, our sepulchres, and our altars.

Through the same plan of a conformity to nature in our artificial institutions, and by calling in the aid of her unerring and powerful instincts, to fortify the fallible and feeble contrivances of our reason, we have derived several other, and those no small benefits, from considering our liberties in the light of an inheritance. Always acting as if in the presence of canonized forefathers, the spirit of freedom, leading in itself to misrule and excess, is tempered with an awful gravity. This idea of a liberal descent inspires us with a sense of habitual native dignity, which prevents that upstart insolence almost inevitably adhering to and disgracing those who are the first acquirers of any distinction. By this means our liberty becomes a noble freedom. It carries an imposing and majestic aspect. It has a pedigree, and illustrating ancestors. It has its bearings, and its ensigns armorial. It has its gallery

---

[14]   Literally, a 'dead hand': lands held permanently by a corporate body, commonly ecclesiastical.

of portraits; its monumental inscriptions; its records, evidences, and titles. We procure reverence to our civil institutions on the principle upon which nature teaches us to revere individual men; on account of their age; and on account of those from whom they are descended. All your sophisters cannot produce any thing better adapted to preserve a rational and manly freedom than the course that we have pursued, who have chosen our nature rather than our speculations, our breasts rather than our inventions, for the great conservatories and magazines of our rights and privileges.

You might, if you pleased, have profited of our example, and have given to your recovered freedom a correspondent dignity. Your privileges, though discontinued, were not lost to memory. Your constitution, it is true, whilst you were out of possession, suffered waste and dilapidation; but you possessed in some parts the walls, and in all the foundations of a noble and venerable castle. You might have repaired those walls; you might have built on those old foundations. Your constitution was suspended before it was perfected; but you had the elements of a constitution very nearly as good as could be wished. In your old states you possessed that variety of parts corresponding with the various descriptions of which your community was happily composed; you had all that combination, and all that opposition of interests, you had that action and counteraction which, in the natural and in the political world, from the reciprocal struggle of discordant powers, draws out the harmony of the universe. These opposed and conflicting interests, which you considered as so great a blemish in your old and in our present constitution, interpose a salutary check to all precipitate resolutions; They render deliberation a matter not of choice, but of necessity; they make all change a subject of *compromise*; which naturally begets moderation; they produce *temperaments*, preventing the sore evil of harsh, crude, unqualified reformations; and rendering all the headlong exertions of arbitrary power, in the few or in the many, for ever impracticable. Through that diversity of members and interests, general liberty had as many securities as there were separate views in the several orders; whilst by pressing down the whole by the weight of a real monarchy, the separate parts would have been prevented from warping and starting from their allotted places.

[Their blow was aimed at an hand holding out graces, favours, and immunities]

France, by the perfidy of her leaders, has utterly disgraced the tone of lenient council in the cabinets of princes, and disarmed it of its most potent topics. She has sanctified the dark suspicious maxims of tyrannous distrust; and taught kings to tremble at (what will hereafter be called) the delusive plausibilities, of moral politicians. Sovereigns will consider those who advise them to place an unlimited confidence in their people, as subverters of their thrones; as traitors who aim at their destruction, by leading their easy good-nature, under specious pretences, to admit combinations of bold and faithless men into a participation of their power. This alone (if there were nothing else) is an irreparable calamity to you and to mankind. Remember that your parliament of Paris told your king, that in calling the states together, he had nothing to fear but the prodigal excess of their zeal in providing for the support of the throne. It is right that these men should hide their heads. It is right that they should bear their part in the ruin which their counsel has brought on their sovereign and their country. Such sanguine declarations tend to lull authority asleep; to encourage it rashly to engage in perilous adventures of untried policy; to neglect those provisions, preparations, and precautions, which distinguish benevolence from imbecility; and without which no man can answer for the salutary effect of any abstract plan of government or of freedom. For want of these, they have seen the medicine of the state corrupted into its poison. They have seen the French rebel against a mild and lawful monarch, with more fury, outrage, and insult, than ever any people has been known to rise against the most illegal usurper, or the most sanguinary tyrant. Their resistance was made to concession; their revolt was from protection; their blow was aimed at an hand holding out graces, favours, and immunities.

This was unnatural. The rest is in order. They have found their punishment in their success. Laws overturned; tribunals subverted; industry without vigour; commerce expiring; the revenue unpaid, yet the people impoverished; a church pillaged,[15] and a state not relieved; civil and military anarchy made the constitution of the kingdom; every thing human and divine sacrificed to the idol of public credit, and national bankruptcy the consequence; and to crown all, the paper securities of new, precarious, tottering power, the discredited paper securities of impoverished fraud, and beggared rapine,[16] held out as a currency for the support of an empire, in lieu of the two great recognized species that represent the lasting conventional credit of mankind, which disappeared and hid themselves in the earth from whence they came, when the principle of property, whose creatures and representatives they are, was systematically subverted.

Were all these dreadful things necessary? were they the inevitable results of the desperate struggle of determined patriots, compelled to wade through blood and tumult, to the quiet shore of a tranquil and prosperous liberty? No! nothing like it. The fresh ruins of France, which shock our feelings wherever we can turn our eyes, are not the devastation of civil war; they are the sad but instructive monuments of rash and ignorant counsel in time of profound peace. They are

---

[15]   On 4 August and 2 November 1789 respectively, the Constituent assembly abolished tithes and appropriated church land and property to the government. Under the Civil Constitution of the Clergy, passed in July 1790, the French Catholic Church and its ministers were subordinated to the state.

[16]   With the nation effectively bankrupt, the French government used confiscated church properties as the basis of paper bonds, to redeem the national debt. Soon treated as currency and called 'assignats', they became rapidly subject to hyperinflation.

the display of inconsiderate and presumptuous, because unresisted and irresistible authority. The persons who have thus squandered away the precious treasure of their crimes, the persons who have made this prodigal and wild waste of public evils (the last stake reserved for the ultimate ransom of the state) have met in their progress with little, or rather with no opposition at all. Their whole march was more like a triumphal procession than the progress of a war. Their pioneers have gone before them, and demolished and laid everything level at their feet. Not one drop of *their* blood have they shed in the cause of the country they have ruined. They have made no sacrifices to their projects of greater consequence than their shoebuckles,[17] whilst they were imprisoning their king, murdering their fellow citizens, and bathing in tears, and plunging in poverty and distress, thousands of worthy men and worthy families. Their cruelty has not even been the base result of fear. It has been the effect of their sense of perfect safety, in authorizing treasons, robberies, rapes, assassinations, slaughters, and burnings throughout their harassed land. But the cause of all was plain from the beginning.

[A profligate disregard of a dignity which they partake with others]

To observing men it must have appeared from the beginning, that the majority of the Third Estate, in conjunction with such a deputation from the clergy as I have described, whilst it pursued the destruction of the nobility, would inevitably become subservient to the worst designs of individuals in that class. In the spoil and humiliation of their own order these individuals would possess a sure fund for the pay of their new followers. To squander away the objects which made the happiness of their fellows, would be to them no sacrifice at all. Turbulent, discontented men of quality, in proportion as they are puffed up with personal pride and arrogance, generally despise their own order. One of the first symptoms they discover of a selfish and mischievous ambition, is a profligate disregard of a dignity which they partake with others. To be attached to the subdivision, to love the little platoon we belong to in society, is the first principle (the germ as it were) of public affections. It is the first link in the series by which we proceed towards a love to our country and to mankind. The interests of that portion of social arrangement is a trust in the hands of all those who compose it; and as none but bad men would justify it in abuse, none but traitors would barter it away for their own personal advantage.[18]

---

[17]   French citizens were encouraged to finance the Revolution by donating valuables, including shoebuckles.

[18]   Burke refers to nobles who had joined the revolutionary cause, including the Duke d'Orléans, the Marquis de Lafayette, as well as *Abbés* such as Sièyes and Talleyrand, who sanctioned the reforms of the church.

[The *real* rights of men]

It is no wonder therefore, that with these ideas of every thing in their constitution and government at home, either in church or state, as illegitimate and usurped, or, at best as a vain mockery, they[19] look abroad with an eager and passionate enthusiasm. Whilst they are possessed by these notions, it is vain to talk to them of the practice of their ancestors, the fundamental laws of their country, the fixed form of a constitution, whose merits are confirmed by the solid test of long experience, and an increasing public strength and national prosperity. They despise experience as the wisdom of unlettered men; and as for the rest, they have wrought underground a mine that will blow up, at one grand explosion all examples of antiquity, all precedents, charters, and acts of parliament.[20] They have 'the rights of men'. Against these there can be no prescription; against these no agreement is binding: these admit no temperament, and no compromise: any thing withheld from their full demand is so much of fraud and injustice. Against these their rights of men let no government look for security in the length of its continuance, or in the justice and lenity of its administration. The objections of these speculatists, if its forms do not quadrate with their theories, are as valid against such an old and beneficent government as against the most violent tyranny, or the greenest usurpation. They are always at issue with governments, not on a question of abuse, but a question of competency and a question of title. I have nothing to say to the clumsy subtilty of their political metaphysics. Let them be their amusement in the schools. – 'Illa *se jactet in aula* – *Æolus, et clauso ventorum carcere regnet.'*[21] – But let them not break prison to burst like a *Levanter*[22] to sweep the earth with their hurricane and to break up the fountains of the great deep to overwhelm us.

Far am I from denying in theory; full as far is my heart from withholding in practice (if I were of power to give or to withhold) the *real* rights of men. In denying their false claims of right, I do not mean to injure those which are real, and are such as their pretended rights would totally destroy. If civil society be made for the advantage of man, all the advantages for which it is made become his right. It is an institution of beneficence; and law itself is only beneficence acting by a rule. Men have a right to live by that rule; they have a right to justice; as between their fellows, whether their fellows are in politic function or in ordinary occupation. They have a right to the fruits of their industry; and to the means of making their industry fruitful. They have a right to the acquisitions of their parents; to the nourishment

---

[19] English supporters of the French Revolution.

[20] Burke appears to allude to a controversial passage in Priestley's *The Importance and Extent of Free Enquiry in Matters of Religion* (London: J. Johnson, 1785), in which Priestley asserted that Unitarian reformers were 'laying gunpowder, grain by grain, under the old building of error and superstition, which a single spark may hereafter inflame, so as to produce an instantaneous explosion' (p. 40).

[21] Virgil, *Aeneid* I.140–1: 'in that hall let Aeolus strut and rule in the prison of the winds'.

[22] A strong wind from the east, in the Mediterranean.

and improvement of their offspring; to instruction in life, and to consolation in death. Whatever each man can separately do, without trespassing upon others, he has a right to do for himself; and he has a right to a fair portion of all which society, with all its combinations of skill and force, can do in his favour.[23] But as to the share of power, authority, and direction which each individual ought to have in the management of the state, that I must deny to be amongst the direct original rights of man in civil society; for I have in my contemplation the civil social man, and no other. It is a thing to be settled by convention.

If civil society be the offspring of convention, that convention must be its law. That convention must limit and modify all the descriptions of constitution which are formed under it. Every sort of legislative, judicial, or executory power are its creatures. They can have no being in any other state of things; and how can any man claim, under the conventions of civil society, rights which do not so much as suppose its existence? Rights which are absolutely repugnant to it? One of the first motives to civil society, and which becomes one of its fundamental rules, is *that no man should be judge in his own cause.* By this each person has at once divested himself of the first fundamental right of uncovenanted man, that is, to judge for himself, and to assert his own cause. He abdicates all right to be his own governor. He inclusively, in a great measure, abandons the right of self-defence, the first law of nature. Men cannot enjoy the rights of an uncivil and of a civil state together. That he may obtain justice he gives up his right of determining what it is in points the most essential to him. That he may secure some liberty, he makes a surrender in trust of the whole of it.

Government is not made in virtue of natural rights, which may and do exist in total independence of it; and exist in much greater clearness, and in a much greater degree of abstract perfection: but their abstract perfection is their practical defect. By having a right to every thing they want every thing. Government is a contrivance of human wisdom to provide for human *wants.* Men have a right that these wants should be provided for by this wisdom. Among these wants is to be reckoned the want, out of civil society, of a sufficient restraint upon their passions. Society requires not only that the passions of individuals should be subjected, but that even in the mass and body as well as in the individuals, the inclinations of men should frequently be thwarted, their will controlled, and their passions brought into subjection. This can only be done *by a power out of themselves*; and not, in the exercise of its function, subject to that will and to those passions which it is its office to bridle and subdue. In this sense the restraints on men, as well as their liberties, are to be reckoned among their rights. But as the liberties and the restrictions vary with times and circumstances, and admit of infinite modifications, they cannot be settled upon any abstract rule; and nothing is so foolish as to discuss them upon that principle.

---

[23]   From the fourth edition onwards, Burke added the following: 'In this partnership all men have equal rights; but not to equal things. He that has but five shillings in the partnership, has as good a right to it, as he that has five hundred pounds has to his larger proportion. But he has not a right to an equal dividend in the product of the joint stock; and as to …'

The moment you abate any thing from the full rights of men, each to govern himself, and suffer any artificial positive limitation upon those rights, from that moment the whole organization of government becomes a consideration of convenience. This it is which makes the constitution of a state, and the due distribution of its powers, a matter of the most delicate and complicated skill. It requires a deep knowledge of human nature and human necessities, and of the things which facilitate or obstruct the various ends which are to be pursued by the mechanism of civil institutions. The state is to have recruits to its strength, and remedies to its distempers. What is the use of discussing a man's abstract right to food or medicine? The question is upon the method of procuring and administering them. In that deliberation I shall always advise to call in the aid of the farmer and the physician, rather than the professor of metaphysics. The science of constructing a commonwealth, or renovating it, or reforming it, is, like every other experimental science, not to be taught *à priori*.[24]

[But the age of chivalry is gone. – That of sophisters, œconomists, and calculators, has succeeded]

Yielding to reasons, at least as forcible as those which were so delicately urged in the compliment on the new year, the king of France will probably endeavour to forget these events, and that compliment.[25] But history, who keeps a durable record of all our acts, and exercises her awful censure over the proceedings of all sorts of sovereigns, will not forget, either those events, or the æra of this liberal refinement in the intercourse of mankind. History will record, that on the morning of the 6th of October 1789, the king and queen of France, after a day of confusion, alarm, dismay, and slaughter, lay down, under the pledged security of public faith, to indulge nature in a few hours of respite and troubled, melancholy repose. From this sleep the queen was first startled by the voice of the centinel at her door, who cried out to her, to save herself by flight – that this was the last proof of fidelity he could give – that they were upon him, and he was dead. Instantly he was cut down. A band of cruel ruffians and assassins, reeking with his blood, rushed into the chamber of the queen, and pierced with a hundred strokes of bayonets and poniards the bed, from whence this persecuted woman had but just time to fly almost naked, and through ways unknown to the murderers had escaped to seek refuge at the feet of a king and husband, not secure of his own life for a moment.[26]

---

[24] In philosophical terms, 'a priori' refers to a type of knowledge prior to or independent of experience, hence innate to the mind.

[25] Burke has just described how members of the Assembly addressed the king for the new year, requesting him to 'forget the stormy period of the last, on account of the great good which *he* was likely to produce to his people'.

[26] The accuracy of Burke's dramatic account of events on 6 October 1789 was the focus of considerable subsequent debate.

This king, to say no more of him, and this queen, and their infant children (who once would have been the pride and hope of a great and generous people) were then forced to abandon the sanctuary of the most splendid palace in the world,[27] which they left swimming in blood, polluted by massacre, and strewed with scattered limbs and mutilated carcasses. Thence they were conducted into the capital of their kingdom. Two had been selected from the unprovoked, unresisted, promiscuous slaughter, which was made of the gentlemen of birth and family who composed the king's body guard. These two gentlemen, with all the parade of an execution of justice, were cruelly and publicly dragged to the block and beheaded in the great court of the palace. Their heads were stuck upon spears, and led the procession; whilst the royal captives who followed in the train were slowly moved along, amidst the horrid yells, and shrilling screams, and frantic dances, and infamous contumelies, and all the unutterable abominations of the furies of hell, in the abused shape of the vilest of women.[28] After they had been made to taste, drop by drop, more than the bitterness of death, in the slow torture of a journey of twelve miles, protracted to six hours, they were, under a guard, composed of those very soldiers who had thus conducted them through this famous triumph, lodged in one of the old palaces of Paris, now converted into a Bastile for kings.[29]

Is this a triumph to be consecrated at altars? To be commemorated with grateful thanksgiving? To be offered to the divine humanity with fervent prayer and enthusiastick ejaculation? – These Theban and Thracian Orgies,[30] acted in France, and applauded only in the Old Jewry, I assure you, kindle prophetic enthusiasm in the minds but of very few people in this kingdom; although a saint and apostle, who may have revelations of his own, and who has so completely vanquished all the mean superstitions of the heart, may incline to think it pious and decorous to compare it with the entrance into the world of the Prince of Peace, proclaimed in a holy temple by a venerable sage, and not long before not worse announced by the voice of angels to the quiet innocence of shepherds.[31]

At first I was at a loss to account for this fit of unguarded transport. I knew, indeed, that the sufferings of monarchs make a delicious repast to some sort of palates. There were reflections which might serve to keep this appetite within some bounds of temperance. But when I took one circumstance into my consideration, I was obliged to confess, that much allowance ought to be made for the Society, and that the temptation was too strong for common discretion; I mean, the circumstance of the Io Pæan of the triumph, the animating cry which called

---

[27] Versailles.

[28] Thousands of poor women gathered at Paris markets, collected arms, and marched on Versailles to confront the king and take the royal family to Paris.

[29] The Tuileries.

[30] This is a reference to ancient rituals celebrated in various parts of the Greek world and related to Dionysus, the Greek god of wine. According to the myth vividly staged in Euripides' play *The Bacchae*, at Thebes Dionysus's female followers, the Maenads, tore apart King Pentheus, who had banned Dionysian worship. Thracean Maenads killed and dismembered the legendary Orpheus (Ovid, *Metamorphoses* XI.1–67).

[31] Luke 2: 8–18.

'for *all* the BISHOPS to be hanged on the lamp-posts',[32] might well have brought forth a burst of enthusiasm on the foreseen consequences of this happy day. I allow to so much enthusiasm some little deviation from prudence. I allow this prophet to break forth into hymns of joy and thanksgiving on an event which appears like the precursor of the Millennium, and the projected fifth monarchy,[33] in the destruction of all church establishments. There was, however (as in all human affairs there is) in the midst of this joy something to exercise the patience of these worthy gentlemen, and to try the long-suffering of their faith. The actual murder of the king and queen, and their child, was wanting to the other auspicious circumstances of this '*beautiful day*'. The actual murder of the bishops, though called for by so many holy ejaculations, was also wanting. A groupe of regicide and sacrilegious slaughter, was indeed boldly sketched, but it was only sketched. It unhappily was left unfinished, in this great history-piece of the massacre of innocents. What hardy pencil of a great master, from the school of the rights of men, will finish it, is to be seen hereafter. The age has not yet the compleat benefit of that diffusion of knowledge that has undermined superstition and error; and the king of France wants another object or two, to consign to oblivion, in consideration of all the good which is to arise from his own sufferings, and the patriotic crimes of an enlightened age.[34]

Although this work of our new light and knowledge, did not go to the length, that in all probability it was intended it should be carried; yet I must think, that such treatment of any human creatures must be shocking to any but those who are made for accomplishing Revolutions. But I cannot stop here. Influenced by the inborn feelings of my nature, and not being illuminated by a single ray of this new-sprung modern light, I confess to you, Sir, that the exalted rank of the persons suffering, and particularly the sex, the beauty, and the amiable qualities of the descendant of so many kings and emperors, with the tender age of royal infants, insensible only through infancy and innocence of the cruel outrages to which their parents were exposed, instead of being a subject of exultation, adds not a little to my sensibility on that most melancholy occasion.

I hear that the august person, who was the principal object of our preacher's triumph, though he supported himself, felt much on that shameful occasion. As a man, it became him to feel for his wife and his children, and the faithful guards of his person, that were massacred in cold blood about him; as a prince, it became him to feel for the strange and frightful transformation of his civilized subjects, and to be more grieved for them, than sollicitous for himself. It derogates little from his fortitude, while it adds infinitely to the honour of his humanity. I am very

---

[32]   {Tous les Eveques à la lanterne} 'All the bishops to the lantern', where revolutionary mobs hanged their enemies. In ancient Greek lyric poetry, the Io Pæan was a shout in a song of joy or victory addressed to Apollo.

[33]   The Fifth Monarchy Men: a radical millenarian sect during the English Republic, whose members believed that Daniel 2: 44 predicted the imminent end of earthly monarchy and the rule of Christ as 'Fifth Monarch'.

[34]   Burke adds here a long footnote, containing a letter from M. de Lally Tollendal, a former moderate member of the National Assembly, again, as eyewitness evidence of Parisian violence.

sorry to say it, very sorry indeed, that such personages are in a situation in which it is not unbecoming to praise the virtues of the great.

I hear, and I rejoice to hear, that the great lady,[35] the other object of the triumph, has borne that day (one is interested that beings made for suffering should suffer well) and that she bears all the succeeding days, that she bears the imprisonment of her husband, and her own captivity, and the exile of her friends, and the insulting adulation of addresses, and the whole weight of her accumulated wrongs, with a serene patience, in a manner suited to her rank and race, and becoming the offspring of a sovereign distinguished for her piety and her courage; that, like her, she has lofty sentiments; that she feels with the dignity of a Roman matron; that in the last extremity she will save herself from the last disgrace, and that if she must fall, she will fall by no ignoble hand.

It is now sixteen or seventeen years since I saw the queen of France, then the dauphiness, at Versailles; and surely never lighted on this orb, which she hardly seemed to touch, a more delightful vision. I saw her just above the horizon, decorating and cheering the elevated sphere she just began to move in, – glittering like the morning-star, full of life, and splendour, and joy. Oh! what a revolution! and what an heart must I have, to contemplate without emotion that elevation and that fall! Little did I dream that, when she added titles of veneration to those of enthusiastic, distant, respectful love, that she should ever be obliged to carry the sharp antidote against disgrace concealed in that bosom; little did I dream that I should have lived to see such disasters fallen upon her in a nation of gallant men, in a nation of men of honour and of cavaliers. I thought ten thousand swords must have leaped from their scabbards to avenge even a look that threatened her with insult. – But the age of chivalry is gone. – That of sophisters, œconomists, and calculators, has succeeded; and the glory of Europe is extinguished forever. Never, never more, shall we behold that generous loyalty to rank and sex, that proud submission, that dignified obedience, that subordination of the heart, which kept alive, even in servitude itself, the spirit of an exalted freedom. The unbought grace of life, the cheap defence of nations, the nurse of manly sentiment and heroic enterprize is gone! It is gone, that sensibility of principle, that chastity of honour, which felt a stain like a wound, which inspired courage whilst it mitigated ferocity, which ennobled whatever it touched, and under which vice itself lost half its evil, by losing all its grossness.

This mixed system of opinion and sentiment had its origin in the antient chivalry; and the principle, though varied in its appearance by the varying state of human affairs, subsisted and influenced through a long succession of generations, even to the time we live in. If it should ever be totally extinguished, the loss I fear will be great. It is this which has given its character to modern Europe. It is this which has distinguished it under all its forms of government, and distinguished it to its advantage, from the states of Asia, and possibly from those states which

[35]   The Queen of France, Marie Antoinette (1755–93), daughter of Emperor Francis I and Empress Maria-Theresa. Burke had seen her as the Dauphiness on his visit to Paris in 1773.

flourished in the most brilliant periods of the antique world. It was this, which, without confounding ranks, had produced a noble equality, and handed it down through all the gradations of social life. It was this opinion which mitigated kings into companions, and raised private men to be fellows with kings. Without force, or opposition, it subdued the fierceness of pride and power; it obliged sovereigns to submit to the soft collar of social esteem, compelled stern authority to submit to elegance, and gave a domination vanquisher of laws, to be subdued by manners.

But now all is to be changed. All the pleasing illusions, which made power gentle, and obedience liberal, which harmonized the different shades of life, and which, by a bland assimilation, incorporated into politics the sentiments which beautify and soften private society, are to be dissolved by this new conquering empire of light and reason. All the decent drapery of life is to be rudely torn off. All the superadded ideas, furnished from the wardrobe of a moral imagination, which the heart owns, and the understanding ratifies, as necessary to cover the defects of our naked shivering nature, and to raise it to dignity in our own estimation, are to be exploded as a ridiculous, absurd, and antiquated fashion.

On this scheme of things, a king is but a man; a queen is but a woman; a woman is but an animal; and an animal not of the highest order. All homage paid to the sex in general as such, and without distinct views, is to be regarded as romance and folly. Regicide, and parricide, and sacrilege, are but fictions of superstition, corrupting jurisprudence by destroying its simplicity. The murder of a king, or a queen, or a bishop, or a father, are only common homicide; and if the people are by any chance, or in any way gainers by it, a sort of homicide much the most pardonable, and into which we ought not to make too severe a scrutiny.

On the scheme of this barbarous philosophy, which is the offspring of cold hearts and muddy understandings, and which is as void of solid wisdom, as it is destitute of all taste and elegance, laws are to be supported only by their own terrors, and by the concern, which each individual may find in them, from his own private speculations, or can spare to them from his own private interests. In the groves of *their* academy, at the end of every visto,[36] you see nothing but the gallows. Nothing is left which engages the affections on the part of the commonwealth. On the principles of this mechanic philosophy, our institutions can never be embodied, if I may use the expression, in persons; so as to create in us love, veneration, admiration, or attachment. But that sort of reason which banishes the affections is incapable of filling their place. These public affections, combined with manners, are required sometimes as supplements, sometimes as correctives, always as aids to law. The precept given by a wise man, as well as a great critic, for the construction of poems, is equally true as to states. *Non satis est pulchra esse poemata, dulcia sunto.*[37] There ought to be a system of manners in every nation which a well-informed mind would be disposed to relish. To make us love our country, our country ought to be lovely.

---

[36]   A view through a long and narrow opening.

[37]   Horace, *Ars Poetica* 99–100: 'It is not enough for poems to be beautiful; they must also be pleasing.'

But power, of some kind or other, will survive the shock in which manners and opinions perish; and it will find other and worse means for its support. The usurpation which, in order to subvert antient institutions, has destroyed antient principles, will hold power by arts similar to those by which it has acquired it. When the old feudal and chivalrous spirit of *Fealty*, which, by freeing kings from fear, freed both kings and subjects from the precautions of tyranny, shall be extinct in the minds of men, plots and assassinations will be anticipated by preventive murder and preventive confiscation, and that long roll of grim and bloody maxims, which form the political code of all power, not standing on its own honour and the honour of those who are to obey it. Kings will be tyrants from policy when subjects are rebels from principle.

When antient opinions and rules of life are taken away, the loss cannot possibly be estimated. From that moment we have no compass to govern us; nor can we know distinctly to what port we steer. Europe undoubtedly, taken in a mass, was in a flourishing condition the day on which your Revolution was compleated. How much of that prosperous state was owing to the spirit of our old manners and opinions is not easy to say; but as such causes cannot be indifferent in their operation, we must presume, that on the whole, their operation was beneficial.

We are but too apt to consider things in the state in which we find them, without sufficiently adverting to the causes by which they have been produced, and possibly may be upheld. Nothing is more certain, than that our manners, our civilization, and all the good things which are connected with manners, and with civilization, have, in this European world of ours, depended for ages upon two principles; and were indeed the result of both combined; I mean the spirit of a gentleman, and the spirit of religion. The nobility and the clergy, the one by profession, the other by patronage, kept learning in existence, even in the midst of arms and confusions, and whilst governments were rather in their causes than formed. Learning paid back what it received to nobility and to priesthood; and paid it with usury, by enlarging their ideas, and by furnishing their minds. Happy if they had all continued to know their indissoluble union, and their proper place! Happy if learning, not debauched by ambition, had been satisfied to continue the instructor, and not aspired to be the master! Along with its natural protectors and guardians, learning will be cast into the mire, and trodden down under the hoofs of a swinish multitude.[38]

If, as I suspect, modern letters owe more than they are always willing to own to ancient manners, so do other interests which we value full as much as they are worth. Even commerce, and trade, and manufacture, the gods of our œconomical politicians, are themselves perhaps but creatures; are themselves but effects, which, as first causes, we choose to worship. They certainly grew under the same shade in which learning flourished. They too may decay with their

---

[38]   The concluding phrase was ironized by radicals: see Thomas Spence's periodical *Pig's Meat; or, Lessons for the Swinish Multitude* (1793–5) and Daniel Isaac Eaton's *Hog's Wash, or, A Salmagundy for Swine* (1793–5).

natural protecting principles. With you, for the present at least, they all threaten to disappear together. Where trade and manufactures are wanting to a people, and the spirit of nobility and religion remains, sentiment supplies, and not always ill supplies their place; but if commerce and the arts should be lost in an experiment to try how well a state may stand without these old fundamental principles, what sort of a thing must be a nation of gross, stupid, ferocious, and at the same time, poor and sordid barbarians, destitute of religion, honour, or manly pride, possessing nothing at present, and hoping for nothing hereafter.

I wish you may not be going fast, and by the shortest cut, to that horrible and disgustful situation. Already there appears a poverty of conception, a coarseness and vulgarity in all the proceedings of the assembly and of all their instructors. Their liberty is not liberal. Their science is presumptuous ignorance. Their humanity is savage and brutal.

[The real tragedy of this triumphal day]

Why do I feel so differently from the Reverend Dr. Price, and those of his lay flock, who will choose to adopt the sentiments of his discourse? – For this plain reason – because it is *natural* I should; because we are so made as to be affected at such spectacles with melancholy sentiments upon the unstable condition of mortal prosperity, and the tremendous uncertainty of human greatness; because in those natural feelings we learn great lessons; because in events like these our passions instruct our reason; because when kings are hurl'd from their thrones by the Supreme Director of this great drama, and become the objects of insult to the base, and of pity to the good, we behold such disasters in the moral, as we should behold a miracle in the physical order of things. We are alarmed into reflexion; our minds (as it has long since been observed) are purified by terror and pity;[39] our weak unthinking pride is humbled, under the dispensations of a mysterious wisdom. – Some tears might be drawn from me, if such a spectacle were exhibited on the stage. I should be truly ashamed of finding in myself that superficial, theatric sense of painted distress, whilst I could exult over it in real life. With such a perverted mind, I could never venture to show my face at a tragedy. People would think the tears that Garrick formerly, or that Siddons not long since,[40] have extorted from me were the tears of hypocrisy; I should know them to be the tears of folly.

Indeed the theatre is a better school of moral sentiments than churches, where the feelings of humanity are thus outraged. Poets, who have to deal with an audience not yet graduated in the school of the rights of men, and who must apply

---

[39]   Purging or purification through 'fear and pity': part of Aristotle's celebrated definition of the workings of tragedy in his *Poetics*, 1452ª and 1452ᵇ.

[40]   David Garrick (1717–79) and Sarah Siddons (1755–1831): the most famous actors of the time.

themselves to the moral constitution of the heart, would not dare to produce such a triumph as a matter of exultation. There, where men follow their natural impulses, they would not bear the odious maxims of a Machiavelian policy, whether applied to the attainment of monarchical or democratic tyranny. They would reject them on the modern, as they once did on the antient stage, where they could not bear even the hypothetical proposition of such wickedness in the mouth of a personated tyrant, though suitable to the character he sustained. No theatric audience in Athens would bear what has been borne, in the midst of the real tragedy of this triumphal day; a principal actor weighing, as it were, in scales hung in a shop of horrors, – so much actual crime, against so much contingent advantage, – and after putting in and out weights, declaring that the balance was on the side of the advantages. They would not bear to see the crimes of new democracy posted as in a ledger against the crimes of old despotism, and the book-keepers of politics finding democracy still in debt, but by no means unable or unwilling to pay the balance. In the theatre, the first intuitive glance, without any elaborate process of reasoning, would shew, that this method of political computation, would justify every extent of crime. They would see, that on these principles, even where the very worst acts were not perpetrated, it was owing rather to the fortune of the conspirators than to their parsimony in the expenditure of treachery and blood. They would soon see, that criminal means once tolerated are soon preferred. They present a shorter cut to the object than through the highway of the moral virtues. Justifying perfidy and murder for public benefit, public benefit would soon become the pretext, and perfidy and murder the end; until rapacity, malice, revenge, and fear more dreadful than revenge, could satiate their insatiable appetites. Such must be the consequences of losing, in the splendour of these triumphs of the rights of men, all natural sense of wrong and right.

[We have not … lost the generosity and dignity of thinking of the fourteenth century]

I almost venture to affirm, that not one in a hundred amongst us participates in the 'triumph' of the Revolution Society. If the king and queen of France, and their children, were to fall into our hands by the chance of war, in the most acrimonious of all hostilities (I deprecate such an event, I deprecate such hostility) they would be treated with another sort of triumphal entry into London. We formerly have had a king of France in that situation; you have read how he was treated by the victor in the field; and in what manner he was afterwards received in England.[41] Four hundred years have gone over us; but I believe we are not materially changed since that period. Thanks to our sullen resistance to innovation, thanks to the cold

---

41   John II (1319–64) was captured at Poitiers in 1356 and held in England with royal privileges.

sluggishness of our national character, we still bear the stamp of our forefathers. We have not (as I conceive) lost the generosity and dignity of thinking of the four-teenth century; nor as yet have we subtilized ourselves into savages. We are not the converts of Rousseau; we are not the disciples of Voltaire; Helvetius has made no progress amongst us.[42] Atheists are not our preachers; madmen are not our law-givers. We know that *we* have made no discoveries; and we think that no discoveries are to be made, in morality; nor many in the great principles of government, nor in the ideas of liberty, which were understood long before we were born, alto-gether as well as they will be after the grave has heaped its mould upon our pre-sumption, and the silent tomb shall have imposed its law on our pert loquacity. In England we have not yet been completely embowelled of our natural entrails; we still feel within us, and we cherish and cultivate, those inbred sentiments which are the faithful guardians, the active monitors of our duty, the true supporters of all liberal and manly morals. We have not been drawn and trussed, in order that we may be filled, like stuffed birds in a museum, with chaff and rags and paltry, blurred shreds of paper about the rights of man. We preserve the whole of our feelings still native and entire, unsophisticated by pedantry and infidelity. We have real hearts of flesh and blood beating in our bosoms. We fear God; we look up with awe to kings; with affection to parliaments; with duty to magistrates; with reverence to priests; and with respect to nobility.[43] Why? Because when such ideas are brought before our minds, it is *natural* to be so affected; because all other feelings are false and spurious, and tend to corrupt our minds, to vitiate our primary morals, to render us unfit for rational liberty; and, by teaching us a servile, licentious, and abandoned insolence, to be our low sport for a few holidays, to make us perfectly fit for, and justly deserving of slavery, through the whole course of our lives.

You see, Sir, that in this enlightened age I am bold enough to confess, that we are generally men of untaught feelings; that, instead of casting away all our old preju-dices, we cherish them to a very considerable degree, and to take more shame to ourselves, we cherish them because they are prejudices; and the longer they have lasted, and the more generally they have prevailed, the more we cherish them. We are afraid to put men to live and trade each on his own private stock of reason; because we suspect that this stock in each man is small, and that the individuals

---

[42] Major philosophical influences on the French Revolution: Jean-Jacques Rousseau (1712–78), whose *Social Contract* (1762) influenced the French Constitution and especially the radical Jacobins, and to whose primitivist *Discourse on Inequality* (1754) Burke alludes in the comment on 'savages'; Voltaire, pen name of François-Marie Arouet (1694–1778), philosopher, satirist, supporter of civil liberties, and deist critic of the Catholic church; Claude Adrien Helvétius (1715–71), whose *On the Mind* (1758) expounded the natural equality of all human understandings as well as utilitarian and atheist tenets.

[43] {The English are, I conceive, misrepresented in a Letter published in one of the papers, by a gentleman thought to be a dissenting minister. – When writing to Dr. Price, of the spirit which prevails at Paris, he says, 'The spirit of the people in this place has abolished all the proud *distinctions* which the *king* and *nobles* had usurped in their minds; whether they talk of *the king, the noble, or the priest*, their whole language is that of the most *enlight-ened and liberal amongst the English*.' If this gentleman means to confine the terms *enlightened and liberal* to one set of men in England, it may be true. It is not generally so.}

would do better to avail themselves of the general bank and capital of nations, and of ages. Many of our men of speculation, instead of exploding general prejudices, employ their sagacity to discover the latent wisdom which prevails in them. If they find what they seek, and they seldom fail, they think it more wise to continue the prejudice, with the reason involved, than to cast away the coat of prejudice, and to leave nothing but the naked reason; because prejudice, with its reason, has a motive to give action to that reason, and an affection which will give it permanence. Prejudice is of ready application in the emergency; it previously engages the mind in a steady course of wisdom and virtue, and does not leave the man hesitating in the moment of decision, sceptical, puzzled and unresolved. Prejudice renders a man's virtue his habit; and not a series of unconnected acts. Through just prejudice, his duty becomes a part of his nature.

[Society is indeed a contract]

To avoid therefore the evils of inconstancy and versatility,[44] ten thousand times worse than those of obstinacy and the blindest prejudice, we have consecrated the state, that no man should approach to look into its defects or corruptions but with due caution; that he should never dream of beginning its reformation by its subversion; that he should approach to the faults of the state as to the wounds of a father, with pious awe and trembling sollicitude. By this wise prejudice we are taught to look with horror on those children of their country who are prompt rashly to hack that aged parent in pieces, and put him into the kettle of magicians, in hopes that by their poisonous weeds, and wild incantations, they may regenerate the paternal constitution and renovate their father's life.

Society is indeed a contract. Subordinate contracts for objects of mere occasional interest may be dissolved at pleasure – but the state ought not to be considered as nothing better than a partnership agreement in a trade of pepper and coffee, callico or tobacco, or some other such low concern, to be taken up for a little temporary interest, and to be dissolved by the fancy of the parties. It is to be looked on with other reverence; because it is not a partnership in things subservient only to the gross animal existence of a temporary and perishable nature. It is a partnership in all science; a partnership in all art; a partnership in every virtue, and in all perfection. As the ends of such a partnership cannot be obtained in many generations, it becomes a partnership not only between those who are living, but between those who are living, those who are dead, and those who are to be born.[45] Each contract of each particular state is but a clause in the great primæval contract of eternal society, linking the lower with the higher natures, connecting the visible

---

[44] Changeable or fickle conduct.
[45] See Paine, *Rights of Man*, Part I; p. 71 below.

and invisible world, according to a fixed compact sanctioned by the inviolable oath which holds all physical and all moral natures, each in their appointed place. This law is not subject to the will of those, who by an obligation above them, and infinitely superior, are bound to submit their will to that law. The municipal corporations of that universal kingdom are not morally at liberty at their pleasure, and on their speculations of a contingent improvement, wholly to separate and tear asunder the bands of their subordinate community, and to dissolve it into an unsocial, uncivil, unconnected chaos of elementary principles. It is the first and supreme necessity only, a necessity that is not chosen but chooses, a necessity paramount to deliberation, that admits no discussion, and demands no evidence, which alone can justify a resort to anarchy. This necessity is no exception to the rule; because this necessity itself is a part too of that moral and physical disposition of things to which man must be obedient by consent or force; but if that which is only submission to necessity should be made the object of choice, the law is broken, nature is disobeyed, and the rebellious are outlawed, cast forth, and exiled, from this world of reason, and order, and peace, and virtue, and fruitful penitence, into the antagonist world of madness, discord, vice, confusion, and unavailing sorrow.

[The political Men of Letters]

Along with the monied interest, a new description of men had grown up, with whom that interest soon formed a close and marked union; I mean the political Men of Letters. Men of Letters, fond of distinguishing themselves, are rarely averse to innovation. Since the decline of the life and greatness of Lewis the XIVth,[46] they were not so much cultivated either by him, or by the regent,[47] or the successors to the crown; nor were they engaged to the court by favours and emoluments so systematically as during the splendid period of that ostentatious and not impolitic reign. What they lost in the old court protection they endeavoured to make up by joining in a sort of incorporation of their own; to which the two academies of France,[48] and afterwards the vast undertaking of the Encyclopædia,[49] carried on by a society of these gentlemen, did not a little contribute.

The literary cabal had some years ago formed something like a regular plan for the destruction of the Christian religion. This object they pursued with a degree of zeal which hitherto had been discovered only in the propagators of

---

[46] King Louis XIV of France (reigned 1643–1715).

[47] Philippe II, Duke d'Orléans (1674–1723, regent 1715–23).

[48] Two from the Académie Française, the Académie des Beaux-Arts, the Académies des Inscriptions et Belles-Lettres, the Académie des Sciences, and the Académie Royale de Musique.

[49] The *Encyclopédie* (1751–72), edited by Denis Diderot and Jean d'Alembert, focused on the achievements of human reason, with a radical and sceptical emphasis. It featured articles by major Enlightenment figures, including Diderot, Rousseau, and Voltaire.

some system of piety. They were possessed with a spirit of proselytism in the most fanatical degree; and from thence, by an easy progress, with the spirit of persecution according to their means.[50] What was not to be done towards their great end by any direct or immediate act, might be wrought by a longer process through the medium of opinion. To command that opinion, the first step is to establish a dominion over those who direct it. They contrived to possess themselves, with great method and perseverance, of all the avenues to literary fame. Many of them indeed stood high in the ranks of literature and science. The world had done them justice; and in favour of general talents forgave the evil tendency of their peculiar principles. This was true liberality; which they returned by endeavouring to confine the reputation of sense, learning, and taste to themselves or their followers. I will venture to say that this narrow, exclusive spirit has not been less prejudicial to literature and to taste, than to morals and true philosophy. These Atheistical fathers have a bigotry of their own; and they have learned to talk against monks with the spirit of a monk. But in some things they are men of the world. The resources of intrigue are called in to supply the defects of argument and wit. To this system of literary monopoly was joined an unremitting industry to blacken and discredit in every way, and by every means, all those who did not hold to their faction. To those who have observed the spirit of their conduct, it has long been clear that nothing was wanted but the power of carrying the intolerance of the tongue and of the pen into a persecution which would strike at property, liberty, and life.

The desultory and faint persecution carried on against them, more from compliance with form and decency than with serious resentment, neither weakened their strength, nor relaxed their efforts.[51] The issue of the whole was, that what with opposition, and what with success, a violent and malignant zeal, of a kind hitherto unknown in the world, had taken an entire possession of their minds, and rendered their whole conversation, which otherwise would have been pleasing and instructive, perfectly disgusting. A spirit of cabal, intrigue, and proselytism, pervaded all their thoughts, words, and actions. And as controversial zeal soon turns its thoughts on force, they began to insinuate themselves into a correspondence with foreign princes; in hopes, through their authority, which at first they flattered, they might bring about the changes they had in view. To them it was indifferent whether these changes were to be accomplished by the thunderbolt of despotism, or by the earthquake of popular commotion. The correspondence between this cabal, and the late king of Prussia, will throw no small light upon the spirit of all

---

[50]   {This (down to the end of the first sentence in the next paragraph) and some other parts here and there, were inserted, on his reading the manuscript, by my lost son.} Added in 1803 edition; the son is Richard Burke (1758–94).

[51]   Diderot was imprisoned for the materialism of his *Letter on the Blind* (1749). Voltaire was sent to the Bastille for 11 months in 1717 and imprisoned again in 1725. In the furore over his *Philosophical Letters* (1733), he only escaped by being out of Paris. Helvétius had to issue retractions of his *On Mind* (1758), and a number of Rousseau's works, including *Émile* and *The Social Contract*, were condemned by French and Genevan authorities.

their proceedings.[52] For the same purpose for which they intrigued with princes, they cultivated, in a distinguished manner, the monied interest of France; and partly through the means furnished by those whose peculiar offices gave them the most extensive and certain means of communication, they carefully occupied all the avenues to opinion.

Writers, especially when they act in a body, and with one direction, have great influence on the public mind; the alliance therefore of these writers with the monied interest had no small effect in removing the popular odium and envy which attended that species of wealth. These writers, like the propagators of all novelties, pretended to a great zeal for the poor, and the lower orders, whilst in their satires they rendered hateful, by every exaggeration, the faults of courts, of nobility, and of priesthood. They became a sort of demagogues. They served as a link to unite, in favour of one object, obnoxious wealth to restless and desperate poverty.

[We do not draw the moral lessons we might from history]

Nobility is a graceful ornament to the civil order. It is the Corinthian capital[53] of polished society. *Omnes boni nobilitati semper favemus*, was the saying of a wise and good man.[54] It is indeed one sign of a liberal and benevolent mind to incline to it with some sort of partial propensity. He feels no ennobling principle in his own heart who wishes to level all the artificial institutions which have been adopted for giving a body to opinion, and permanence to fugitive esteem. It is a sour, malignant, envious disposition, without taste for the reality or for any image or representation of virtue, that sees with joy the unmerited fall of what had long flourished in splendour and in honour. I do not like to see anything destroyed; any void produced in society; any ruin on the face of the land. It was therefore with no disappointment or dissatisfaction, that my inquiries and observation did not present to me any incorrigible vices in the noblesse of France, or any abuse which could not be removed by a reform very short of abolition. Your noblesse did not deserve punishment; but to degrade is to punish.

It was with the same satisfaction I found that the result of my enquiry concerning your clergy was not dissimilar. It is no soothing news to my ears, that great bodies of men are incurably corrupt. It is not with much credulity I listen to any, when they speak evil of those whom they are going to plunder. I rather suspect that vices are feigned or exaggerated, when profit is looked for in their punishment. An enemy is a bad witness: a robber is a worse. Vices and abuses there were

---

[52]   Frederick II (1712–86), King of Prussia (1740–86). 'Frederick the Great' advocated 'enlightened despotism' and was a correspondent of and a host to Voltaire, d'Alembert, and La Mettrie.
[53]   Corinthian: one of the three major orders of classical architecture. Corinthian capitals are the most elaborate form of pillar tops.
[54]   Cicero, *Pro Sestio* IX.xxi: 'All virtuous men always look with favour on noble birth.'

undoubtedly in that order, and must be. It was an old establishment, and not frequently revised. But I saw no crimes in the individuals that merited confiscation of
their substance, nor those cruel insults and degradations, and that unnatural persecution which have been substituted in the place of meliorating regulation.

If there had been any just cause for this new religious persecution, the atheistic
libellers, who act as trumpeters to animate the populace to plunder, do not love any-
body so much as not to dwell with complacence on the vices of the existing clergy.
This they have not done. They find themselves obliged to rake into the histories of
former ages (which they have ransacked with a malignant and profligate industry) for
every instance of oppression and persecution which has been made by that body or
in its favour, in order to justify, upon very iniquitous, because very illogical principles
of retaliation, their own persecutions, and their own cruelties. After destroying all
other genealogies and family distinctions, they invent a sort of pedigree of crimes. It
is not very just to chastise men for the offences of their natural ancestors; but to take
the fiction of ancestry in a corporate succession, as a ground for punishing men who
have no relation to guilty acts, except in names and general descriptions, is a sort of
refinement in injustice belonging to the philosophy of this enlightened age. The
assembly punishes men, many, if not most, of whom abhor the violent conduct of
ecclesiastics in former times as much as their present persecutors can do, and who
would be as loud and as strong in the expression of that sense, if they were not well
aware of the purposes for which all this declamation is employed.

Corporate bodies are immortal for the good of the members, but not for their
punishment. Nations themselves are such corporations. As well might we in
England think of waging inexpiable war upon all Frenchmen for the evils which
they have brought upon us in the several periods of our mutual hostilities. You
might, on your part, think yourselves justified in falling upon all Englishmen on
account of the unparalleled calamities brought upon the people of France by the
unjust invasions of our Henries and our Edwards.[55] Indeed, we should be mutually
justified in this exterminatory war upon each other, full as much as you are in the
unprovoked persecution of your present countrymen, on account of the conduct
of men of the same name in other times.

We do not draw the moral lessons we might from history. On the contrary,
without care it may be used to vitiate our minds and to destroy our happiness. In
history a great volume is unrolled for our instruction, drawing the materials of
future wisdom from the past errors and infirmities of mankind. It may, in the perversion, serve for a magazine, furnishing offensive and defensive weapons for parties in church and state, and supplying the means of keeping alive, or reviving
dissensions and animosities, and adding fuel to civil fury. History consists, for the
greater part, of the miseries brought upon the world by pride, ambition, avarice,

---

[55]   Burke refers to the Hundred Years War (1337–1453), a series of conflicts caused by English claims to the
French throne. The first phase involved Edward III's invasion of France; the later phases were continued by Henry
V and Henry VI.

revenge, lust, sedition, hypocrisy, ungoverned zeal, and all the train of disorderly appetites which shake the public with the same

> — troublous storms that toss
> The private state, and render life unsweet.[56]

These vices are the *causes* of those storms. Religion, morals, laws, prerogatives, privileges, liberties, rights of men, are the *pretexts*. The pretexts are always found in some specious appearance of a real good. You would not secure men from tyranny and sedition, by rooting out of the mind the principles to which these fraudulent pretexts apply? If you did, you would root out everything that is valuable in the human breast. As these are the pretexts, so the ordinary actors and instruments in great public evils are kings, priests, magistrates, senates, parliaments, national assemblies, judges, and captains. You would not cure the evil by resolving, that there should be no more monarchs, nor ministers of state, nor of the gospel; no interpreters of law; no general officers; no public councils. You might change the names. The things in some shape must remain. A certain *quantum* of power must always exist in the community, in some hands, and under some appellation. Wise men will apply their remedies to vices, not to names; to the causes of evil which are permanent, not to the occasional organs by which they act, and the transitory modes in which they appear. Otherwise you will be wise historically, a fool in practice. Seldom have two ages the same fashion in their pretexts and the same modes of mischief. Wickedness is a little more inventive. Whilst you are discussing fashion, the fashion is gone by. The very same vice assumes a new body. The spirit transmigrates; and, far from losing its principle of life by the change of its appearance, it is renovated in its new organs with the fresh vigour of a juvenile activity. It walks abroad; it continues its ravages; whilst you are gibbeting the carcass, or demolishing the tomb. You are terrifying yourselves with ghosts and apparitions, whilst your house is the haunt of robbers. It is thus with all those, who, attending only to the shell and husk of history, think they are waging war with intolerance, pride, and cruelty, whilst, under colour of abhorring the ill principles of antiquated parties, they are authorizing and feeding the same odious vices in different factions, and perhaps in worse.

[By hating vices too much, they come to love men too little]

To proceed in this manner, that is, to proceed with a presiding principle, and a prolific energy, is with me the criterion of profound wisdom. What your politicians think the marks of a bold, hardy genius, are only proofs of a deplorable want of ability. By their violent haste, and their defiance of the process of nature, they are delivered

---

[56] Edmund Spenser, *The Faerie Queene* (1589–96), II.vii.14.

over blindly to every projector and adventurer, to every alchymist and empiric.[57] They despair of turning to account anything that is common. Diet is nothing in their system of remedy. The worst of it is, that this their despair of curing common distempers by regular methods, arises not only from defect of comprehension, but, I fear, from some malignity of disposition. Your legislators seem to have taken their opinions of all professions, ranks, and offices, from the declamations and buffooneries of satirists; who would themselves be astonished if they were held to the letter of their own descriptions. By listening only to these, your leaders regard all things only on the side of their vices and faults, and view those vices and faults under every colour of exaggeration. It is undoubtedly true, though it may seem paradoxical; but in general, those who are habitually employed in finding and displaying faults, are unqualified for the work of reformation: because their minds are not only unfurnished with patterns of the fair and good, but by habit they come to take no delight in the contemplation of those things. By hating vices too much, they come to love men too little. It is therefore not wonderful, that they should be indisposed and unable to serve them. From hence arises the complexional disposition of some of your guides to pull every thing in pieces. At this malicious game they display the whole of their *quadrimanous*[58] activity. As to the rest, the paradoxes of eloquent writers, brought forth purely as a sport of fancy, to try their talents, to rouze attention, and excite surprise, are taken up by these gentlemen, not in the spirit of the original authors, as means of cultivating their taste and improving their style. These paradoxes become with them serious grounds of action, upon which they proceed in regulating the most important concerns of the state. Cicero ludicrously describes Cato as endeavouring to act in the commonwealth upon the school paradoxes which exercised the wits of the junior students in the stoic philosophy.[59] If this was true of Cato, these gentlemen copy after him in the manner of some persons who lived about his time – *pede nudo Catonem*.[60] Mr. Hume told me that he had from Rousseau himself the secret of his principles of composition.[61] That acute, though eccentric, observer had perceived, that to strike and interest the public, the marvellous must be produced; that the marvellous of the heathen mythology had long since lost its effect; that the giants, magicians, fairies, and heroes of romance which succeeded, had exhausted the portion of credulity which belonged to their age; that now nothing was left to a writer but that species of the marvellous, which might still be produced, and with as great an effect as ever, though in another way; that is, the marvellous in life, in manners, in characters, and in extraordinary situations, giving

---

[57] At this period, 'empiricism' denoted unscientific and superstitious quackery.
[58] Using four hands; like an ape or monkey.
[59] In *Pro Murena*, xxix–xxxi.
[60] That is, they would copy 'Cato in being barefooted', an allusion to Horace's point at *Epistles* I.xix.12–14: 'What? Suppose a man imitates Cato in his rough and stern-faced manner, in being barefooted, and down to copying the weaver of his scanty toga: would he reproduce Cato's virtues and character?'
[61] David Hume (1711–76), Scottish philosopher and historian. In 1766 he met Rousseau in Paris and brought him to England for refuge, but their relationship became strained and ended in acrimony.

rise to new and unlooked-for strokes in politics and morals. I believe, that were Rousseau alive, and in one of his lucid intervals, he would be shocked at the practical phrenzy of his scholars, who in their paradoxes are servile imitators; and even in their incredulity discover an implicit faith.

[Old establishments … are the results of various necessities and expediencies]

Old establishments are tried by their effects. If the people are happy, united, wealthy, and powerful, we presume the rest. We conclude that to be good from whence good is derived. In old establishments various correctives have been found for their aberrations from theory. Indeed they are the results of various necessities and expediencies. They are not often constructed after any theory; theories are rather drawn from them. In them we often see the end best obtained, where the means seem not perfectly reconcileable to what we may fancy was the original scheme. The means taught by experience may be better suited to political ends than those contrived in the original project. They again re-act upon the primitive constitution, and sometimes improve the design itself from which they seem to have departed. I think all this might be curiously exemplified in the British constitution. At worst, the errors and deviations of every kind in reckoning are found and computed, and the ship proceeds in her course. This is the case of old establishments; but in a new and merely theoretic system, it is expected that every contrivance shall appear, on the face of it, to answer its end; especially where the projectors are no way embarrassed with an endeavour to accommodate the new building to an old one, either in the walls or on the foundations.

[Some popular general … shall draw the eyes of all men upon himself]

It is besides to be considered, whether an assembly like yours, even supposing that it was in possession of another sort of organ through which its orders were to pass, is fit for promoting the obedience and discipline of an army. It is known, that armies have hitherto yielded a very precarious and uncertain obedience to any senate, or popular authority; and they will least of all yield it to an assembly which is to have only a continuance of two years.[62] The officers must totally lose the

---

[62]   The National Assembly convened from June 1789 to September 1791 to debate and establish the new constitution, and was superseded by the Legislative Assembly in October 1791.

characteristic disposition of military men, if they see with perfect submission and due admiration, the dominion of pleaders; especially when they find, that they have a new court to pay to an endless succession of those pleaders, whose military policy, and the genius of whose command (if they should have any) must be as uncertain as their duration is transient. In the weakness of one kind of authority, and in the fluctuation of all, the officers of an army will remain for some time mutinous and full of faction, until some popular general, who understands the art of conciliating the soldiery, and who possesses the true spirit of command, shall draw the eyes of all men upon himself. Armies will obey him on his personal account. There is no other way of securing military obedience in this state of things. But the moment in which that event shall happen, the person who really commands the army is your master; the master (that is little) of your king, the master of your assembly, the master of your whole republic.

3

Mary Wollstonecraft

A Vindication of the Rights of Men,
in a Letter to the Right Honourable
Edmund Burke

2nd edn (London: J. Johnson, 1792)

Mary Wollstonecraft (1759–97) was the eldest of seven children born to an Irish mother and to a volatile, often violent, English father. This unstable background meant that, from early on in life, she had to fend for herself and assume much of the responsibility for her siblings. During her teenage years, she developed a passionate friendship with a young woman, Fanny Blood, whose family she also ended up trying to support. Wollstonecraft's first attempt at economic independence was running a school for girls in Islington, north London, soon moved to nearby Newington Green. Fanny and Wollestonecraft's sisters were also involved. The arrangement was broken up when Fanny accepted a marriage proposal from a British merchant in Lisbon and sailed for Portugal. Wollstonecraft followed her to help with the birth of the first child, but Fanny passed away soon afterwards. When Wollstonecraft returned to London, she found her sisters quarrelling over the management of the school. Economic necessity forced her to take up work in Ireland as a governess for Lady Kingsborough, but she had to return to London in 1787 after being dismissed, apparently for encouraging the eldest daughter to rebel against her parents. Although born into the established church, when Wollstonecraft had moved to Newington Green, a stronghold for religious dissenters, she came into contact with progressive nonconformist thinkers, particularly Richard Price. Through Price and other dissenting contacts, Wollstonecraft met the bookseller Joseph Johnson, who published her early writings – mainly concerned with the education of

Romanticism and Revolution: A Reader.
Edited by Jon Mee and David Fallon.   © 2011 Blackwell Publishing Ltd.

women – *Thoughts on the Education of Daughters* (1787), *Original Stories from Real Life* (1788), and *The Female Reader* (1789). After she was dismissed by Lady Kingsborough, Wollstonecraft was supported by Johnson with work translating and reviewing for his new journal *The Analytical Review*. She also produced *Mary: A Fiction* (1788), a novel partly drawing on her own experience in Ireland. Events in France in 1789, however, transformed Wollstonecraft's reputation and ambitions. Although she remained fascinated by educational issues, she turned her attention towards political events. Most of the writers of Johnson's circle welcomed the French Revolution as a major change in the course of human affairs. Burke's *Reflections* was on sale from 1 November 1790. Wollstonecraft's reaction was available in Johnson's shop before the end of the same month. What distinguishes it as a political answer to Burke, apart from the speed at which it was written, is the way it immediately pitches on the question of morals as the key to Burke's thinking about the French Revolution. The relation between the ways in which members of a society conducted their domestic and other kind of relationships defined for Burke the nature of that society's politics. Wollstonecraft immediately attacked Burke on the central role of feeling in his account of social cohesion and questioned whether there might not be a more natural or rational way to understand its operation in society than his emotional veneration of the traditional order of Church and State.

Advertisement

Mr. Burke's Reflections on the French Revolution first engaged my attention as the transient topic of the day; and reading it more for amusement than information, my indignation was roused by the sophistical arguments, that every moment crossed me, in the questionable shape of natural feelings and common sense.

Many pages of the following letter were the effusions of the moment; but, swelling imperceptibly to a considerable size, the idea was suggested of publishing a short vindication of *the Rights of Men*.

Not having leisure or patience to follow this desultory writer through all the devious tracks in which his fancy has started fresh game, I have confined my strictures, in a great measure, to the grand principles at which he has levelled many ingenious arguments in a very specious garb.

[I have not yet learned to twist my periods,
nor ... to disguise my sentiments]

Sir,

It is not necessary, with courtly insincerity, to apologise to you for thus intruding on your precious time, not to profess that I think it an honour to discuss an important subject with a man whose literary abilities have raised him to notice in the state. I have not yet learned to twist my periods, nor, in the equivocal idiom of politeness,[1] to disguise my sentiments, and imply what I should be afraid to utter: if, therefore, in the course of this epistle, I chance to express contempt, and even indignation, with some emphasis, I beseech you to believe that it is not a flight of fancy; for truth, in morals, has ever appeared to me the essence of the sublime; and, in taste, simplicity the only criterion of the beautiful.[2] But I war not with an individual when I contend for the *rights of men* and the liberty of reason. You see I do not condescend to cull my words to avoid the invidious phrase, nor shall I be prevented from giving a manly definition[3] of it, by the flimsy ridicule which a lively fancy has interwoven with the present acceptation of the term. Reverencing the rights of humanity, I shall dare to assert them; not intimidated by the horse laugh that you have raised, or waiting till time has wiped away the compassionate tears which you have elaborately laboured to excite.

[I perceive ... that you have a mortal antipathy to reason]

And though some dry reasoner might whisper that the arguments were superficial, and should even add, that the feelings which are thus ostentatiously displayed are often the cold declamation of the head, and not the effusions of the heart – what will these shrewd remarks avail, when the witty arguments and ornamental feelings are on a level with the comprehension of the fashionable world, and a book is found very amusing? Even the Ladies, Sir, may repeat your sprightly sallies, and retail in theatrical attitudes many of your sentimental

---

[1] 'Politeness' was a crucial concept in the eighteenth century, associated especially with the refinements brought by commercial society and the easy or agreeable manner of interaction between its citizens. By the end of the century, however, politeness was increasingly open to attacks from evangelicals and radicals as a species of hypocrisy privileging manners over sincerity. See Jenny Davidson, *Hypocrisy and the Politics of Politeness* (Cambridge: Cambridge University Press, 2004), pp. 76–80 on Wollstonecraft in this regard.

[2] Wollstonecraft alludes to Burke's *Philosophical Enquiry* (see above, p. 19). She challenges his definitions repeatedly in both *Vindications*.

[3] Wollstonecraft accepts the gendering of terms like 'virtue' and 'truth', but insists that they are not biologically determined; she emphasises her own ability to reason upon the 'manly' issues of truth and justice.

exclamations. Sensibility is the *manie*[4] of the day, and compassion the virtue which is to cover a multitude of vices, whilst justice is left to mourn in sullen silence, and balance truth in vain.

In life, an honest man with a confined understanding is frequently the slave of his habits and the dupe of his feelings, whilst the man with a clearer head and colder heart makes the passions of others bend to his interest; but truly sublime is the character that acts from principle, and governs the inferior springs of activity without slackening their vigour; whose feelings give vital heat to his resolves, but never hurry him into feverish eccentricities.

However, as you have informed us that respect chills love, it is natural to con-clude, that all your pretty flights arise from your pampered sensibility; and that, vain of this fancied pre-eminence of organs, you foster every emotion till the fumes, mounting to your brain, dispel the sober suggestions of reason. It is not in this view surprising, that when you should argue you become impassioned, and that reflection inflames your imagination, instead of enlightening your understanding.

Quitting now the flowers of rhetoric, let us, Sir, reason together; and, believe me, I should not have meddled with these troubled waters, in order to point out your inconsistencies, if your wit had not burnished up some rusty, baneful opin-ions, and swelled the shallow current of ridicule till it resembled the flow of reason, and presumed to be the test of truth.

I shall not attempt to follow you through 'horse-way and foot-path';[5] but, attacking the foundation of your opinions, I shall leave the superstructure to find a centre of gravity on which it may lean till some strong blast puffs it into the air; or your teeming fancy, which the ripening judgment of sixty years has not tamed, produces another Chinese erection,[6] to stare, at every turn, the plain country people in the face, who bluntly call such an airy edifice – a folly.

The birthright of man, to give you, Sir, a short definition of this disputed right, is such a degree of liberty, civil and religious, as is compatible with the liberty of every other individual with whom he is united in a social compact,[7] and the contin-ued existence of that compact.

---

[4]   'Sensibility' was another key term in eighteenth-century writing on taste and culture. It described the suscep-tibility to feeling, increasingly associated with the physiology of nerves developed earlier in the century by medi-cal science. From being identified with the virtues of sympathy and benevolence in writers of the Scottish Enlightenment, it was taken up by novelists and poets as a fashionable trait. For Wollstonecraft and many others it was potentially a form of self-indulgence, a fad or mania ('*manie*') for feeling in itself, especially for young women encouraged to feed their sensitive nerves on a diet of novels with fainting heroines and gallant heroes.

[5]   *King Lear*, IV.i.55.

[6]   Burke was 60 in 1790. There was a fashion for Chinese pagodas in the 1770s and 1780s, but Wollstonecraft might be having a sly joke at Burke's passionate defence of the *ancien régime*, especially at his gallantry towards the French queen.

[7]   In his *Two Treatises of Government* (1690), II.§97, John Locke had written of the 'original Compact, whereby [each man] with others incorporates into one Society'.

Liberty, in this simple, unsophisticated sense, I acknowledge, is a fair idea that has never yet received a form in the various governments that have been established on our beauteous globe; the demon of property[8] has ever been at hand to encroach on the sacred rights of men, and to fence round with awful pomp laws that war with justice. But that it results from the eternal foundation of right – from immutable truth – who will presume to deny, that pretends to rationality – if reason has led them to build their morality[9] and religion on an everlasting foundation – the attributes of God?

I glow with indignation when I attempt, methodically, to unravel your slav-ish paradoxes, in which I can find no fixed first principle to refute; I shall not, therefore, condescend to shew where you affirm in one page what you deny in another; and how frequently you draw conclusions without any previous premises: – it would be something like cowardice to fight with a man who had never exercised the weapons with which his opponent chose to combat, and irksome to refute sentence after sentence in which the latent spirit of tyranny appeared.

I perceive, from the whole tenor of your Reflections, that you have a mortal antipathy to reason; but, if there is any thing like argument, or first principles, in your wild declamation, behold the result: – that we are to reverence the rust of antiquity, and term the unnatural customs, which ignorance and mistaken self-interest have consolidated, the sage fruit of experience: nay, that, if we do discover some errors, our *feelings* should lead us to excuse, with blind love, or unprincipled filial affection, the venerable vestiges of ancient days. These are gothic[10] notions of beauty – the ivy is beautiful, but, when it insidiously destroys the trunk from which it receives support, who would not grub it up?

Further, that we ought cautiously to remain for ever in frozen inactivity, because a thaw, whilst it nourishes the soil, spreads a temporary inundation; and the fear of risking any personal present convenience should prevent a struggle for the most estimable advantages. This is sound reasoning, I grant, in the mouth of the rich and short-sighted.

Yes, Sir, the strong gained riches, the few have sacrificed the many to their vices; and, to be able to pamper their appetites, and supinely exist without exercising mind or body, they have ceased to be men. – Lost to the relish of true pleasure, such beings would, indeed, deserve compassion, if injustice was not softened by

---

[8] Jean-Jacques Rousseau's *Discourse on Inequality* (1754) represented property as a cursed fall from the happy equality of the state of nature. Wollstonecraft was deeply indebted to Rousseau's ideas, but in *Vindication of the Rights of Woman* fiercely attacks the gendered assumptions of his philosophy of education.

[9] {As religion is included in my idea of morality, I should not have mentioned the term without specifying all the simple ideas which that comprehensive word generalizes; but as the charge of atheism has been very freely banded about in the letter I am considering, I wish to guard against misrepresentation.}

[10] Gothic architecture and literature became fashionable in the late eighteenth century. The Gothic was associ-ated with medieval values, obscurity, and superstition (and the delight of a modern reader in these qualities). Wollstonecraft represents Burke's veneration of Christian Europe as the inappropriate application of such a taste to political matters, which ought to be judged by questions of reason and justice.

the tyrant's plea – necessity;[11] if prescription was not raised as an immortal bound-ary against innovation. Their minds, in fact, instead of being cultivated, have been so warped by education, that it may require some ages to bring them back to nature, and enable them to see their true interest, with that degree of conviction which is necessary to influence their conduct.

The civilization which has taken place in Europe has been very partial, and, like every custom that an arbitrary point of honour has established, refines the man-ners at the expence of morals, by making sentiments and opinions current in con-versation that have no root in the heart, or weight in the cooler resolves of the mind. – And what has stopped its progress? – hereditary property – hereditary honours. The man has been changed into an artificial monster by the station in which he was born, and the consequent homage that benumbed his faculties like the torpedo's touch;[12] – or a being, with a capacity of reasoning, would not have failed to discover, as his faculties unfolded, that true happiness arose from the friendship and intimacy which can only be enjoyed by equals; and that charity is not a condescending distribution of alms, but an intercourse of good offices and mutual benefits, founded on respect for justice and humanity.

Governed by these principles, the poor wretch, whose *inelegant* distress extorted from a mixed feeling of disgust and animal sympathy present relief, would have been considered as a man, whose misery demanded a part of his birthright, sup-posing him to be industrious; but should his vices have reduced him to poverty, he could only have addressed his fellow-men as weak beings, subject to like passions, who ought to forgive, because they expect to be forgiven, for suffering the impulse of the moment to silence the suggestions of conscience, or reason, which you will; for, in my view of things, they are synonymous terms.

Will Mr. Burke be at the trouble to inform us, how far we are to go back to dis-cover the rights of men, since the light of reason is such a fallacious guide that none but fools trust to its cold investigation?

In the infancy of society, confining our view to our own country, customs were established by the lawless power of an ambitious individual; or a weak prince was obliged to comply with every demand of the licentious barbarous insurgents, who disputed his authority with irrefragable arguments at the point of their swords; or the more specious requests of the Parliament, who only allowed him conditional supplies.

Are these the venerable pillars of our constitution? And is Magna Charta[13] to rest for its chief support on a former grant, which reverts to another, till chaos becomes the base of the mighty structure – or we cannot tell what? – for coher-ence, without some pervading principle of order, is a solecism.

---

[11]   *Paradise Lost*, IV.393–4: 'So spake the Fiend, and with necessity, / The tyrant's plea, excused his devilish deed.'
[12]   Torpedoes or electric rays are fish that can numb by delivering an electric shock.
[13]   See above, p. 26, n. 13.

[The champion of property, the adorer of the golden image which power has set up]

A Roman Catholic, it is true, enlightened by the reformation, might, with singular propriety, celebrate the epoch that preceded it, to turn our thoughts from former atrocious enormities; but a Protestant must acknowledge that this faint dawn of liberty only made the subsiding darkness more visible; and that the boasted virtues of that century all bear the stamp of stupid pride and headstrong barbarism.[14] Civility was then called condescension, and ostentatious almsgiving humanity; and men were content to borrow their virtues, or, to speak with more propriety, their consequence, from posterity, rather than undertake the arduous task of acquiring it for themselves.

The imperfection of all modern governments must, without waiting to repeat the trite remark, that all human institutions are unavoidably imperfect, in a great measure have arisen from this simple circumstance, that the constitution, if such an heterogeneous mass deserve that name, was settled in the dark days of ignorance, when the minds of men were shackled by the grossest prejudices and most immoral superstition. And do you, Sir, a sagacious philosopher, recommend night as the fittest time to analyze a ray of light?

Are we to seek for the rights of men in the ages when a few marks were the only penalty imposed for the life of a man, and death for death when the property of the rich was touched? when – I blush to discover the depravity of our nature – when a deer was killed! Are these the laws that it is natural to love, and sacrilegious to invade? – Were the rights of men understood when the law authorized or tolerated murder? – or is power and right the same in your creed?

But in fact all your declamation leads so directly to this conclusion, that I beseech you to ask your own heart, when you call yourself a friend of liberty, whether it would not be more consistent to style yourself the champion of property, the adorer of the golden image which power has set up? – And, when you are examining your heart, if it would not be too much like mathematical drudgery, to which a fine imagination very reluctantly stoops, enquire further, how it is consistent with the vulgar notions of honesty, and the foundation of morality – truth; for a man to boast of his virtue and independence, when he cannot forget that he is at the moment enjoying the wages of falsehood;[15] and that, in a skulking, unmanly way, he has secured himself a pension of fifteen hundred pounds per annum on

---

[14]   Although raised a Protestant, Burke was regularly attacked as a crypto-Catholic. See, for instance, *The Knight of the Woeful Countenance* – a satire shown on the cover of the present book, which is one out of many representing him as a quixotic inquisitor riding to the defence of the Papacy.

[15]   {See Mr. Burke's Bills for œconomical reform.} Burke's speech to the House of Commons in 1780 calling for economic reform had exhorted the House to vote on the basis of virtue and independence rather than self-interest. When Wollstonecraft was writing, Burke was not yet in receipt of the government pension he was granted later.

the Irish establishment? Do honest men, Sir, for I am not rising to the refined principle of honour, ever receive the reward of their public services, or secret assistance, in the name of *another*?

But to return from a digression which you will more perfectly understand than any of my readers – on what principle you, Sir, can justify the reformation, which tore up by the roots an old establishment, I cannot guess – but, I beg your pardon, perhaps you do not wish to justify it – and have some mental reservation to excuse you, to yourself, for not openly avowing your reverence. Or, to go further back; – had you been a Jew – you would have joined in the cry, crucify him! – crucify him![16] The promulgator of a new doctrine, and the violator of old laws and customs, that not melting, like ours, into darkness and ignorance, rested on Divine authority, must have been a dangerous innovator, in your eyes, particularly if you had not been informed that the Carpenter's Son was of the stock and lineage of David. But there is no end to the arguments which might be deduced to combat such palpable absurdities, by shewing the manifest inconsistencies which are necessarily involved in a direful train of false opinions.

It is necessary emphatically to repeat, that there are rights which men inherit at their birth, as rational creatures, who were raised above the brute creation by their improvable faculties; and that, in receiving these, not from their forefathers but from God, prescription can never undermine natural rights.

A father may dissipate his property without his child having any right to complain; – but should he attempt to sell him for a slave, or fetter him with laws contrary to reason; nature, in enabling him to discern good from evil, teaches him to break the ignoble chain, and not to believe that bread becomes flesh, and wine blood, because his parents swallowed the Eucharist with this blind persuasion.

There is no end to this implicit submission to authority – some where it must stop, or we return to barbarism; and the capacity of improvement, which gives us a natural sceptre on earth, is a cheat, an ignis-fatuus,[17] that leads us from inviting meadows into bogs and dung-hills. And if it be allowed that many of the precautions, with which any alteration was made, in our government, were prudent, it rather proves its weakness than substantiates an opinion of the soundness of the stamina, or the excellence of the constitution.

But on what principle Mr. Burke could defend American independence, I cannot conceive;[18] for the whole tenor of his plausible arguments settles slavery on an everlasting foundation. Allowing his servile reverence for antiquity, and prudent attention to self-interest, to have the force which he insists on, the slave

---

[16] Mark 15: 13, Luke 23: 21. The attack on Burke as an inquisitor is extended to imagining him as one of those who condemned Christ as a heretic.
[17] Latin phrase (literally 'foolish fire') for the phosphorescent light produced at night over marshland, known in English as 'will-o'-the-wisp' or 'friar's lantern'; metaphor for any misleading idea or thing.
[18] Burke's *Speech on Conciliation with the America* (1775) had taken the view that the American colonists were asserting traditional British liberties in their struggle against the Crown. Many others found it difficult to reconcile Burke's reputation as a defender of liberty with his attitude towards the French Revolution.

trade ought never to be abolished;[19] and, because our ignorant forefathers, not understanding the native dignity of man, sanctioned a traffic that outrages every suggestion of reason and religion, we are to submit to the inhuman custom, and term an atrocious insult to humanity the love of our country, and a proper submission to the laws by which our property is secured. – Security of property! Behold, in a few words, the definition of English liberty. And to this selfish principle every nobler one is sacrificed. – The Briton takes place of the man, and the image of God is lost in the citizen! But it is not that enthusiastic flame which in Greece and Rome consumed every sordid passion: no, self is the focus; and the disparting rays rise not above our foggy atmosphere. But softly – it is only the property of the rich that is secure; the man who lives by the sweat of his brow has no asylum from oppression; the strong man may enter – when was the castle of the poor sacred? and the base informer steal him from the family that depend on his industry for subsistence.

[Misery, to reach your heart, I perceive, must have its cap and bells]

Our penal laws punish with death the thief who steals a few pounds; but to take by violence, or trepan, a man, is no such heinous offence. – For who shall dare to complain of the venerable vestige of the law that rendered the life of a deer more sacred than that of a man?[20] But it was the poor man with only his native dignity who was thus oppressed – and only metaphysical sophists and cold mathematicians can discern this insubstantial form; it is a work of abstraction – and a *gentleman* of lively imagination must borrow some drapery[21] from fancy before he can love or pity a *man*. – Misery, to reach your heart, I perceive, must have its cap and bells; your tears are reserved, very *naturally* considering your character, for the declamation of the theatre, or for the downfall of queens, whose rank alters the nature of folly, and throws a graceful veil over vices that degrade humanity; whilst the distress of many industrious mothers, whose *helpmates* have been torn from them, and the hungry cry of helpless babes, were vulgar sorrows that could not move your commiseration, though they might extort an alms. 'The tears that are shed for fictitious sorrow are admirably adapted', says Rousseau, 'to make us proud of all the virtues which we do not possess.'[22]

---

[19] The campaign for the abolition of slave trade, spearheaded by William Wilberforce MP, was gathering widespread support in the 1790s, although vested interests in Parliament would delay abolition until 1807.

[20] The eighteenth-century game laws in Britain were notoriously brutal. Under the Black Act of 1723 it was a hanging offence to hunt deer with the face blackened, or in disguise.

[21] A riposte to Burke's famous line on 'decent drapery'; see above p. 37.

[22] *A Letter from M. Rousseau, of Geneva, to M. D'Alembert, of Paris*, trans. anon. (London: J. Nourse, 1759), pp. 24–5.

[In reprobating Dr. Price's opinions you
might have spared the man]

I agree with you, Sir, that the pulpit is not the place for political discussions[23] though it might be more excusable to enter on such a subject, when the day was set apart merely to commemorate a political revolution, and no stated duty was encroached upon. I will, however, wave this point, and allow that Dr. Price's zeal may have carried him further than sound reason can justify. I do also most cordially coincide with you, that till we can see the remote consequences of things, present calamities must appear in the ugly form of evil, and excite our commiseration. The good that time slowly educes from them may be hid from mortal eye, or dimly seen; whilst sympathy compels man to feel for man, and almost restrains the hand that would amputate a limb to save the whole body. But, after making this concession, allow me to expostulate with you, and calmly hold up the glass which will shew you your partial feelings.

In reprobating Dr. Price's opinions you might have spared the man; and if you had had but half as much reverence for the grey hairs of virtue as for the accidental distinctions of rank, you would not have treated with such indecent familiarity and supercilious contempt, a member of the community whose talents and modest virtues place him high in the scale of moral excellence. I am not accustomed to look up with vulgar awe, even when mental superiority exalts a man above his fellows; but still the sight of a man whose habits are fixed by piety and reason, and whose virtues are consolidated into goodness, commands my homage – and I should touch his errors with a tender hand when I made a parade of my sensibility. Granting, for a moment, that Dr. Price's political opinions are Utopian reveries, and that the world is not yet sufficiently civilized to adopt such a sublime system of morality; they could, however, only be the reveries of a benevolent mind. Tottering on the verge of the grave, that worthy man in his whole life never dreamt of struggling for power or riches; and, if a glimpse of the glad dawn of liberty rekindled the fire of youth in his veins, you, who could not stand the fascinating glance of a *great* Lady's eyes,[24] when neither virtue nor sense beamed in them, might have pardoned his unseemly transport, – if such it must be deemed.

I could almost fancy that I now see this respectable old man, in his pulpit, with hands clasped, and eyes devoutly fixed, praying with all the simple energy of unaffected piety; or, when more erect, inculcating the dignity of virtue, and enforcing the doctrines his life adorns; benevolence animated each feature, and persuasion attuned his accents; the preacher grew eloquent, who only laboured

---

[23]   See above, p. 24, for Burke's objection to politics in the pulpit. Wollstonecraft's defence of Price is based on personal acquaintance.
[24]   A reference to Burke's set-piece description of Marie Antoinette; see above p. 36. This passage parodies Burke's vision of the Dauphiness.

to be clear; and the respect that he extorted, seemed only the respect due to personified virtue and matured wisdom. – Is this the man you brand with so many opprobrious epithets? he whose private life will stand the test of the strictest enquiry – away with such unmanly sarcasms, and puerile conceits. – But, before I close this part of my animadversions, I must convict you of wilful misrepresentation and wanton abuse.

[The younger children have been sacrificed to the eldest son]

Who can recount all the unnatural crimes which the *laudable, interesting* desire of perpetuating a name has produced? The younger children have been sacrificed to the eldest son; sent into exile, or confined in convents, that they might not encroach on what was called, with shameful falsehood, the *family* estate.[25] Will Mr Burke call this parental affection reasonable or virtuous? – No; it is the spurious offspring of over-weening, mistaken pride – and not that first source of civilization, natural parental affection, that makes no difference between child and child, but what reason justifies by pointing out superior merit.

Another pernicious consequence which unavoidably arises from this artificial affection is, the insuperable bar which it puts in the way of early marriages. It would be difficult to determine whether the minds or bodies of our youth are most injured by this impediment. Our young men become selfish coxcombs, and gallantry with modest women, and intrigues with those of another description, weaken both mind and body, before either has arrived at maturity. The character of a master of a family, a husband, and a father, forms the citizen imperceptibly, by producing a sober manliness of thought, and orderly behaviour; but, from the lax morals and depraved affections of the libertine, what results? – a finical man of taste, who is only anxious to secure his own private gratifications, and to maintain his rank in society.[26]

The same system has an equally pernicious effect on female morals. – Girls are sacrificed to family convenience, or else marry to settle themselves in a superior rank, and coquet, without restraint, with the fine gentleman whom I have already described. And to such lengths has this vanity, this desire of shining, carried them, that it is not now necessary to guard girls against imprudent love matches; for if some widows did not now and then *fall* in love, Love and Hymen would seldom meet, unless at a village church.

---

[25] Primogeniture, the legal system through which the eldest son inherits all his father's estate, was a primary target of radical critiques. Despite all Burke's rhetoric about the ties of nature and family, Wollstonecraft suggests that primogeniture forced parents to sacrifice the claims of their other children to the eldest. Likewise, she suggests, Burke sacrifices to the authority of aristocracy the claims of the people at large.

[26] *Vindication of the Rights of Woman* is deeply concerned with the question of what domestic arrangements are best adduced to the education of a good citizen.

[The respect paid to rank and fortune damps every generous purpose of the soul]

The only security of property that nature authorizes and reason sanctions is, the right a man has to enjoy the acquisitions which his talents and industry have acquired; and to bequeath them to whom he chooses. Happy would it be for the world if there were no other road to wealth or honour; if pride, in the shape of parental affection, did not absorb the man, and prevent friendship from having the same weight as relationship. Luxury and effeminacy would not then introduce so much idiotism into the noble families which form one of the pillars of our state:[27] the ground would not lie fallow, nor would undirected activity of mind spread the contagion of restless idleness, and its concomitant, vice, through the whole mass of society.

Instead of gaming they might nourish a virtuous ambition, and love might take place of the gallantry which you, with knightly fealty, venerate. Women would probably then act like mothers, and the fine lady, become a rational woman, might think it necessary to superintend her family and suckle her children, in order to fulfil her part of the social compact.[28] But vain is the hope, whilst great masses of property are hedged round by hereditary honours; for numberless vices, forced in the hot-bed of wealth, assume a sightly form to dazzle the senses and cloud the understanding. The respect paid to rank and fortune damps every generous purpose of the soul, and stifles the natural affections on which human contentment ought to be built. Who will venturously ascend the steeps of virtue, or explore the great deep for knowledge, when *the one thing needful*,[29] attained by less arduous exertions, if not inherited, procures the attention man naturally pants after, and vice 'loses half its evil by losing all its grossness'.[30] – What a sentiment to come from a moral pen!

A surgeon would tell you that by skinning over a wound you spread disease through the whole frame; and, surely, they indirectly aim at destroying all purity of morals, who poison the very source of virtue, by smearing a sentimental varnish over vice, to hide its natural deformity. Stealing, whoring, and drunkenness, are gross vices, I presume, though they may not obliterate every moral sentiment, and have a vulgar brand that makes them appear with all their native deformity; but

---

[27] Possibly a sly allusion to George III, whose mental illness over 1788–9 had been the focus of a constitutional dispute between Pitt and the Whig supporters of the Prince of Wales. 'Luxury and effeminacy' are more generally part of Wollstonecraft's republican critique of the moral decay caused by the self-indulgence fostered by an aristocracy of birth rather than of merit.

[28] 'Parental Affection', Chapter x of *Vindication of the Rights of Woman*, promotes breastfeeding as 'equally calculated to inspire maternal and filial affection'; see below, p. 115. Only through the exercise of such 'mutual sympathy' are the values inculcated which, Wollstonecraft believes, make a good citizen.

[29] Luke 10: 42.

[30] See above, p. 36.

over-reaching, adultery, and coquetry, are venial offences, though they reduce virtue to an empty name, and make wisdom consist in saving appearances.

'On this scheme of things[31] a king *is* but a man; a queen *is* but a woman; a woman *is* but an animal, and an animal not of the highest order.' – All true, Sir; if she is not more attentive to the duties of humanity than queens and fashionable ladies in general are. I will still further accede to the opinion you have so justly conceived of the spirit which begins to animate this age. – 'All homage paid to the sex in general, as such, and without distinct views, is to be regarded as *romance* and folly.' Undoubtedly; because such homage vitiates them, prevents their endeavouring to obtain solid personal merit; and, in short, makes those beings vain inconsiderate dolls, who ought to be prudent mothers and useful members of society. 'Regicide and sacrilege are but fictions of superstition corrupting jurisprudence, by destroying its simplicity. The murder of a king, or a queen, or a bishop, are only common homicide.' – Again I agree with you; but you perceive, Sir, that by leaving out the word *father*, I think the whole extent of the comparison invidious.

[The spirit of romance and chivalry is in the wane; and reason will gain by its extinction]

It is a proverbial observation, that a very thin partition divides wit and madness.[32] Poetry therefore naturally addresses the fancy, and the language of passion is with great felicity borrowed from the heightened picture which the imagination draws of sensible objects concentred by impassioned reflection. And, during this 'fine phrensy',[33] reason has no right to rein-in the imagination, unless to prevent the introduction of supernumerary images; if the passion is real, the head will not be ransacked for stale tropes and cold rodomontade. I now speak of the genuine enthusiasm of genius, which, perhaps, seldom appears, but in the infancy of civilization; for as this light becomes more luminous reason clips the wing of fancy – the youth becomes a man.

Whether the glory of Europe is set, I shall not now enquire; but probably the spirit of romance and chivalry is in the wane; and reason will gain by its extinction.

From observing several cold romantic characters I have been led to confine the term romantic to one definition – false, or rather artificial, feelings. Works of genius are read with a prepossession in their favour, and sentiments imitated, because they were fashionable and pretty, and not because they were forcibly felt.

---

[31] {As you ironically observe, p. 114.} See above, p. 37.
[32] John Dryden, *Absalom and Achitophel*, I.163–4: 'Great wits are sure to madness near allied, / And thin partitions do their bounds divide.'
[33] *A Midsummer Night's Dream*, V.i.12.

In modern poetry the understanding and memory often fabricate the pretended effusions of the heart, and romance destroys all simplicity; which, in works of taste, is but a synonymous word for truth. This romantic spirit has extended to our prose, and scattered artificial flowers over the most barren heath; or a mixture of verse and prose producing the strangest incongruities. The turgid bombast of some of your periods fully proves these assertions; for when the heart speaks we are seldom shocked by hyperbole, or dry raptures.

I speak in this decided tone, because from turning over the pages of your late publication, with more attention than I did when I first read it cursorily over; and comparing the sentiments it contains with your conduct on many important occasions, I am led very often to doubt your sincerity, and to suppose that you have said many things merely for the sake of saying them well; or to throw some pointed obloquy on characters and opinions that jostled with your vanity.

It is an arduous task to follow the doublings of cunning, or the subterfuges of inconsistency; for in controversy, as in battle, the brave man wishes to face his enemy, and fight on the same ground. Knowing, however, the influence of a ruling passion, and how often it assumes the form of reason when there is much sensibility in the heart, I respect an opponent, though he tenaciously maintains opinions in which I cannot coincide; but, if I once discover that many of those opinions are empty rhetorical flourishes, my respect is soon changed into that pity which borders on contempt; and the mock dignity and haughty stalk, only reminds me of the ass in the lion's skin.[34]

A sentiment of this kind glanced across my mind when I read the following exclamation. 'Whilst the royal captives, who followed in the train, were slowly moved along, amidst the horrid yells, and shrilling screams, and frantic dances, and infamous contumelies, and all the unutterable abominations of the furies of hell, in the abused shape of the vilest of women.'[35] Probably you mean women who gained a livelihood by selling vegetables or fish, who never had had any advantages of education; or their vices might have lost part of their abominable deformity, by losing part of their grossness. The queen of France – the great and small vulgar, claim our pity; they have almost insuperable obstacles to surmount in their progress towards true dignity of character; still I have such a plain downright understanding that I do not like to make a distinction without a difference. But it is not very extraordinary that *you* should, for throughout your letter you frequently advert to a sentimental jargon, which has long been current in conversation, and even in books of morals, though it never received the *regal* stamp of reason. A kind of mysterious instinct is *supposed* to reside in the soul, that instantaneously discerns truth, without the tedious labour of ratiocination. This instinct, for I know not what other name to give it, has been termed *common*

---

[34]   A reference to Aesop's fable of the ass who puts on a lion's skin and frightens the village, but gives himself away when he brays.

[35]   {Page 106.} See above, p. 34.

sense, and more frequently *sensibility;* and, by a kind of *indefeasible* right, it has been *supposed*, for rights of this kind are not easily proved, to reign paramount over the other faculties of the mind, and to be an authority from which there is no appeal.

This subtle magnetic fluid,[36] that runs around the whole circle of society, is not subject to any known rule, or, to use an obnoxious phrase, in spite of the sneers of mock humility, or the timid fears of some well-meaning Christians, who shrink away from any freedom of thought, lest they should rouse the old serpent, to the *eternal fitness of things.*[37] It dips, we know not why, granting it to be an infallible instinct, and, though supposed always to point to truth, its pole-star, the point is always shining, and seldom stands due north.

It is to this instinct, without doubt, that you allude, when you talk of the 'moral constitution of the heart'.[38]

[Reason at second-hand]

But the cultivation of reason is an arduous task, and men of lively fancy, finding it easier to follow the impulse of passion, endeavour to persuade themselves and others that it is most *natural*. And happy is it for those, who indolently let that heaven-lighted spark rest like the ancient lamps in sepulchres, that some virtuous habits, with which the reason of others shackled them, supplies its place. – Affection for parents, reverence for superiors or antiquity, notions of honour, or that worldly self-interest that shrewdly shews them that honesty is the best policy: all proceed from the reason for which they serve as substitutes; – but it is reason at second-hand.

Children are born ignorant, consequently innocent; the passions, are neither good nor evil dispositions, till they receive a direction, and either bound over the feeble barrier raised by a faint glimmering of unexercised reason, called con-science, or strengthen her wavering dictates till sound principles are deeply rooted, and able to cope with the headstrong passions that often assume her awful form. What moral purpose can be answered by extolling good dispositions, as they are called, when these good dispositions are described as instincts: for instinct moves in a direct line to its ultimate end, and asks not for guide or support. But if virtue is to be acquired by experience, or taught by example, reason, perfected by reflec-tion, must be the director of the whole host of passions, which produce a fructify-ing heat, but no light, that you would exalt into her place. – She must hold the

---

[36]   One eighteenth-century explanation for the power of sympathy was through recourse to the idea of a 'mag-netic fluid' in the body, which was responsible for animation in the individual and acted as a force of attraction between members of society more generally.

[37]   Henry Fielding, *Tom Jones* (1749), II.iv.4.

[38]   See above, p. 40.

rudder, or, let the wind blow which way it list, the vessel will never advance smoothly to its destined port; for the time lost in tacking about would dreadfully impede its progress.

[This fear of God makes me reverence myself]

I reverence the rights of men. – Sacred rights! for which I acquire a more profound respect, the more I look into my own mind; and, professing these heterodox opinions, I still preserve my bowels; my heart is human, beats quick with human sympathies – and I FEAR God!

I bend with awful reverence when I enquire on what my fear is built. – I fear that sublime power, whose motive for creating me must have been wise and good; and I submit to the moral laws which my reason deduces from this view of my dependence on him. – It is not his power that I fear – it is not to an arbitrary will, but to unerring *reason* I submit. – Submit – yes; I disregard the charge of arrogance, to the law that regulates his just resolves; and the happiness I pant after must be the same in kind, and produced by the same exertions as his – though unfeigned humility overwhelms every idea that would presume to compare the goodness which the most exalted created being could acquire, with the grand source of life and bliss.

This fear of God makes me reverence myself. – Yes, Sir, the regard I have for honest fame, and the friendship of the virtuous, falls far short of the respect which I have for myself. And this, enlightened self-love, if an epithet the meaning of which has been grossly perverted will convey my idea, forces me to see; and, if I may venture to borrow a prostituted term, to *feel*, that happiness is reflected, and that, in communicating good, my soul receives its noble aliment. – I do not trouble myself, therefore, to enquire whether this is the fear the *people* of England feel: – and, if it be *natural* to include all the modifications which you have annexed – it is not.[39]

Besides, I cannot help suspecting that, if you had the *enlightened* respect for yourself, which you affect to despise, you would not have said that the constitution of our church and state, formed, like most other modern ones, by degrees, as Europe was emerging out of barbarism, was formed 'under the auspices, and was confirmed by the sanctions, of religion and piety'. You have turned over the historic page; have been hackneyed in the ways of men, and must know that private cabals and public feuds, private virtues and vices, religion and superstition, have all concurred to foment the mass and swell it to its present form; nay more, that it in part owes its sightly appearance to bold rebellion and insidious innovation. Factions, Sir, have been the leaven, and private interest has produced public good.

---

[39]   {*Vide* Reflections, p. 128. 'We fear God; we look up with *awe* to kings; with *affection* to parliaments; with *duty* to magistrates; with *reverence* to priests; and with *respect* to nobility.'} See above, p. 41.

[The cold arguments of reason, that give no sex to virtue]

Where is the dignity, the infallibility of sensibility, in the fair ladies, whom, if the voice of rumour is to be credited, the captive negroes curse in all the agony of bodily pain, for the unheard of tortures they invent? It is probable that some of them, after the sight of a flagellation, compose their ruffled spirits and exercise their tender feelings by the perusal of the last imported novel. – How true these tears are to nature, I leave you to determine. But these ladies may have read your Enquiry concerning the origin of our ideas of the Sublime and Beautiful, and, convinced by your arguments, may have laboured to be pretty, by counterfeiting weakness.[40]

You may have convinced them that *littleness* and *weakness* are the very essence of beauty; and that the Supreme Being, in giving women beauty in the most supereminent degree, seemed to command them, by the powerful voice of Nature, not to cultivate the moral virtues that might chance to excite respect, and interfere with the pleasing sensations they were created to inspire. Thus confining truth, fortitude, and humanity, within the rigid pale of manly morals, they might justly argue, that to be loved, women's high end and great distinction! they should 'learn to lisp, to totter in their walk, and nick-name God's creatures'.[41] Never, they might repeat after you, was any man, much less a woman, rendered amiable by the force of those exalted qualities, fortitude, justice, wisdom, and truth; and thus forewarned of the sacrifice they must make to those austere, unnatural virtues, they would be authorized to turn all their attention to their persons, systematically neglecting morals to secure beauty. – Some rational old woman indeed might chance to stumble at this doctrine, and hint, that in avoiding atheism you had not steered clear of the mussulman's creed;[42] but you could readily exculpate yourself by turning the charge on Nature, who made our idea of beauty independent of reason. Nor would it be necessary for you to recollect, that if virtue has any other foundation than worldly utility, you have clearly proved that one half of the human species, at least, have not souls; and that Nature, by making women *little, smooth, delicate, fair* creatures, never designed that they should exercise their reason to acquire the virtues that produce opposite, if not contradictory, feelings. The affection they excite, to be uniform and perfect, should not be tinctured with the respect which moral virtues inspire, lest pain should be blended with pleasure, and admiration disturb the soft intimacy of love. This laxity of morals in the female world is certainly more captivating to a libertine imagination than the cold arguments of reason, that give no sex to virtue. If beautiful weakness be interwoven in a woman's frame, if the chief business of her life be (as you insinuate) to

---

[40] Burke's *Philosophical Enquiry*, III.ix and xvi.

[41] *Hamlet*, III.i.146–8.

[42] Wollstonecraft alludes to the widespread misconception that Muslims believed women had no souls.

inspire love, and Nature has made an eternal distinction between the qualities that dignify a rational being and this animal perfection, her duty and happiness in this life must clash with any preparation for a more exalted state. So that Plato and Milton were grossly mistaken in asserting that human love led to heavenly, and was only an exaltation of the same affection;[43] for the love of the Deity, which is mixed with the most profound reverence, must be love of perfection, and not compassion for weakness.

To say the truth, I not only tremble for the souls of women, but for the good natured man, whom every one loves. The *amiable* weakness of his mind is a strong argument against its immateriality, and seems to prove that beauty relaxes the *solids* of the soul as well as the body.

It follows then immediately, from your own reasoning, that respect and love are antagonist principles; and that, if we really wish to render men more virtuous, we must endeavour to banish all enervating modifications of beauty from civil society. We must, to carry your argument a little further, return to the Spartan regulations,[44] and settle the virtues of men on the stern foundation of mortification and self-denial; for any attempt to civilize the heart, to make it humane by implanting reasonable principles, is a mere philosophic dream. If refinement inevitably lessens respect for virtue, by rendering beauty, the grand tempter, more seductive; if these relaxing feelings are incompatible with the nervous exertions of morality, the sun of Europe is not set; it begins to dawn, when cold metaphysicians try to make the head give laws to the heart.

But should experience prove that there is a beauty in virtue, a charm in order, which necessarily implies exertion, a depraved sensual taste may give way to a more manly one – and *melting* feelings to rational satisfactions. Both may be equally natural to man; the test is their moral difference, and that point reason alone can decide.

Such a glorious change can only be produced by liberty. Inequality of rank must ever impede the growth of virtue, by vitiating the mind that submits or domineers; that is ever employed to procure nourishment for the body, or amusement for the mind. And if this grand example be set by an assembly of unlettered clowns, if they can produce a crisis that may involve the fate of Europe, and 'more than Europe',[45] you must allow us to respect unsophisticated reason, and reverence the active exertions that were not relaxed by a fastidious respect for the beauty of rank, or a dread of the deformity produced by any *void* in the social structure.

---

[43]   See, for example, Plato, *Symposium*, 178c–85c (the speech of Pausanias) and Milton, *Paradise Lost*, VIII.589–92.

[44]   The classical Spartan state, much admired by Rousseau among other eighteenth-century thinkers, demanded from its citizens an absolute devotion to the welfare of the community and was founded on a regime of military training from early childhood.

[45]   {Page 11. 'It looks to me as if I were in a great crisis, not of the affairs of France alone but of all Europe, perhaps of more than Europe. All circumstances taken together, the French revolution is the most astonishing that has hitherto happened in the world.'} See above, p. 23.

[What were the outrages of a day to these continual miseries?]

Surveying civilized life, and seeing, with undazzled eye, the polished vices of the rich, their insincerity, want of natural affections, with all the specious train that luxury introduces, I have turned impatiently to the poor, to look for man undebauched by riches or power – but, alas! what did I see? a being scarcely above the brutes, over which he tyrannized; a broken spirit, worn-out body, and all those gross vices which the example of the rich, rudely copied, could produce. Envy built a wall of separation, that made the poor hate, whilst they bent to their superiors; who, on their part, stepped aside to avoid the loathsome sight of human misery.

What were the outrages of a day[46] to these continual miseries? Let those sorrows hide their diminished head before the tremendous mountain of woe that thus defaces our globe! Man preys on man; and you mourn for the idle tapestry that decorated a gothic pile, and the dronish bell that summoned the fat priest to prayer. You mourn for the empty pageant of a name, when slavery flaps her wing, and the sick heart retires to die in lonely wilds, far from the abodes of men. Did the pangs you felt for insulted nobility, the anguish that rent your heart when the gorgeous robes were torn off the idol human weakness had set up, deserve to be compared with the long-drawn sigh of melancholy reflection, when misery and vice are thus seen to haunt our steps, and swim on the top of every cheering prospect? Why is our fancy to be appalled by terrific perspectives of a hell beyond the grave? – Hell stalks abroad; – the lash resounds on the slave's naked sides; and the sick wretch, who can no longer earn the sour bread of unremitting labour, steals to a ditch to bid the world a long good night – or, neglected in some ostentatious hospital, breathes his last amidst the laugh of mercenary attendants.

Such misery demands more than tears – I pause to recollect myself; and smother the contempt I feel rising for your rhetorical flourishes and infantine sensibility.

- - - - - - - - - - -

- - - - - - - - - - -

---

[46]   {The 6th October.} The day when the king and his family were moved from Versailles to Paris under the protection of the National Guard. See Burke, pp. 33–36 above.

4

Thomas Paine

Rights of Man: Being an Answer to Mr. Burke's Attack on the French Revolution

(London: J. S. Jordan, 1791)

Thomas Paine (1737–1809) was born in Thetford, Norfolk, where, after a basic education, he was apprenticed to his father as a stay-maker. In 1759 he married Mary Lambert, who died in childbirth the following year. Paine turned to a career in the excise and moved to Lewes, on the English south coast, where he married a relatively prosperous local woman, Elizabeth Ollive. In 1774 he was dismissed from his post for organizing a campaign to improve pay and conditions. The same year he formally separated from his wife and left for America, bearing a letter of introduction from Benjamin Franklin.

Paine began a career as a journalist in Philadelphia, a city already famous for the progressive opinions of citizens such as Franklin. Paine became the most outspoken defender of the colonists at the outbreak of the War of Independence. His *Common Sense* (1776) decisively pressed for the radical step of a break with the Crown. The pamphlet anticipated the vigorous and accessible prose of *Rights of Man*. He followed it up with the brilliant series of *Crisis* essays (1776–83), which roused the people to the cause of independence. He was rewarded with the position of Secretary to the Committee for Foreign Affairs in Congress, but ran into trouble when he attacked those profiteering from trade with France. He resigned in 1778, when Congress refused to back his campaign. After the war he was rewarded for his service, bought a farm, and devoted himself to the scientific interests that had first drawn him to Franklin. He developed an iron bridge, and in 1787 went to France looking for investors. There he reacquainted himself with Thomas Jefferson before shifting his project to England. A full-scale version of the

Romanticism and Revolution: A Reader.
Edited by Jon Mee and David Fallon.   © 2011 Blackwell Publishing Ltd.

bridge was put on display in 1790, but by that stage Paine had already started to interest himself in politics again. Jefferson had kept him up to date with events in France. Paine seems to have already begun writing an account of events in France when he heard that Burke planned to attack the Revolution. The first part of *Rights of Man* was printed in February 1791, but withdrawn by the publisher Joseph Johnson from fear of prosecution. J. S. Jordan brought it out a month later, with immediate popular success, although its circulation has always been exaggerated.

Part I of *Rights of Man* does not call for France to become a republic. At this stage, Paine seems to have hoped that Louis XVI ('friend of the nation', p. 74 below) would fulfil his promises to lead the Revolution. With regard to Britain, Paine was dismissive of its claim to represent a state based on the liberties of the people enshrined in the Bill of Rights. Paine mocked the reverence shown even by most reformers for the Glorious Revolution of 1688 and represented it as a fraud, practised on the people in the interests of the aristocracy. The irreverence of Paine's writing upset many who agreed with his political principles, but it was an intrinsic part of his attempt to shake the English out of their respect for precedent (which was so powerful a part of Burke's case) and into a political discourse whose terms they could define for themselves. Much of Part I is taken up with contradicting Burke's account of events in France, but this part is also vitally concerned to dislodge his account of English liberty and the basic vocabulary of most British writing about politics at the time.

[The vanity and presumption of governing beyond the grave]

There never did, there never will, and there never can exist a parliament, or any description of men, or any generation of men, in any country, possessed of the right or the power of binding and controlling posterity to the *'end of time,'* or of commanding for ever how the world shall be governed, or who shall govern it: and therefore all such clauses, acts or declarations, by which the makers of them attempt to do what they have neither the right nor the power to do, nor the power to execute, are in themselves null and void. – Every age and generation must be as free to act for itself, *in all cases*, as the ages and generations which preceded it. The vanity and presumption of governing beyond the grave is the most ridiculous and insolent of all tyrannies. Man has no property in man;[1] neither has any generation

---

[1]   Paine immediately attacks Burke's claim that the settlement of 1689 meant that the British people had entered a compact to accept in perpetuity the political arrangements agreed there (see above, p. 42).

a property in the generations which are to follow. The parliament or the people of 1688, or of any other period, had no more right to dispose of the people of the present day, or to bind or to controul them *in any shape whatever*, than the parliament or the people of the present day have to dispose of, bind or controul those who are to live a hundred or a thousand years hence. Every generation is and must be competent to all the purposes which its occasions require. It is the living, and not the dead, that are to be accommodated. When man ceases to be, his power and his wants cease with him; and having no longer any participation in the concerns of this world, he has no longer any authority in directing who shall be its governors, or how its government shall be organized, or how administered.

I am not contending for, nor against, any form of government, nor for, nor against, any party here or elsewhere. That which a whole nation chooses to do, it has a right to do. Mr. Burke says, No. Where, then, *does* the right exist? I am contending for the rights of the *living*, and against their being willed away, and controuled and contracted for, by the manuscript assumed authority of the dead; and Mr. Burke is contending for the authority of the dead over the rights and freedom of the living. There was a time when kings disposed of their crowns by will upon their death-beds, and consigned the people, like beasts of the field,[2] to whatever successor they appointed. This is now so exploded as scarcely to be remembered, and so monstrous as hardly to be believed: But the parliamentary clauses upon which Mr. Burke builds his political church, are of the same nature.

The laws of every country must be analogous to some common principle. In England, no parent or master, nor all the authority of parliament, omnipotent as it has called itself, can bind or controul the personal freedom even of an individual beyond the age of twenty-one years: On what ground of right then could the parliament of 1688, or any other parliament, bind all posterity for ever?

Those who have quitted the world, and those who are not yet arrived at it, are as remote from each other as the utmost stretch of mortal imagination can conceive: What possible obligation then can exist between them, what rule or principle can be laid down, that two non-entities, the one out of existence, and the other not in, and who never can meet in this world, that the one should control the other to the end of time?

In England, it is said that money cannot be taken out of the pockets of the people without their consent: But who authorized, and who could authorize, the parliament of 1688 to controul and take away the freedom of posterity, and limit and confine their rights of acting in certain cases for ever, who were not in existence to give or to with-hold their consent?

A greater absurdity cannot present itself to the understanding of man, than what Mr. Burke offers to his readers. He tells them, and he tells the world to come, that a certain body of men, who existed a hundred years ago, made a law, and that there does not now exist in the nation, nor ever will, nor ever can, a power to alter it.

---

[2]   God gives Adam dominion over the 'beasts of the field' in Genesis 2.

Under how many subtilties, or absurdities, has the divine right to govern been imposed on the credulity of mankind! Mr. Burke has discovered a new one, and he has shortened his journey to Rome, by appealing to the power of this infallible parliament of former days;[3] and he produces what it has done, as of divine authority: for that power must certainly be more than human, which no human power to the end of time can alter.

[Mr. Burke has set up a sort of political Adam, in whom all posterity are bound for ever]

From what, or from whence, does Mr. Burke prove the right of any human power to bind posterity for ever? He has produced his clauses; but he must produce also his proofs, that such a right existed, and shew how it existed. If it ever existed, it must now exist; for whatever appertains to the nature of man, cannot be annihilated by man. It is the nature of man to die, and he will continue to die as long as he continues to be born. But Mr. Burke has set up a sort of political Adam, in whom all posterity are bound for ever;[4] he must, therefore, prove that his Adam possessed such a power, or such a right.

The weaker any cord is, the less will it bear to be stretched, and the worse is the policy to stretch it, unless it is intended to break it. Had a person contemplated the overthrow of Mr. Burke's positions, he would have proceeded as Mr. Burke has done. He would have magnified the authorities, on purpose to have called the *right* of them into question; and the instant the question of right was started, the authorities must have been given up.

It requires but a very small glance of thought to perceive, that altho' laws made in one generation often continue in force through succeeding generations, yet that they continue to derive their force from the consent of the living. A law not repealed continues in force, not because it *cannot* be repealed, but because it *is not* repealed; and the non-repealing passes for consent.

But Mr. Burke's clauses have not even this qualification in their favour. They become null, by attempting to become immortal. The nature of them precludes consent. They destroy the right which they *might* have, by grounding it on a right which they *cannot* have. Immortal power is not a human right, and therefore cannot be a right of parliament. The parliament of 1688 might as well have passed an act to have authorised themselves to live for ever, as to make their authority live for ever. All therefore that can be said of them is, that they are a formality of words, of as much import, as if those who used them had addressed a congratulation to themselves, and, in the oriental stile of antiquity, had said, O Parliament, live for ever!

---

[3]   Burke was widely regarded as a crypto-Catholic.
[4]   See note 2 above.

[Mr. Burke does not attend to the distinction between *men* and *principles*]

It was not against Louis XVIth, but against the despotic principles of the government, that the nation revolted. These principles had not their origin in him, but in the original establishment, many centuries back; and they were become too deeply rooted to be removed, and the augean stable[5] of parasites and plunderers too abominably filthy to be cleansed, by any thing short of a complete and universal revolution. When it becomes necessary to do a thing, the whole heart and soul should go into the measure, or not attempt it. That crisis was then arrived, and there remained no choice but to act with determined vigour, or not to act at all. The King was known to be the friend of the nation, and this circumstance was favourable to the enterprise. Perhaps no man bred up in the stile of an absolute King ever possessed a heart so little disposed to the exercise of that species of power as the present King of France. But the principles of the government itself still remained the same. The Monarch and the Monarchy were distinct and separate things; and it was against the established despotism of the latter, and not against the person or principles of the former, that the revolt commenced, and the revolution has been carried.

Mr. Burke does not attend to the distinction between *men* and *principles*, and therefore, he does not see that a revolt may take place against the despotism of the latter, while there lies no charge of despotism against the former.

[The Quixote age of chivalry nonsense is gone]

I know a place in America called Point-no-Point;[6] because as you proceed along the shore, gay and flowery as Mr. Burke's language, it continually recedes and presents itself at a distance a head; and when you have got as far as you can go, there is no point at all. Just thus it is with Mr. Burke's three hundred and fifty-six pages. It is therefore difficult to reply to him. But as the points he wishes to establish may be inferred from what he abuses, it is in his paradoxes that we must look for his arguments.

As to the tragic paintings by which Mr. Burke has outraged his own imagination, and seeks to work upon that of his readers, they are very well calculated for theatrical representation, where facts are manufactured for the sake of show, and accommodated to produce, through the weakness of sympathy, a weeping effect.

---

[5]   One of the labours of Hercules was to clean out the stables of Augeas, purging in one single day the filth left by vast numbers of cattle. He performed this by diverting the rivers Alpheus and Peneus.

[6]   Point no Point (or Dietrick's Hook) is on the Hudson River.

But Mr. Burke should recollect that he is writing History, and not *Plays*; and that his readers will expect truth, and not the spouting rant of high-toned exclamation.

When we see a man dramatically lamenting in a publication intended to be believed, that, '*The age of chivalry is gone! that The glory of Europe is extinguished for ever!* that *The unbought grace of life,* (if anyone knows what it is), *the cheap defence of nations, the nurse of manly sentiment and heroic enterprize, is gone!*' and all this because the Quixote age of chivalry nonsense is gone, What opinion can we form of his judgment, or what regard can we pay to his facts? In the rhapsody of his imagination, he has discovered a world of wind-mills, and his sorrows are, that there are no Quixotes to attack them.[7] But if the age of aristocracy, like that of chivalry, should fall, and they had originally some connection, Mr. Burke, the trumpeter of the Order, may continue his parody to the end, and finish with exclaiming – '*Othello's occupation's gone!*'[8]

Notwithstanding Mr. Burke's horrid paintings, when the French Revolution is compared with that of other countries, the astonishment will be, that it is marked with so few sacrifices; but this astonishment will cease when we reflect that it was *principles*, and not *persons*, that were the meditated objects of destruction. The mind of the nation was acted upon by a higher stimulus than what the consideration of persons could inspire, and sought a higher conquest than could be produced by the downfall of an enemy. Among the few who fell, there do not appear to be any that were intentionally singled out. They all of them had their fate in the circumstances of the moment, and were not pursued with that long, cold-blooded, unabated revenge which pursued the unfortunate Scotch in the affair of 1745.[9]

Through the whole of Mr. Burke's book I do not observe that the Bastille is mentioned more than once, and that with a kind of implication as if he were sorry it is pulled down, and wished it were built up again.[10] 'We have rebuilt Newgate (says he) and tenanted the mansion; and we have prisons almost as strong as the Bastille for those who dare to libel the Queens of France.'[11] As to what a madman, like the person called Lord George Gordon, might say, and to whom Newgate is

---

[7] This comparison was made in many of the attacks on Burke, including the caricature shown on the cover of this book. See Burke, above, p. 22.

[8] *Othello*, III.iii.357.

[9] Paine refers to the brutal treatment of those who supported the Jacobite rising of 1745 under Charles Edward Stuart after their defeat at the Battle of Culloden.

[10] See Burke, above, p. 44.

[11] {Since writing the above, two other places occur in Mr. Burke's pamphlet, in which the name of the Bastille is mentioned, but in the same manner. In the one, he introduces in it a sort of obscure question, and asks – 'Will any ministers now serve such a king, with but a decent appearance of respect, cordially obey the orders of those whom but the other day, *in his name*, they had committed to the Bastille?' In the other, the taking it is mentioned as implying criminality in the French guards who assisted in demolishing it. – 'They have not (says he) forgot the taking the king's castles at Paris.' – This is Mr. Burke, who pretends to write on constitutional freedom.} The taking of the Bastille on 14 July 1789 was, and still is, regarded as the key event of the French Revolution, not least because it had long been seen across Europe as a symbol of the arbitrary powers of the French monarchy to arrest and imprison its enemies. The attack on the Bastille was sparked by fears that an army was being deployed around Paris to cut off the city from the National Assembly in Versailles. On the following day, regular troops were withdrawn from Paris and Lafayette was elected commander of the National Guard.

rather a bedlam than a prison, it is unworthy a rational consideration.[12] It was a madman that libelled – and that is sufficient apology; and it afforded an opportunity for confining him, which was the thing that was wished for: But certain it is that Mr. Burke, who does not call himself a madman, whatever other people may do, has libelled, in the most unprovoked manner, and in the grossest stile of the most vulgar abuse, the whole representative authority of France; and yet Mr. Burke takes his seat in the British House of Commons! From his violence and his grief, his silence on some points and his excess on others, it is difficult not to believe that Mr. Burke is sorry, extremely sorry, that arbitrary power, the power of the Pope, and the Bastille, are pulled down.

Not one glance of compassion, not one commiserating reflection, that I can find throughout his book, has he bestowed on those who lingered out the most wretched of lives, a life without hope, in the most miserable of prisons. It is painful to behold a man employing his talents to corrupt himself. Nature has been kinder to Mr. Burke than he is to her. He is not affected by the reality of distress touching upon his heart, but by the showy resemblance of it striking his imagination. He pities the plumage, but forgets the dying bird. Accustomed to kiss the aristocratical hand that hath purloined him from himself, he degenerates into a composition of art, and the genuine soul of nature forsakes him. His hero or his heroine must be a tragedy-victim expiring in show, and not the real prisoner of misery, sliding into death in the silence of a dungeon.[13]

[Lay then the axe to the root, and teach governments humanity]

More of the citizens fell in this struggle[14] than of their opponents: but four or five persons were seized by the populace, and instantly put to death; the Governor of the Bastille, and the Mayor of Paris, who was detected in the act of betraying them; and afterwards Foulon, one of the new ministry, and Berthier, his son-in-law,

---

[12] Paine is reacting to Burke's comparison of Richard Price with Lord George Gordon (1751–93) in *Reflections* (London: J. Dodsley, 1790), pp. 124–5, not excerpted above). Gordon, a fanatical anti-Catholic, had been leader of the Protestant Association, which petitioned against government proposals to extend a degree of toleration towards Catholics. This culminated in riots which convulsed London from 2 to 10 June 1780, causing immense damage. Gordon was acquitted of treason, but in 1787 he was imprisoned for libelling the Queen of France and for publishing a pamphlet attacking the administration of justice. He converted to Judaism while in Newgate, where he died. Gordon was popular among some radicals, who visited him in prison, but Paine takes the more common view that he was insane. 'Bedlam' was Bethlehem Hospital in Moorfields, the house for the insane in London.

[13] This whole passage may play on one of the most famous ones in Burke's *Philosophical Enquiry* (I.xv), where he compares the relatively weak effects of tragedy to the excitement generated by the real execution of a state criminal of high rank.

[14] Paine is discussing the struggle for the Bastille.

who had accepted the office of intendant of Paris.[15] Their heads were stuck upon spikes, and carried about the city; and it is upon this mode of punishment that Mr. Burke builds a great part of his tragic scenes. Let us therefore examine how men came by the idea of punishing in this manner.

They learn it from the governments they live under, and retaliate the punishments they have been accustomed to behold. The heads stuck upon spikes, which remained for years upon Temple-Bar,[16] differed nothing in the horror of the scene from those carried about upon spikes at Paris: yet this was done by the English government. It may perhaps be said, that it signifies nothing to a man what is done to him after he is dead; but it signifies much to the living: it either tortures their feelings, or hardens their hearts; and in either case, it instructs them how to punish when power falls into their hands.

Lay then the axe to the root,[17] and teach governments humanity. It is their sanguinary punishments which corrupt mankind. In England the punishment in certain cases, is by *hanging, drawing,* and *quartering*; the heart of the sufferer is cut out, and held up to the view of the populace. In France, under the former government, the punishments were not less barbarous. Who does not remember the execution of Damien, torn to pieces by horses?[18] The effect of those cruel spectacles exhibited to the populace, is to destroy tenderness, or excite revenge; and by the base and false idea of governing men by terror, instead of reason, they become precedents. It is over the lowest class of mankind that government by terror is intended to operate, and it is on them that it operates to the worst effect. They have sense enough to feel they are the objects aimed at; and they inflict in their turn the examples of terror they have been instructed to practise.

There is in all European countries, a large class of people of that description, which in England is called the '*mob*'. Of this class were those who committed the burnings and devastations in London in 1780,[19] and of this class were those who carried the heads upon spikes in Paris. Foulon and Berthier were taken up in the country, and sent to Paris, to undergo their examination at the Hotel de Ville; for the National Assembly, immediately on the new ministry coming into office, passed a decree, which they communicated to the King and Cabinet, that they (the National Assembly) would hold the ministry, of which Foulon was one,

---

[15]   The governor of the Bastille, Bernard-René Jourdan de Launay (1740–89), had succeeded his father in 1776. Jacques de Flesselles (1721–89), head of the municipal government (rather than mayor), was killed on the steps of the Hôtel de Ville on 14 July. Joseph François Foulon (1715–89) had the key role in the build-up of troops around Paris over June–July 1789. His son-in-law, Louis-Bénigne-François Bertier de Sauvigny (1737–89), was responsible for organizing food supplies to the army around Paris. They were both killed by the angry crowd whilst being led to trial on 22 July.

[16]   Temple-Bar marks the boundary between the City of London and Westminster. The heads of executed traitors were still displayed there in the eighteenth century.

[17]   'And now also the axe is laid unto the root of the trees: therefore every tree which bringeth not forth good fruit is hewn down, and cast into the fire': John the Baptist's words in Matthew 3: 10.

[18]   Robert-François Damiens (1714–57) attempted to assassinate Louis XV in 1757. He was tortured and then horribly executed.

[19]   See p. 76 above.

responsible for the measures they were advising and pursuing; but the mob, incensed at the appearance of Foulon and Berthier, tore them from their conductors before they were carried to the Hotel de Ville, and executed them on the spot. Why then does Mr. Burke charge outrages of this kind on a whole people? As well may he charge the riots and outrages of 1780 on all the people of London, or those in Ireland on all his country.

But every thing we see or hear offensive to our feelings, and derogatory to the human character, should lead to other reflections than those of reproach. Even the beings who commit them have some claim to our consideration. How then is it that such vast classes of mankind as are distinguished by the appellation of the vulgar, or the ignorant mob, are so numerous in all old countries? The instant we ask ourselves this question, reflection feels an answer. They arise, as an unavoidable consequence, out of the ill construction of all the old governments in Europe, England included with the rest. It is by distortedly exalting some men, that others are distortedly debased, till the whole is out of nature. A vast mass of mankind are degradedly thrown into the back-ground of the human picture, to bring forward, with greater glare, the puppet-show of state and aristocracy. In the commencement of a Revolution, those men are rather the followers of the *camp* than of the *standard* of liberty, and have yet to be instructed how to reverence it.

[We are now got at the origin of man, and at the origin of his rights]

I have now to follow Mr. Burke through a pathless wilderness of rhapsodies, and a sort of descant upon governments, in which he asserts whatever he pleases, on the presumption of its being believed, without offering either evidence or reasons for so doing.

Before anything can be reasoned upon to a conclusion, certain facts, principles, or data, to reason from, must be established, admitted, or denied. Mr. Burke, with his usual outrage, abuses the *Declaration of the Rights of Man*, published by the National Assembly of France as the basis on which the constitution of France is built.[20] This he calls 'paltry and blurred sheets of paper about the rights of man.' – Does Mr. Burke mean to deny that *man* has any rights? If he does, then he must mean that there are no such things as rights any where, and that he has none himself; for who is there in the world but man? But if Mr. Burke means to admit that man has rights, the question then will be, What are those rights, and how came man by them originally?

---

[20]   The Declaration of the Rights of Man was decreed by the National Assembly on 26 August 1789. Louis XVI refused to ratify it in September. For Burke's description of these rights as 'paltry and blurred', see p. 41 above.

The error of those who reason by precedents drawn from antiquity, respecting the rights of man, is that they do not go far enough into antiquity. They do not go the whole way. They stop in some of the intermediate stages of an hundred or a thousand years, and produce what was then done as a rule for the present day. This is no authority at all. If we travel still farther into antiquity, we shall find a direct contrary opinion and practice prevailing; and if antiquity is to be authority, a thousand such authorities may be produced, successively contradicting each other: But if we proceed on, we shall at last come out right; we shall come to the time when man came from the hand of his Maker. What was he then? Man. Man was his high and only title, and a higher cannot be given him. – But of titles I shall speak hereafter.

We are now got at the origin of man, and at the origin of his rights. As to the manner in which the world has been governed from that day to this, it is no farther any concern of ours than to make a proper use of the errors or the improvements which the history of it presents. Those who lived an hundred or a thousand years ago, were then moderns as we are now. They had *their* ancients, and those ancients had others, and we also shall be ancients in our turn. If the mere name of antiquity is to govern in the affairs of life, the people who are to live an hundred or a thousand years hence, may as well take us for a precedent, as we make a precedent of those who lived an hundred or a thousand years ago. The fact is, that portions of antiquity, by proving every thing, establish nothing. It is authority against authority all the way, till we come to the divine origin of the rights of man at the creation. Here our enquiries find a resting-place, and our reason finds a home. If a dispute about the rights of man had arisen at the distance of an hundred years from the creation, it is to this source of authority they must have referred, and it is to this same source of authority that we must now refer.

Though I mean not to touch upon any sectarian principle of religion, yet it may be worth observing, that the genealogy of Christ is traced to Adam. Why then not trace the rights of man to the creation of man? I will answer the question. Because there have been upstart governments, thrusting themselves between, and presumptuously working to *un-make* man.

If any generation of men ever possessed the right of dictating the mode by which the world should be governed for ever, it was the first generation that existed; and if that generation did not do it, no succeeding generation can shew any authority for doing it, nor set any up. The illuminating and divine principle of the equal rights of man, (for it has its origin from the Maker of man) relates, not only to the living individuals, but to generations of men succeeding each other. Every generation is equal in rights to the generations which preceded it, by the same rule that every individual is born equal in rights with his contemporary.

Every history of the creation, and every traditionary account, whether from the lettered or unlettered world, however they may vary in their opinion or belief of certain particulars, all agree in establishing one point, *the unity of man*; by which I mean that men is all of *one degree*, and consequently that all men are born equal, and with equal natural rights, in the same manner as if posterity had been continued by *creation* instead of *generation*, the latter being the only mode by which the former is carried forward; and consequently, every child born into the world must be considered as deriving its existence from God. The world is as new to him as it was to the first man that existed, and his natural right in it is of the same kind.

[The natural rights of man ... the civil rights of man]

The duty of man is not a wilderness of turnpike gates,[21] through which he is to pass by tickets from one to the other. It is plain and simple, and consists but of two points. His duty to God, which every man must feel; and with respect to his neighbour, to do as he would be done by. If those to whom power is delegated do well, they will be respected; if not, they will be despised: and with regard to those to whom no power is delegated, but who assume it, the rational world can know nothing of them.

Hitherto we have spoken only (and that but in part) of the natural rights of man. We have now to consider the civil rights of man, and to shew how the one originates from the other. Man did not enter into society to become *worse* than he was before, nor to have fewer rights than he had before, but to have those rights better secured. His natural rights are the foundation of all his civil rights. But in order to pursue this distinction with more precision, it will be necessary to mark the different qualities of natural and civil rights.

A few words will explain this. Natural rights are those which appertain to man in right of his existence. Of this kind are all the intellectual rights, or rights of the mind, and also all those rights of acting as an individual for his own comfort and happiness, which are not injurious to the natural rights of others. – Civil rights are those which appertain to man in right of his being a member of society. Every civil right has for its foundation some natural right pre-existing in the individual, but to which his individual power is not, in all cases, sufficiently competent. Of this kind are all those which relate to security and protection.

From this short review, it will be easy to distinguish between that class of natural rights which man retains after entering into society, and those which he throws into the common stock as a member of society.

The natural rights which he retains, are all those in which the *power* to execute is as perfect in the individual as the right itself. Among this class, as is before mentioned, are all the intellectual rights, or rights of the mind: consequently, religion is one of those rights. The natural rights which are not retained, are all those in which, though the right is perfect in the individual, the power to execute them is defective. They answer not his purpose. A man, by natural right, has a right to

---

21 The barriers on a toll road.

judge in his own cause; and so far as the right of the mind is concerned, he never surrenders it: But what availeth it him to judge, if he has not power to redress? He therefore deposits this right in the common stock of society, and takes the arm of society, of which he is a part, in preference and in addition to his own. Society *grants* him nothing. Every man is a proprietor in society, and draws on the capital as a matter of right.

From these premises, two or three certain conclusions will follow.

First; That every civil right grows out of a natural right; or, in other words, is a natural right exchanged.

Secondly, That civil power, properly considered as such, is made up of the aggregate of that class of the natural rights of man, which becomes defective in the individual in point of power, and answers not his purpose; but when collected to a focus, becomes competent to the purpose of every one.

Thirdly, That the power produced from the aggregate of natural rights, imperfect in power in the individual, cannot be applied to invade the natural rights which are retained in the individual, and in which the power to execute is as perfect as the right itself.

We have now, in a few words, traced man from a natural individual to a member of society, and shewn, or endeavoured to shew, the quality of the natural rights retained, and of those which are exchanged for civil rights. Let us now apply these principles to governments.

In casting our eyes over the world, it is extremely easy to distinguish the governments which have arisen out of society, or out of the social compact, from those which have not: but to place this in a clearer light than what a single glance may afford, it will be proper to take a review of the several sources from which governments have arisen, and on which they have been founded.

They may be all comprehended under three heads. First, Superstition. Secondly, Power. Thirdly, the common interest of society, and the common rights of man.

The first was a government of priestcraft, the second of conquerors, and the third of reason.

[Governments must have arisen, either *out* of the people, or *over* the people]

To possess ourselves of a clear idea of what government is, or ought to be, we must trace it to its origin. In doing this, we shall easily discover that governments must have arisen, either *out* of the people, or *over* the people. Mr. Burke has made no distinction. He investigates nothing to its source, and therefore he confounds every thing: but he has signified his intention of undertaking at some future opportunity, a comparison between the constitutions of England and France. As he thus renders it a subject of controversy by throwing the gauntlet, I take him up on his own ground. It is in high challenges that high truths have the right of appearing; and I accept it with the more readiness, because it affords me, at the same time, an opportunity of pursuing the subject with respect to governments arising out of society.

But it will be first necessary to define what is meant by a *constitution*. It is not sufficient that we adopt the word; we must fix also a standard signification to it.

A constitution is not a thing in name only, but in fact. It has not an ideal, but a real existence; and wherever it cannot be produced in a visible form, there is none. A constitution is a thing *antecedent* to a government, and a government is only the creature of a constitution. The constitution of a country is not the act of its government, but of the people constituting a government. It is the body of elements, to which you can refer, and quote article by article; and which contains the principles on which the government shall be established, the manner in which it shall be organized, the powers it shall have, the mode of elections, the duration of parliaments, or by what other name such bodies may be called; the powers which the executive part of the government shall have; and, in fine, every thing that relates to the compleat organization of a civil government, and the principles on which it shall act, and by which it shall be bound. A constitution, therefore, is to a government, what the laws made afterwards by that government are to a court of judicature. The court of judicature does not make the laws, neither can it alter them; it only acts in conformity to the laws made; and the government is in like manner governed by the constitution.

Can then Mr. Burke produce the English Constitution? If he cannot, we may fairly conclude that though it has been so much talked about, no such thing as a constitution exists, or ever did exist, and consequently that the people have yet a constitution to form.

Mr. Burke will not, I presume, deny the position I have already advanced; namely, that governments arise either *out* of the people, or *over* the people. The English government is one of those which arose out of a conquest, and not out of society, and consequently it arose over the people; and though it has been much modified from the opportunity of circumstances since the time of William the Conqueror, the country has never yet regenerated itself, and is therefore without a constitution.

[Titles are but nick-names … a sort of foppery in the human character which degrades it]

The French Constitution says, *There shall be no titles*; and of consequence, all that class of equivocal generation, which in some countries is called '*aristocracy*', and in others '*nobility*', is done away, and the *peer* is exalted into MAN.

Titles are but nick-names, and every nick-name is a title. The thing is perfectly harmless in itself, but it marks a sort of foppery in the human character which degrades it. It renders man into the diminutive of man in things which are great, and the counterfeit of woman in things which are little. It talks about its fine *blue ribbon* like a girl, and shews its new *garter* like a child.[22] A certain writer, of some antiquity, says: 'When I was a child, I thought as a child; but when I became a man, I put away childish things.'[23]

It is, properly, from the elevated mind of France, that the folly of titles has fallen. It has outgrown the baby-cloaths of *Count* and *Duke*, and breeched itself in man-hood. France has not levelled; it has exalted. It has put down the dwarf, to set up the man. The punyism of a senseless word like *Duke*, or *Count*, or *Earl*, has ceased to please. Even those who possessed them have disowned the gibberish, and, as they outgrew the rickets, have despised the rattle. The genuine mind of man, thirsting for its native home, society, contemns the gewgaws that separate him from it.[24] Titles are like circles drawn by the magician's wand, to contract the sphere of man's felicity. He lives immured within the Bastille of a word, and surveys at a distance the envied life of man.

[Toleration is not the *opposite* of Intolerance, but is the *counterfeit* of it]

The French constitution hath abolished or renounced *Toleration*, and *Intolerance* also, and hath established UNIVERSAL RIGHT OF CONSCIENCE.[25]

Toleration is not the *opposite* of Intolerance, but is the *counterfeit* of it. Both are despotisms. The one assumes to itself the right of with-holding Liberty of Conscience, and the other of granting it. The one is the pope, armed with fire and faggot, and the other is the pope selling or granting indulgences. The former is church and state, and the latter is church and traffic.[26]

But Toleration may be viewed in a much stronger light. Man worships not him-self, but his Maker; and the liberty of conscience which he claims, is not for the service of himself, but of his God. In this case, therefore, we must necessarily have the associated idea of two beings; the *mortal* who renders the worship, and the

---

[22]   Paine mocks the regalia of the knights of the garter.

[23]   Saint Paul, 1 Corinthians 13: 11.

[24]   Paine refers to the titles and feudal privileges put aside by those aristocrats who joined the National Assembly. 'Rickets': a common childhood disease causing softening of the bones. 'Gewgaw': a showy trifle or bauble without value.

[25]   Decreed in the Declaration of the Rights of Man (see note 20 above).

[26]   The Toleration Act of 1689 exempted Protestant Dissenters from various penalties and allowed them their own places of worship and education. It was a widely praised achievement of British liberty and Paine shows some daring in attacking it.

IMMORTAL BEING who is worshipped. Toleration, therefore, places itself, not between man and man, nor between church and church, nor between one denomination of religion and another, but between God and man; between the being who worships, and the BEING who is worshipped; and by the same act of assumed authority by which it tolerates man to pay his worship, it presumptuously and blasphemously sets itself up to tolerate the Almighty to receive it.

[The church with the state, a sort of mule animal]

All religions are in their nature mild and benign, and united with principles of morality. They could not have made proselytes at first, by professing any thing that was vicious, cruel, persecuting, or immoral. Like every thing else, they had their beginning; and they proceeded by persuasion, exhortation, and example. How then is it that they lose their native mildness, and become morose and intolerant?

It proceeds from the connection which Mr. Burke recommends. By engendering the church with the state, a sort of mule animal, capable only of destroying, and not of breeding up, is produced, called *The Church established by Law*. It is a stranger, even from its birth, to any parent mother on which it is begotten, and whom in time it kicks out and destroys.

The inquisition[27] in Spain does not proceed from the religion originally professed, but from this mule-animal, engendered between the church and the state. The burnings in Smithfield[28] proceeded from the same heterogeneous production; and it was the regeneration of this strange animal in England afterwards, that renewed rancour and irreligion among the inhabitants, and that drove the people called Quakers and Dissenters to America.[29] Persecution is not an original feature in *any* religion; but it is always the strongly-marked feature of all law-religions, or religions established by law. Take away the law-establishment, and every religion reassumes its original benignity. In America, a Catholic Priest[30] is a good citizen, a good character, and a good neighbour; an Episcopalian[31] Minister is of the same description: and this proceeds independent of the men, from there being no law-establishment in America.

---

[27]   The Spanish Inquisition (1479–1814) was closely associated with state power and directed against suspected heretics, who were frequently tortured and burnt at the stake if convicted.

[28]   A London marketplace, used for burning Protestant martyrs in the reign of Mary I (1553–8).

[29]   The Quakers were a sect founded in the 1650s. Their refusal to take oaths and to pay tithes led to their persecution at the Restoration in 1660. The most famous Quaker migrants to America were those who founded Pennsylvania with William Penn.

[30]   Opponents of Catholics' full rights in Britain often claimed that allegiance to the pope would interfere with their loyalty as British subjects.

[31]   Part of the Anglican communion in America, but, unlike the Church of England, not part of the state.

Miscellaneous Chapter

To prevent interrupting the argument in the preceding part of this work, or the narrative that follows it, I reserved some observations to be thrown together in a Miscellaneous Chapter; by which variety might not be censured for confusion. Mr. Burke's book is *all* Miscellany. His intention was to make an attack on the French Revolution; but instead of proceeding with an orderly arrangement, he has stormed it with a Mob of ideas, tumbling over and destroying one another.

But this confusion and contradiction in Mr. Burke's Book is easily accounted for. – When a man in a long cause attempts to steer his course by any thing else than some polar truth or principle, he is sure to be lost. It is beyond the compass of his capacity, to keep all the parts of an argument together, and make them unite in one issue, by any other means than having this guide always in view. Neither memory nor invention will supply the want of it. The former fails him, and the latter betrays him.

Notwithstanding the nonsense, for it deserves no better name, that Mr. Burke has asserted about hereditary rights, and hereditary succession, and that a Nation has not a right to form a Government for itself; it happened to fall in his way to give some account of what Government is. '*Government*, says he, *is a contrivance of human wisdom.*'[32]

Admitting that Government is a contrivance of human *wisdom*, it must necessarily follow, that hereditary succession, and hereditary rights, (as they are called), can make no part of it, because it is impossible to make wisdom hereditary; and on the other hand, *that* cannot be a wise contrivance, which in its operation may commit the government of a nation to the wisdom of an ideot. The ground which Mr. Burke now takes is fatal to every part of his cause. The argument changes from hereditary rights to hereditary wisdom; and the question is, Who is the wisest man? He must now shew that every one in the line of hereditary succession was a Solomon, or his title is not good to be a king. – What a stroke has Mr. Burke now made! To use a sailor's phrase, he has *swabbed the deck*, and scarcely left a name legible in the list of kings; and he has mowed down and thinned the House of Peers, with a scythe as formidable as Death and Time.

But, Mr. Burke appears to have been aware of this retort; and he has taken care to guard against it, by making government to be not only a *contrivance* of human wisdom, but a *monopoly* of wisdom. He puts the nation as fools on one side, and places his government of wisdom, all wise men of Gotham,[33] on the other side; and he then proclaims, and says, that '*Men have a* RIGHT *that their* WANTS *should be provided for by this wisdom.*'[34] Having thus made proclamation, he next proceeds to explain to them what their *wants* are, and also what their *rights* are. In this he has

---

[32] See above, p. 32.
[33] The village of Gotham in Nottinghamshire was proverbial for its foolishness.
[34] See above, p. 32.

succeeded dextrously, for he makes their wants to be a *want* of wisdom; but as this is but cold comfort, he then informs them, that they have a *right* (not to any of the wisdom) but to be governed by it: and in order to impress them with a solemn reverence for this monopoly-government of wisdom, and of its vast capacity for all purposes, possible or impossible, right or wrong, he proceeds with astrological mysterious importance, to tell to them its powers, in these words:

> The Rights of men in government are their advantages; and these are often in balances between differences of good; and in compromises sometimes between *good* and *evil*, and sometimes between *evil* and *evil*. Political reason is a *computing principle*; adding – subtracting – multiplying – and dividing, morally and not meta-physically or mathematically, true moral demonstrations.[35]

As the wondering audience whom Mr. Burke supposes himself talking to, may not understand all this learned jargon, I will undertake to be its interpreter. The mean-ing then, good people, of all this, is: *That government is governed by no principle what-ever; that it can make evil good, or good evil, just as it pleases. In short, that government is arbitrary power.*

Conclusion

Reason and Ignorance, the opposites of each other, influence the great bulk of mankind. If either of these can be rendered sufficiently extensive in a country, the machinery of Government goes easily on. Reason obeys itself; and Ignorance sub-mits to whatever is dictated to it.

The two modes of Government which prevail in the world, are, *first*, Government by election and representation: *Secondly*, Government by hereditary succession. The former is generally known by the name of republic; the latter by that of mon-archy and aristocracy.

Those two distinct and opposite forms, erect themselves on the two distinct and opposite bases of Reason and Ignorance. – As the exercise of Government requires talents and abilities, and as talents and abilities cannot have hereditary descent, it is evident that hereditary succession requires a belief from man, to which his reason cannot subscribe, and which can only be established upon his ignorance; and the more ignorant any country is, the better it is fitted for this species of Government.

On the contrary, Government in a well constituted republic, requires no belief from man beyond what his reason can give. He sees the *rationale* of the whole system, its origin and its operation; and as it is best supported when best

---

[35]   See Burke's *Reflections*, p. 92, not excerpted here.

understood, the human faculties act with boldness, and acquire, under this form of Government, a gigantic manliness.

[In mixed Governments there is no responsibility]

In mixed Governments there is no responsibility: the parts cover each other till responsibility is lost; and the corruption which moves the machine, contrives at the same time its own escape. When it is laid down as a maxim, that *a King can do no wrong*, it places him in a state of similar security with that of ideots and persons insane, and responsibility is out of the question with respect to himself. It then descends upon the Minister, who shelters himself under a majority in Parliament, which, by places, pensions, and corruption, he can always command; and that majority justifies itself by the same authority with which it protects the Minister. In this rotatory motion, responsibility is thrown off from the parts, and from the whole.

[The Revolutions of America and France, are a renovation of the natural order of things]

What were formerly called Revolutions, were little more than a change of persons, or an alteration of local circumstances. They rose and fell like things of course, and had nothing in their existence or their fate that could influence beyond the spot that produced them. But what we now see in the world, from the Revolutions of America and France, are a renovation of the natural order of things, a system of principles as universal as truth and the existence of man, and combining moral with political happiness and national prosperity.

I   *Men are born and always continue free, and equal in respect of their rights. Civil distinctions, therefore, can be founded only on public utility.*

II   *The end of all political associations is the preservation of the natural and imprescriptible rights of man; and these rights are liberty, property, security, and resistance of oppression.*

III   *The Nation is essentially the source of all Sovereignty; nor can any* INDIVIDUAL, *or* ANY BODY OF MEN, *be entitled to any authority which is not expressly derived from it.*

In these principles, there is nothing to throw a Nation into confusion by inflaming ambition. They are calculated to call forth wisdom and abilities, and to exercise them for the public good, and not for the emolument or aggrandizement of particular descriptions of men or families. Monarchical sovereignty, the enemy of mankind, and the source of misery, is abolished; and sovereignty itself is restored to its natural and original place, the Nation. Were this the case throughout Europe, the cause of wars would be taken away.

[It is an age of Revolutions, in which every thing may be looked for]

As it is not difficult to perceive, from the enlightened state of mankind, that hereditary Governments are verging to their decline, and that Revolutions on the broad basis of national sovereignty, and Government by representation, are making their way in Europe, it would be an act of wisdom to anticipate their approach, and produce Revolutions by reason and accommodation, rather than commit them to the issue of convulsions.

From what we now see, nothing of reform in the political world ought to be held improbable. It is an age of Revolutions, in which every thing may be looked for. The intrigue of Courts, by which the system of war is kept up, may provoke a confederation of Nations to abolish it: and a European Congress to patronize the progress of free Government, and promote the civilization of Nations with each other, is an event nearer in probability, than once were the revolutions and alliance of France and America.

5

Mary Wollstonecraft
A Vindication of the Rights of Woman: with Strictures on Political and Moral Subjects

(London: J. Johnson, 1792)

Originally published in January 1792, *Vindication of the Rights of Woman* is a key text in the history of feminist thinking. Its initial occasion was debates in France about whether women should be granted full rights as citizens and the associated question of the appropriate level of education; hence the address to Talleyrand, with which the work opens. This piece also bears the stamp of the kind of thinking about educational issues that had characterized Wollstonecraft's writing before the revolution, in the books published by Joseph Johnson. For many of the Rational Dissenters associated with Johnson, reason and the soul were unsexed. Consequently there was a long-standing emphasis in such circles on rational education for women as 'moral beings', as Wollstonecraft puts it, especially if they were to contribute politically to 'those glorious principles that give a substance to morality'. Politics and education were also crucially linked for Wollstonecraft in terms of the question of how 'children are to be educated to understand the true principle of patriotism' (see p. 91 below). A patriot, for her, was the independent citizen who placed the welfare of the commonwealth before self or other interests. She engages directly with Rousseau, a writer whom in many ways she admired as an inspired republican, to contradict the theories of education set out in *Émile* (1762). Rousseau's call for a return to nature in education did not extend to little girls, who, he thought, should be encouraged into a compliance that would make them helpmeets for their husbands. Wollstonecraft wanted Rousseau's ideas, in so far as she agreed with them, to be extended to both sexes. Most writers on education known to Wollstonecraft from her

Romanticism and Revolution: A Reader.
Edited by Jon Mee and David Fallon.   © 2011 Blackwell Publishing Ltd.

liberal and dissenting circles advocated a much more active encouragement of female intellect. In this respect, *Vindication* was not particularly out of the ordinary when it appeared, which may account for its relatively positive reception, at least initially. Where she struck out more deliberately in a new direction was in her insistence that 'manly' virtues of political 'independence' (p. 113 below) should be aspirations for women as well as for men. Women should aim not just to exist as companions of active republican spouses, but also to 'unfold their own faculties and acquire the dignity of conscious virtue' (p. 98 below). At the same time, *Vindication of the Rights of Woman* places domestic duties at the centre of the political virtues. Breastfeeding and a close involvement with the family are recommended for women as part of the active benevolence expected of any citizen. The aristocratic woman who indulges her sensibility but keeps herself distant from her children is represented as unnatural. The father who would rather play the libertine or gallant is represented as effeminate and unmanly. Only after the revelations about her private life made by her (by then) husband William Godwin in his *Memoir* (1798) did the representation of Wollstonecraft herself as an 'unsex'd female' really begin to take hold, as part of the cultural backlash against Jacobin intellectual life in the second half of the 1790s.

To M. Talleyrand-Périgord, Late Bishop of Autun[1]

Sir,

Having read with great pleasure a pamphlet, which you have lately published, on National Education,[2] I dedicate this volume to you – to induce you to read it with attention; and, because I think that you will understand me, which I do not suppose many pert witlings will, who may ridicule the arguments they are unable to answer. But, Sir, I carry my respect for your understanding still farther; so far, that I am confident you will not throw my work aside, and hastily conclude that I am wrong, because you did not view the subject in the same light yourself. – And, pardon my frankness, but I must observe, that you treated it in too cursory a manner, contented to consider it as it had been considered formerly, when the rights of man, not to advert to woman, were trampled on as chimerical – I call upon you,

---

[1]   Charles-Maurice de Talleyrand-Périgord (1754–1838) was to prove one of the great survivors of the French Revolution. He resigned his bishopric in 1791 to concentrate on politics. After 1792 he was involved in foreign affairs, and eventually served under Napoleon and the restored monarchy after 1815 in this capacity.

[2]   Talleyrand's *Rapport sur l'instruction publique* (Paris: Imprimerie Nationale, 1791) called for free education for boys and girls, but followed Rousseau's view that women should be educated as helpmates for their future spouses.

therefore, now to[3] weigh what I have advanced respecting the rights of woman, and national education – and I call with the firm tone of humanity. For my arguments, Sir, are dictated by a disinterested spirit – I plead for my sex – not for myself. Independence I have long considered as the grand blessing of life, the basis of every virtue – and independence I will ever secure by contracting my wants, though I were to live on a barren heath.

It is then an affection for the whole human race that makes my pen dart rapidly along to support what I believe to be the cause of virtue: and the same motive leads me earnestly to wish to see woman placed in a station in which she would advance, instead of retarding, the progress of those glorious principles that give a substance to morality. My opinion, indeed, respecting the rights and duties of woman, seems to flow so naturally from these simple principles, that I think it scarcely possible, but that some of the enlarged minds who formed your admirable constitution, will coincide with me.

[The prevailing notion respecting a sexual character was subversive of morality]

Contending for the rights of woman, my main argument is built on this simple principle, that if she be not prepared by education to become the companion of man, she will stop the progress of knowledge,[4] for truth must be common to all, or it will be inefficacious with respect to its influence on general practice. And how can woman be expected to co-operate unless she know why she ought to be virtuous? unless freedom strengthen her reason till she comprehend her duty, and see in what manner it is connected with her real good? If children are to be educated to understand the true principle of patriotism, their mother must be a patriot; and the love of mankind, from which an orderly train of virtues spring, can only be produced by considering the moral and civil interest of mankind; but the education and situation of woman, at present, shuts her out from such investigations.

In this work I have produced many arguments, which to me were conclusive, to prove that the prevailing notion respecting a sexual character was subversive of morality, and I have contended, that to render the human body and mind more perfect, chastity must more universally prevail, and that chastity will never be respected in the male world till the person of a woman is not, as it were, idolized, when little virtue or sense embellish it with the grand traces of mental beauty, or the interesting simplicity of affection.

---

[3]   Second edition: 'to read it with attention … therefore, now to' was replaced with 'reconsider the subject, and maturely'.

[4]   Second edition: 'knowledge and virtue'.

Consider, Sir, dispassionately, these observations – for a glimpse of this truth seemed to open before you when you observed, 'that to see one half of the human race excluded by the other from all participation of government, was a political phænomenon that, according to abstract principles, it was impossible to explain'.[5] If so, on what does your constitution rest? If the abstract rights of man will bear discussion and explanation, those of woman, by a parity of reasoning, will not shrink from the same test: though a different opinion prevails in this country, built on the very arguments which you use to justify the oppression of woman – prescription.

Introduction

After considering the historic page, and viewing the living world with anxious solicitude, the most melancholy emotions of sorrowful indignation have depressed my spirits, and I have sighed when obliged to confess, that either nature has made a great difference between man and man, or that the civilization which has hitherto taken place in the world has been very partial. I have turned over various books written on the subject of education,[6] and patiently observed the conduct of parents and the management of schools; but what has been the result? – a profound conviction that the neglected education of my fellow-creatures is the grand source of the misery I deplore; and that women, in particular, are rendered weak and wretched by a variety of concurring causes, originating from one hasty conclusion. The conduct and manners of women, in fact, evidently prove that their minds are not in a healthy state; for, like the flowers which are planted in too rich a soil, strength and usefulness are sacrificed to beauty; and the flaunting leaves, after having pleased a fastidious eye, fade, disregarded on the stalk, long before the season when they ought to have arrived at maturity. – One cause of this barren blooming I attribute to a false system of education, gathered from the books written on this subject by men who, considering females rather as women than human creatures, have been more anxious to make them alluring mistresses than rational wives;[7] and the understanding of the sex has been so bubbled by this specious homage, that the civilized women of the present century, with a few exceptions, are only anxious to inspire love, when they ought to cherish a nobler ambition, and by their abilities and virtues exact respect.

In a treatise, therefore, on female rights and manners, the works which have been particularly written for their improvement must not be overlooked; especially when it is asserted, in direct terms, that the minds of women are enfeebled by false

---

[5]   Talleyrand, *Rapport sur l'instruction publique*, p. 118.
[6]   Wollstonecraft already had an established reputation as a writer on education herself, and she reviewed in the area regularly for the *Analytical Review*. These contributions included a long notice in the November 1790 issue of Catherine Macaulay's *Letters on Education*, referred to below, p. 111.
[7]   Second edition: 'affectionate wives and rational mothers'.

refinement; that the books of instruction, written by men of genius, have had the same tendency as more frivolous productions; and that, in the true style of Mahometanism, they are only considered as females, and not as a part of the human species, when improvable reason is allowed to be the dignified distinction which raises men above the brute creation, and puts a natural sceptre in a feeble hand.[8]

Yet, because I am a woman, I would not lead my readers to suppose that I mean violently to agitate the contested question respecting the equality or inferiority of the sex; but as the subject lies in my way, and I cannot pass it over without subjecting the main tendency of my reasoning to misconstruction, I shall stop a moment to deliver, in a few words, my opinion. – In the government of the physical world it is observable that the female[9] is, in general, inferior to the male. The male pursues, the female yields – this is the law of nature; and it does not appear to be suspended or abrogated in favour of woman. This physical superiority cannot be denied – and it is a noble prerogative! But not content with this natural pre-eminence, men endeavour to sink us still lower, merely to render us alluring objects for a moment; and women, intoxicated by the adoration which men, under the influence of their senses, pay them, do not seek to obtain a durable interest in their hearts, or to become the friends of the fellow creatures who find amusement in their society.

I am aware of an obvious inference: – from every quarter have I heard exclamations against masculine women;[10] but where are they to be found? If by this appellation men mean to inveigh against their ardour in hunting, shooting, and gaming, I shall most cordially join in the cry; but if it be against the imitation of manly virtues, or, more properly speaking, the attainment of those talents and virtues, the exercise of which ennobles the human character, and which raise females in the scale of animal being, when they are comprehensively termed mankind; – all those who view them with a philosophical eye must, I should think, wish with me, that they may every day grow more and more masculine.

[I shall disdain to cull my phrases or polish my style]

My own sex, I hope, will excuse me, if I treat them like rational creatures, instead of flattering their *fascinating* graces, and viewing them as if they were in a state of perpetual childhood, unable to stand alone. I earnestly wish to point out in what

---

[8]   See note 8 to p. 55 above (Chapter 3). For an analysis of Wollstonecraft's use of the idea of oriental despotism, especially towards women, as part of her republican critique, see Saree Makdisi, *William Blake and the Impossible History of the 1790s* (Chicago: University of Chicago Press, 2003), pp. 214–32.

[9]   Second edition adds: 'in point of strength,'.

[10]   Wollstonecraft was to become an object of satire in this regard. Especially after Godwin's *Memoir* (1798), a host of novels represented the figure of a female philosopher as inappropriately manly, sexually predatory, and generally grotesque. See for instance Bridgetina Botherim in Elizabeth Hamilton's *Memoirs of Modern Philosophers* (1800) and Harriet Freke in Maria Edgeworth's *Belinda* (1801).

true dignity and human happiness consists – I wish to persuade women to endeavour to acquire strength, both of mind and body, and to convince them that the soft phrases, susceptibility of heart, delicacy of sentiment, and refinement of taste, are almost synonymous with epithets of weakness, and that those beings who are only the objects of pity and that kind of love, which has been termed its sister, will soon become objects of contempt.

Dismissing then those pretty feminine phrases, which the men condescendingly use to soften our slavish dependence, and despising that weak elegancy of mind, exquisite sensibility, and sweet docility of manners, supposed to be the sexual characteristics of the weaker vessel, I wish to shew that elegance is inferior to virtue, that the first object of laudable ambition is to obtain a character as a human being, regardless of the distinction of sex; and that secondary views should be brought to this simple touchstone.

This is a rough sketch of my plan; and should I express my conviction with the energetic emotions that I feel whenever I think of the subject, the dictates of experience and reflection will be felt by some of my readers. Animated by this important object, I shall disdain to cull my phrases or polish my style; – I aim at being useful, and sincerity will render me unaffected; for, wishing rather to persuade by the force of my arguments, than dazzle by the elegance of my language, I shall not waste my time in rounding periods, nor in fabricating the turgid bombast of artificial feelings, which, coming from the head, never reach the heart. – I shall be employed about things, not words! – and, anxious to render my sex more respectable members of society, I shall try to avoid that flowery diction which has slided from essays into novels, and from novels into familiar letters and conversation.

These pretty nothings – these caricatures of the real beauty of sensibility,[11] dropping glibly from the tongue, vitiate the taste, and create a kind of sickly delicacy that turns away from simple unadorned truth; and a deluge of false sentiments and overstretched feelings, stifling the natural emotions of the heart, render the domestic pleasures insipid, that ought to sweeten the exercise of those severe duties, which educate a rational and immortal being for a nobler field of action.

Chap. II   The Prevailing Opinion of a Sexual Character Discussed

To account for, and excuse the tyranny of man, many ingenious arguments have been brought forward to prove, that the two sexes, in the acquirement of virtue, ought to aim at attaining a very different character: or, to speak explicitly, women are not allowed to have sufficient strength of mind to acquire what really deserves the name of virtue. Yet it should seem, allowing them to have souls,

---

[11]   Second edition: 'These pretty superlatives, dropping…'.

that there is but one way appointed by Providence to lead *mankind* to either virtue or happiness.

If then women are not a swarm of ephemeron triflers, why should they be kept in ignorance under the specious name of innocence? Men complain, and with reason, of the follies and caprices of our sex, when they do not keenly satirize our head-strong passions and groveling vices. – Behold, I should answer, the natural effect of ignorance! The mind will ever be unstable that has only prejudices to rest on, and the current will run with destructive fury when there are no barriers to break its force. Women are told from their infancy, and taught by the example of their mothers, that a little knowledge of human weakness, justly termed cunning, softness of temper, *outward* obedience, and a scrupulous attention to a puerile kind of propriety, will obtain for them the protection of man; and should they be beautiful, every thing else is needless, for, at least, twenty years of their lives.

Thus Milton describes our first frail mother; though when he tells us that women are formed for softness and sweet attractive grace, I cannot comprehend his meaning, unless, in the true Mahometan strain, he meant to deprive us of souls, and insinuate that we were beings only designed by sweet attractive grace, and docile blind obedience, to gratify the senses of man when he can no longer soar on the wing of contemplation.[12]

How grossly do they insult us who thus advise us only to render ourselves gentle, domestic brutes! For instance, the winning softness so warmly, and frequently, recommended, that governs by obeying. What childish expressions, and how insignificant is the being – can it be an immortal one? who will condescend to govern by such sinister methods! 'Certainly,' says Lord Bacon, 'man is of kin to the beasts by his body; and if he be not of kin to God by his spirit, he is a base and ignoble creature!'[13] Men, indeed, appear to me to act in a very unphilosophical manner when they try to secure the good conduct of women by attempting to keep them always in a state of childhood. Rousseau was more consistent when he wished to stop the progress of reason in both sexes, for if men eat of the tree of knowledge, women will come in for a taste; but, from the imperfect cultivation which their understandings now receive, they only attain a knowledge of evil.[14]

Children, I grant, should be innocent; but when the epithet is applied to men, or women, it is but a civil term for weakness. For if it be allowed that women were destined by Providence to acquire human virtues, and by the exercise of their understandings, that stability of character which is the firmest ground to rest our future hopes upon, they must be permitted to turn to the fountain of light, and not

---

[12] *Paradise Lost* IV.297–8. The lines are quoted by James Fordyce in his *Sermons to Young Women* (3rd corrected edn, 1766), II, 221. See Wollstonecraft's criticism of Fordyce, p. 106 below.

[13] Francis Bacon, 'Of Atheism', *Essays* (London: Penguin, 1985 [1625]), p. 110.

[14] Rousseau's *Émile* was translated by William Kenrick as *Emilius and Sophia; or A New System of Education* (1762, 1763). Wollstonecraft's quotations are from the 3rd edn of 1783, which is used in these notes. In it Rousseau begins by asserting (I, 1): 'All things are good as their Creator made them, but every thing degenerates in the hands of man.'

forced to shape their course by the twinkling of a mere satellite. Milton, I grant, was of a very different opinion; for he only bends to the indefeasible right of beauty, though it would be difficult to render two passages which I now mean to contrast, consistent. But into similar inconsistencies are great men often led by their senses.

> To whom thus Eve with *perfect beauty* adorn'd.
> My Author and Disposer, what thou bidst
> *Unargued* I obey; so God ordains;
> God is *thy law, thou mine:* to know no more
> Is Woman's *happiest* knowledge and her *praise*.[15]

These are exactly the arguments that I have used to children; but I have added, your reason is now gaining strength, and, till it arrives at some degree of maturity, you must look up to me for advice – then you ought to *think,* and only rely on God.

Yet in the following lines Milton seems to coincide with me; when he makes Adam thus expostulate with his Maker.

> Hast thou not made me here thy substitute,
> And these inferior far beneath me set?
> Among *unequals* what society
> Can sort, what harmony or true delight?
> Which must be mutual, in proportion due
> Giv'n and receiv'd; but in *disparity*
> The one intense, the other still remiss
> Cannot well suit with either, but soon prove
> Tedious alike: of *fellowship* I speak
> Such as I seek, fit to participate
> All rational delight –[16]

In treating, therefore, of the manners of women, let us, disregarding sensual arguments, trace what we should endeavour to make them in order to co-operate, if the expression be not too bold, with the supreme Being.

By individual education, I mean, for the sense of the word is not precisely defined, such an attention to a child as will slowly sharpen the senses, form the temper, regulate the passions, as they begin to ferment, and set the understanding to work before the body arrives at maturity; so that the man may only have to proceed, not to begin, the important task of learning to think and reason.

To prevent any misconstruction, I must add, that I do not believe that a private education[17] can work the wonders which some sanguine writers have attributed to

---

[15]   *Paradise Lost*, IV.634–8. Wollstonecraft's italics.
[16]   Ibid., VIII.381–92. Wollstonecraft's italics.
[17]   By 'private education' Wollstonecraft means education given by a tutor in the home, as many aristocratic families preferred.

it. Men and women must be educated, in a great degree, by the opinions and manners of the society they live in. In every age there has been a stream of popular opinion that has carried all before it, and given a family character, as it were, to the century. It may then fairly be inferred, that, till society be differently constituted, much cannot be expected from education. It is, however, sufficient for my present purpose to assert, that, whatever effect circumstances have on the abilities, every being may become virtuous by the exercise of its own reason; for if but one being was created with vicious inclinations, that is positively bad, what can save us from atheism? or if we worship a God, is not that God a devil?

Consequently, the most perfect education, in my opinion, is such an exercise of the understanding as is best calculated to strengthen the body and form the heart. Or, in other words, to enable the individual to attain such habits of virtue as will render it independent. In fact, it is a farce to call any being virtuous whose virtues do not result from the exercise of its own reason. This was Rousseau's opinion respecting men:[18] I extend it to women, and confidently assert that they have been drawn out of their sphere by false refinement, and not by an endeavour to acquire masculine qualities. Still the regal homage which they receive is so intoxicating, that till the manners of the times are changed, and formed on more reasonable principles, it may be impossible to convince them that the illegitimate power, which they obtain, by degrading themselves, is a curse, and that they must return to nature and equality, if they wish to secure the placid satisfaction that unsophisticated affections impart. But for this epoch we must wait – wait, perhaps, till kings and nobles, enlightened by reason, and, preferring the real dignity of man to childish state, throw off their gaudy hereditary trappings: and if then women do not resign the arbitrary power of beauty – they will prove that they have *less* mind than man.

[The grand end of their exertions should be to unfold their own faculties]

Let us examine this question. Rousseau declares that a woman should never, for a moment, feel herself independent, that she should be governed by fear to exercise her *natural* cunning, and made a coquetish slave in order to render her a more alluring object of desire, a *sweeter* companion to man, whenever he chooses to relax himself. He carries the arguments, which he pretends to draw from the indications of nature, still further, and insinuates that truth and fortitude, the corner stones of all human virtue, should be cultivated with certain restrictions, because, with respect to the female character, obedience is the grand lesson which ought to be impressed with unrelenting rigour.[19]

---

[18]   'Reason only teaches us to know good from evil' (Rousseau, *Emilius*, I, 78).
[19]   See for instance *Emilius*, III, 191.

What nonsense! when will a great man arise with sufficient strength of mind to puff away the fumes which pride and sensuality have thus spread over the subject! If women are by nature inferior to men, their virtues must be the same in quality, if not in degree, or virtue is a relative idea; consequently, their conduct should be founded on the same principles, and have the same aim.

Connected with man as daughters, wives, and mothers, their moral character may be estimated by their manner of fulfilling those simple duties; but the end, the grand end of their exertions should be to unfold their own faculties and acquire the dignity of conscious virtue. They may try to render their road pleasant; but ought never to forget, in common with man, that life yields not the felicity which can satisfy an immortal soul.

[To endeavour to reason love out of the world, would be to out Quixote Cervantes]

To speak disrespectfully of love is, I know, high treason against sentiment and fine feelings; but I wish to speak the simple language of truth, and rather to address the head than the heart. To endeavour to reason love out of the world, would be to out Quixote Cervantes, and equally offend against common sense; but an endeavour to restrain this tumultuous passion, and to prove that it should not be allowed to dethrone superior powers, or to usurp the sceptre which the understanding should ever coolly wield, appears less wild.

Youth is the season for love in both sexes; but in those days of thoughtless enjoyment provision should be made for the more important years of life, when reflection takes place of sensation. But Rousseau, and most of the male writers who have followed his steps, have warmly inculcated that the whole tendency of female education ought to be directed to one point: – to render them pleasing.[20]

[Surely she has not an immortal soul who can loiter life away]

Women ought to endeavour to purify their heart; but can they do so when their uncultivated understandings make them entirely dependent on their senses for employment and amusement, when no noble pursuit sets them above the little vanities of the day, or enables them to curb the wild emotions that agitate a reed over which every passing breeze has power? To gain the affections of a virtuous

---

[20]   *Emilius*, III, 178.

man is affectation necessary? Nature has given woman a weaker frame than man; but, to ensure her husband's affections, must a wife, who by the exercise of her mind and body whilst she was discharging the duties of a daughter, wife, and mother, has allowed her constitution to retain its natural strength, and her nerves a healthy tone, is she, I say, to condescend to use art and feign a sickly delicacy in order to secure her husband's affection? Weakness may excite tenderness, and gratify the arrogant pride of man;[21] but the lordly caresses of a protector will not gratify a noble mind that pants for, and deserves to be respected. Fondness is a poor substitute for friendship!

In a seraglio, I grant, that all these arts are necessary; the epicure must have his palate tickled, or he will sink into apathy; but have women so little ambition as to be satisfied with such a condition? Can they supinely dream life away in the lap of pleasure, or the languor of weariness, rather than assert their claim to pursue reasonable pleasures and render themselves conspicuous by practising the virtues which dignify mankind? Surely she has not an immortal soul who can loiter life away merely employed to adorn her person, that she may amuse the languid hours, and soften the cares of a fellow-creature who is willing to be enlivened by her smiles and tricks, when the serious business of life is over.

Besides, the woman who strengthens her body and exercises her mind will, by managing her family and practising various virtues, become the friend, and not the humble dependent of her husband, and if she deserves his regard by possessing such substantial qualities, she will not find it necessary to conceal her affection, nor to pretend to an unnatural coldness of constitution to excite her husband's passions. In fact, if we revert to history, we shall find that the women who have distinguished themselves have neither been the most beautiful nor the most gentle of their sex.

Chap. III   The Same Subject Continued

[…] Women, as well as despots, have now, perhaps, more power than they would have if the world, divided and subdivided into kingdoms and families, was governed by laws deduced from the exercise of reason; but in obtaining it, to carry on the comparison, their character is degraded, and licentiousness spread through the whole aggregate of society. The many become pedestal to the few. I, therefore, will venture to assert, that till women are more rationally educated, the progress of human virtue and improvement in knowledge must receive continual checks. And if it be granted that woman was not created merely to gratify the appetite of man,

---

[21]   This idea is reiterated in James Fordyce's *Sermons*; this is one of the reasons why Wollstonecraft is more hostile to it than to Gregory's *A Father's Advice to his Daughters* (1774), a point made by Vivien Jones in 'Mary Wollstonecraft and the literature of advice and instruction', in Claudia Johnson (ed.), *The Cambridge Companion to Mary Wollstonecraft* (Cambridge: Cambridge University Press, 2002), pp. 119–40.

nor to be the upper servant, who provides his meals and takes care of his linen, it must follow, that the first care of those mothers or fathers, who really attend to the education of females, should be, if not to strengthen the body, at least, not to destroy the constitution by mistaken notions of beauty and female excellence; nor should girls ever be allowed to imbibe the pernicious notion that a defect can, by any chemical process of reasoning, become an excellence.[22]

[It is time to effect a revolution in female manners]

It is time to effect a revolution in female manners – time to restore to them their lost dignity – and make them, as a part of the human species, labour by reforming themselves to reform the world. It is time to separate unchangeable morals from local manners. – If men be demi-gods – why let us serve them! And if the dignity of the female soul be as disputable as that of animals – if their reason does not afford sufficient light to direct their conduct whilst unerring instinct is denied – they are surely of all creatures the most miserable! and, bent beneath the iron hand of destiny, must submit to be a *fair defect* in creation. But to justify the ways of Providence respecting them,[23] by pointing out some irrefragable reason for thus making such a large portion of mankind accountable and not accountable, would puzzle the subtilest casuist.

The only solid foundation for morality appears to be the character of the supreme Being; the harmony of which arises from a balance of attributes; – and, to speak with reverence, one attribute seems to imply the *necessity* of another. He must be just, because he is wise, he must be good, because he is omnipotent. For to exalt one attribute at the expence of another equally noble and necessary, bears the stamp of the warped reason of man – the homage of passion. Man, accustomed to bow down to power in his savage state, can seldom divest himself of this barbarous prejudice, even when civilization determines how much superior mental is to bodily strength; and his reason is clouded by these crude opinions, even when he thinks of the Deity. – His omnipotence is made to swallow up, or preside over his other attributes, and those mortals are supposed to limit his power irreverently, who think that it must be regulated by his wisdom.

I disclaim that specious humility which, after investigating nature, stops at the author. – The High and Lofty One, who inhabiteth eternity, doubtless possesses many attributes of which we can form no conception; but reason tells me that they cannot clash with those I adore – and I am compelled to listen to her voice.

---

[22] At this point, Wollstonecraft comments on and quotes from Thomas Day's novel *Sandford and Merton*, (6th edn, 1791), III, 207–9, respecting gender difference as a product of education and upbringing. Day was Britain's best-known advocate of Rousseau's educational principles.

[23] Wollstonecraft echoes *Paradise Lost*, I.26, where Milton defines his task in terms of justifying 'the ways of God to men'.

It seems natural for man to search for excellence, and either to trace it in the object that he worships, or blindly to invest it with perfection, as a garment. But what good effect can the latter mode of worship have on the moral conduct of a rational being? He bends to power; he adores a dark cloud, which may open a bright prospect to him, or burst in angry, lawless fury, on his devoted head – he knows not why. And, supposing that the Deity acts from the vague impulse of an undirected will, man must also follow his own, or act according to rules, deduced from principles which he disclaims as irreverent. Into this dilemma have both enthusiasts and cooler thinkers fallen, when they laboured to free men from the wholesome restraints which a just conception of the character of God imposes.

It is not impious thus to scan the attributes of the Almighty: in fact, who can avoid it that exercises his faculties? For to love God as the fountain of wisdom, goodness, and power, appears to be the only worship useful to a being who wishes to acquire either virtue or knowledge. A blind unsettled affection may, like human passions, occupy the mind and warm the heart, whilst, to do justice, love mercy, and walk humbly with our God, is forgotten. I shall pursue this subject still further, when I consider religion in a light opposite to that recommended by Dr. Gregory, who treats it as a matter of sentiment or taste.[24]

To return from this apparent digression. It were to be wished that women would cherish an affection for their husbands, founded on the same principle that devotion ought to rest upon. No other firm base is there under heaven – for let them beware of the fallacious light of sentiment; too often used as a softer phrase for sensuality. It follows then, I think, that from their infancy women should either be shut up like eastern princes, or educated in such a manner as to be able to think and act for themselves.

Chap. IV　Observations on the State of Degradation to Which Woman Is Reduced by Various Causes

[…] But, dismissing these fanciful theories, and considering woman as a whole, let it be what it will, instead of a part of man, the inquiry is whether she has reason or not. If she has, which, for a moment, I will take for granted, she was not created merely to be the solace of man, and the sexual should not destroy the human character.

Into this error men have, probably, been led by viewing education in a false light; not considering it as the first step to form a being advancing gradually

---

[24]　Gregory, *A Father's Legacy to his Daughters*, 2nd edn (London: Strahan and Cadell, 1774), p. 13: 'Religion is rather a matter of sentiment than reasoning.' This question was much disputed in Wollstonecraft's circles. On the importance of religion to Wollstonecraft's ideas, see Barbara Taylor, *Mary Wollstonecraft and the Female Imagination* (Cambridge: Cambridge University Press, 2003), pp. 95–142.

towards perfection;[25] but only as a preparation for life. On this sensual error, for I must call it so, has the false system of female manners been reared, which robs the whole sex of its dignity, and classes the brown and fair with the smiling flowers that only adorn the land. This has ever been the language of men, and the fear of departing from a supposed sexual character, has made even women of superior sense adopt the same sentiments.[26] Thus understanding, strictly speaking, has been denied to woman; and instinct, sublimated into wit and cunning, for the purposes of life, has been substituted in its stead.

The power of generalizing ideas, of drawing comprehensive conclusions from individual observations, is the only acquirement, for an immortal being, that really deserves the name of knowledge. Merely to observe, without endeavouring to account for any thing, may (in a very incomplete manner) serve as the common sense of life; but where is the store laid up that is to clothe the soul when it leaves the body?

This power has not only been denied to women; but writers have insisted that it is inconsistent, with a few exceptions, with their sexual character. Let men prove this, and I shall grant that woman only exists for man. I must, however, previously remark, that the power of generalizing ideas, to any great extent, is not very

---

[25]   {This word is not strictly just, but I cannot find a better.}

[26]   {

Pleasure's the portion of th' *inferior* kind;
But glory, virtue, Heaven for *man* design'd.

After writing these lines, how could Mrs. Barbauld write the following ignoble comparison?

To a Lady, with some painted flowers

Flowers to the fair: to you these flowers I bring,
And strive to greet you with an earlier spring.
Flowers SWEET, *and gay, and* DELICATE LIKE YOU;
Emblems of innocence, and beauty too.
With flowers the Graces bind their yellow hair,
And flowery wreaths consenting lovers wear.
Flowers, the sole luxury which nature knew,
In Eden's pure and guiltless garden grew.
To loftier forms are rougher tasks assign'd;
The sheltering oak resists the stormy wind,
The tougher yew repels invading foes,
And the tall pine for future navies grows;
But this soft family, to cares unknown,
Were born for pleasure and delight ALONE.
Gay without toil, and lovely without art,
They spring to CHEER *the sense, and* GLAD *the heart.*
Nor blush, my fair, to own you copy these;
Your BEST, *your* SWEETEST *empire* is—to PLEASE.

So the men tell us; but virtue must be acquired by *rough* toils, and useful struggles with worldly *cares.*}
Wollstonecraft quotes from Barbauld's poem 'To Mary P[riestley]' and then 'To a Lady'. The italics are hers. Barbauld seems to have answered with her poem 'The Rights of Woman'. Wollstonecraft's disappointment reflects her knowledge of Barbauld as a progressive member of the Johnson circle as well as a fellow writer on education and a poet and political pamphleteer.

common amongst men or women. But this exercise is the true cultivation of the understanding; and every thing conspires to render the cultivation of the understanding more difficult in the female than the male world.

[Their senses are inflamed, and their understandings neglected]

In short, women, in general, as well as the rich of both sexes, have acquired all the follies and vices of civilization, and missed the useful fruit. It is not necessary for me always to premise, that I speak of the condition of the whole sex, leaving exceptions out of the question. Their senses are inflamed, and their understandings neglected, consequently they become the prey of their senses, delicately termed sensibility, and are blown about by every momentary gust of feeling. They are, therefore, in a much worse condition than they would be in were they in a state nearer to nature.[27] Ever restless and anxious, their over exercised sensibility not only renders them uncomfortable themselves, but troublesome, to use a soft phrase, to others. All their thoughts turn on things calculated to excite emotion; and feeling, when they should reason, their conduct is unstable, and their opinions are wavering – not the wavering produced by deliberation or progressive views, but by contradictory emotions. By fits and starts they are warm in many pursuits; yet this warmth, never concentrated into perseverance, soon exhausts itself; exhaled by its own heat, or meeting with some other fleeting passion, to which reason has never given any specific gravity, neutrality ensues. Miserable, indeed, must be that being whose cultivation of mind has only tended to inflame its passions! A distinction should be made between inflaming and strengthening them. The passions thus pampered, whilst the judgment is left unformed, what can be expected to ensue?
– Undoubtedly, a mixture of madness and folly!

This observation should not be confined to the *fair* sex; however, at present, I only mean to apply it to them.

Novels, music, poetry, and gallantry, all tend to make women the creatures of sensation, and their character is thus formed[28] during the time they are acquiring accomplishments, the only improvement they are excited, by their station in society, to acquire. This overstretched sensibility naturally relaxes the other powers of the mind, and prevents intellect from attaining that sovereignty which it ought to attain to render a rational creature useful to others, and content with its own station: for the exercise of the understanding, as life advances, is the only method pointed out by nature to calm the passions.

---

[27]   'They are ... nearer to nature': second edition reads: 'Civilized women are, therefore, so weakened by false refinement, that, respecting morals, their condition is much below what it would be were they left in a state nearer to nature.'

[28]   Second edition adds 'in the mould of folly'.

Chap. V   Animadversions on Some of the Writers
Who Have Rendered Women Objects of Pity,
Bordering on Contempt – Sect. i   [Rousseau]

[…] I shall begin with Rousseau, and give a sketch of the character of women, in his own words, interspersing comments and reflections. My comments, it is true, will all spring from a few simple principles, and might have been deduced from what I have already said; but the artificial structure has been raised with so much ingenuity, that it seems necessary to attack it in a more circumstantial manner, and make the application myself.

Sophia, says Rousseau, should be as perfect a woman as Emilius is a man, and to render her so, it is necessary to examine the character which nature has given to the sex.[29]

He then proceeds to prove that woman ought to be weak and passive, because she has less bodily strength than man; and, from hence infers, that she was formed to please and to be subject to him; and that it is her duty to render herself *agreeable* to her master – this being the grand end of her existence.[30] Still, however, to give a little mock dignity to lust, he insists that man should not exert his strength, but depend on the will of the woman, when he seeks for pleasure with her.

> Hence we deduce a third consequence from the different constitutions of the sexes; which is, that the strongest should be master in appearance, and be dependent in fact on the weakest; and that not from any frivolous practice of gallantry or vanity of protectorship, but from an invariable law of nature, which, furnishing woman with a greater facility to excite desires than she has given man to satisfy them, makes the latter dependent on the good pleasure of the former, and compels him to endeavour to please in his turn, *in order to obtain her consent that he should be strongest.*[31] On these occasions, the most delightful circumstance a man finds in his victory is, to doubt whether it was the woman's weakness that yielded to his superior strength, or whether her inclinations spoke in his favour: the females are also generally artful enough to leave this matter in doubt. The understanding of women answers in this respect perfectly to their constitution: so far from being ashamed of their weakness, they glory in it; their tender muscles make no resistance; they affect to be incapable of lifting the smallest burthens, and would blush to be thought robust and strong. To what purpose is all this? Not merely for the sake of appearing delicate, but through an artful precaution: it is thus they provide an excuse beforehand, and a right to be feeble when they think it expedient.[32]

I have quoted this passage, lest my readers should suspect that I warped the author's reasoning to support my own arguments. I have already asserted that in educating women these fundamental principles lead to a system of cunning and lasciviousness.

---

[29]   *Emilius*, III, 162.
[30]   {I have already inserted the passage, page 99.} The passage in question is not included in the present selection.
[31]   {What nonsense!}
[32]   {Rousseau's *Emilius*, Vol. III. p. 168.} See above, note 14. Wollstonecraft's references are to the same 1783 edition.

[Is it surprising that some of them hug their chains, and fawn like the spaniel?]

The common attachment and regard of a mother, nay, mere habit, will make her beloved by her children, if she does nothing to incur their hate. Even the constraint she lays them under, if well directed, will increase their affection, instead of lessening it; because a state of dependence being natural to the sex, they perceive themselves formed for obedience.[33]

This is begging the question; for servitude not only debases the individual, but its effects seem to be transmitted to posterity. Considering the length of time that women have been dependent, is it surprising that some of them hug their chains, and fawn like the spaniel? 'These dogs', observes a naturalist, 'at first keep their ears erect; but custom has superseded nature, and a token of fear is become a beauty.'[34]

'For the same reason,' adds Rousseau, 'women have, or ought to have, but little liberty; they are apt to indulge themselves excessively in what is allowed them. Addicted in every thing to extremes, they are even more transported at their diversions than boys.'[35]

The answer to this is very simple. Slaves and mobs have always indulged themselves in the same excesses, when once they broke loose from authority. – The bent bow recoils with violence, when the hand is suddenly relaxed that forcibly held it; and sensibility, the play-thing of outward circumstances, must be subjected to authority, or moderated by reason.

[Let us then ... arrive at perfection of body]

Daughters should be always submissive; their mothers, however, should not be inexorable. To make a young person tractable, she ought not to be made unhappy; to make her modest she ought not to be rendered stupid. On the contrary, I should not be displeased at her being permitted to use some art, not to elude punishment in case of disobedience, but to exempt herself from the necessity of obeying. It is not necessary to make her dependence burdensome, but only to let her feel it. Subtilty is a talent natural to the sex; and, as I am persuaded, all our natural inclinations are right and good in themselves, I am of opinion this should be cultivated as well as the others: it is requisite for us only to prevent its abuse.[36]

---

[33] Ibid., p. 193.
[34] Buffon, *The Natural History of the Dog* (1762), Chapter 4.
[35] Rousseau, *Emilius*, III, 193.
[36] Ibid., p. 195.

'Whatever is, is right,'[37] he then proceeds triumphantly to infer. Granted; – yet, perhaps, no aphorism ever contained a more paradoxical assertion. It is a solemn truth with respect to God. He, reverentially I speak, sees the whole at once, and saw its just proportions in the womb of time; but man, who can only inspect disjointed parts, finds many things wrong; and it is a part of the system, and therefore right, that he should endeavour to alter what appears to him to be so, even while he bows to the Wisdom of his Creator, and respects the darkness he labours to disperse.

The inference that follows is just, supposing the principle to be sound.

> The superiority of address, peculiar to the female sex, is a very equitable indemnification for their inferiority in point of strength: without this, woman would not be the companion of man; but his slave: it is by her superiour art and ingenuity that she preserves her equality, and governs him while she affects to obey. Woman has every thing against her, as well our faults, as her own timidity and weakness; she has nothing in her favour, but her subtilty and her beauty. Is it not very reasonable, therefore, she should cultivate both?[38]

Greatness of mind can never dwell with cunning, or address, for I shall not boggle about words, when their direct signification is insincerity and falsehood; but content myself with observing, that if any class of mankind are to be educated by rules not strictly deducible from truth, virtue is an affair of convention. How could Rousseau dare to assert, after giving this advice, that in the grand end of existence the object of both sexes should be the same, when he well knew that the mind, formed by its pursuits, is expanded by great views swallowing up little ones, or that it becomes itself little?

Men have superiour strength of body; but were it not for mistaken notions of beauty, women would acquire sufficient to enable them to earn their own subsistence, the true definition of independence; and to bear those bodily inconveniencies and exertions that are requisite to strengthen the mind.

Let us then, by being allowed to take the same exercise as boys, not only during infancy, but youth, arrive at perfection of body, that we may know how far the natural superiority of man extends. For what reason or virtue can be expected from a creature when the seed-time of life is neglected? None – did not the winds of heaven casually scatter many useful seeds in the fallow ground.

Sect. ii   [Dr. Fordyce's sermons]

Dr. Fordyce's sermons have long made a part of a young woman's library; nay, girls at school are allowed to read them; but I should instantly dismiss them from my pupil's, if I wished to strengthen her understanding, by leading her to

---

[37]   Ibid., IV, 5. Wollstonecraft follows Kenrick in transforming Rousseau's 'ce qui est, est bien' into Alexander Pope's famous phrase from *Essay on Man* (1733–4), I.294: ' "Whatever IS, is right" '.
[38]   *Emilius*, III, 195.

form sound principles on a broad basis; or, were I only anxious to cultivate her taste; though they must be allowed to contain many sensible observations.[39]

Dr. Fordyce may have had a very laudable end in view; but these discourses are written in such an affected style, that were it only on that account, and had I nothing to object against his *mellifluous* precepts, I should not allow girls to peruse them, unless I designed to hunt every spark of nature out of their composition, melting every human quality into female meekness and artificial grace. I say artificial, for true grace arises from some kind of independence of mind.

[Why are girls to be told that they resemble angels; but to sink them below women?]

Even recommending piety he uses the following argument.

> Never, perhaps, does a fine woman strike more deeply, than when, composed into pious recollection, and possessed with the noblest considerations, she assumes, without knowing it, superiour dignity and new graces; so that the beauties of holiness seem to radiate about her, and the by-standers are almost induced to fancy her already worshipping amongst her kindred angels![40]

Why are women to be thus bred up with a desire of conquest? the very epithet, used in this sense, gives me a sickly qualm! Does religion and virtue offer no stronger motives, no brighter reward? Must they always be debased by being made to consider the sex of their companions? Must they be taught always to be pleasing? And when levelling their small artillery at the heart of man, is it necessary to tell them that a little sense is sufficient to render their attention *incredibly soothing*? 'As a small degree of knowledge entertains in a woman, so from a woman, though for a different reason, a small expression of kindness delights, particularly if she have beauty!'[41] I should have supposed for the same reason.

Why are girls to be told that they resemble angels; but to sink them below women? Or, that a gentle innocent female is an object that comes nearer to the idea which we have formed of angels than any other. Yet they are told, at the same time, that they are only like angels when they are young and beautiful; consequently, it is their persons, not their virtues, that procure them this homage.

---

[39] On Wollstonecraft's attitude to the Scottish clergyman James Fordyce, see above, notes 12 and 21.
[40] Fordyce, *Sermons to Young Women* (1766), II, 163.
[41] Ibid., p. 188.

Chap. VI   The Effect Which an Early Association of Ideas Has upon the Character

[...] This habitual slavery, to first impressions, has a more baneful effect on the female than the male character, because business and other dry employments of the understanding, tend to deaden the feelings and break associations that do violence to reason. But females, who are made women of when they are mere children, and brought back to childhood when they ought to leave the go-cart[42] for ever, have not sufficient strength of mind to efface the superinductions of art that have smothered nature.

Every thing that they see or hear serves to fix impressions, call forth emotions, and associate ideas, that give a sexual character to the mind. False notions of beauty and delicacy stop the growth of their limbs and produce a sickly soreness, rather than delicacy of organs; and thus weakened by being employed in unfolding instead of examining the first associations, forced on them by every surrounding object, how can they attain the vigour necessary to enable them to throw off their factitious character? – where find strength to recur to reason and rise superiour to a system of oppression, that blasts the fair promises of spring? This cruel association of ideas, which every thing conspires to twist into all their habits of thinking, or, to speak with more precision, of feeling, receives new force when they begin to act a little for themselves; for they then perceive that it is only through their address to excite emotions in men, that pleasure and power are to be obtained. Besides, all the books professedly written for their instruction, which make the first impression on their minds, all inculcate the same opinions. Educated in worse than Egyptian bondage,[43] it is unreasonable, as well as cruel, to upbraid them with faults that can scarcely be avoided, unless a degree of native vigour can be supposed, that falls to the lot of very few amongst mankind.

Chap. VII   Modesty. – Comprehensively Considered, and Not as a Sexual Virtue

Modesty! Sacred offspring of sensibility and reason! – true delicacy of mind! – may I unblamed presume to investigate thy nature, and trace to its covert the mild charm, that mellowing each harsh feature of a character, renders what would otherwise only inspire cold admiration – lovely! – Thou that smoothest the wrinkles of wisdom, and softenest the tone of the sublimest virtues till they all melt into humanity; – thou that spreadest the ethereal cloud that surrounding love

---

[42]   A frame on wheels, in which a child can safely learn to walk without falling.
[43]   The enslavement of the Israelites in Egypt: Exodus 1: 8.

heightens every beauty, it half shades, breathing those coy sweets that steal into the heart, and charm the senses – modulate for me the language of persuasive reason, till I rouse my sex from the flowery bed, on which they supinely sleep life away![44]

[Those women who have most improved their reason must have the most modesty]

A modest man is steady, an humble man timid, and a vain one presumptuous: – this is the judgment, which the observation of many characters, has led me to form. Jesus Christ was modest, Moses was humble, and Peter vain.

Thus, discriminating modesty from humility in one case, I do not mean to confound it with bashfulness in the other. Bashfulness, in fact, is so distinct from modesty, that the most bashful lass, or raw country lout, often becomes the most impudent; for their bashfulness being merely the instinctive timidity of ignorance, custom soon changes it into assurance.[45]

The shameless behaviour of the prostitutes, who infest the streets of this metropolis, raising alternate emotions of pity and disgust, may serve to illustrate this remark. They trample on virgin bashfulness with a sort of bravado, and glorying in their shame, become more audaciously lewd than men, however depraved, to whom this sexual quality has not been gratuitously granted, ever appear to be. But these poor ignorant wretches never had any modesty to lose, when they consigned themselves to infamy; for modesty is a virtue, not a quality. No, they were only bashful, shame-faced innocents; and losing their innocence, their shame-facedness was rudely brushed off; a virtue would have left some vestiges in the mind, had it been sacrificed to passion, to make us respect the grand ruin.

Purity of mind, or that genuine delicacy, which is the only virtuous support of chastity, is near akin to that refinement of humanity, which never resides in any but cultivated minds. It is something nobler than innocence; it is the delicacy of

---

[44] Freely based on the address to the Holy Spirit in *Paradise Lost*, III.1–55.
[45] {

> Such is the country-maiden's fright,
> When first a red-coat is in sight;
> Behind the door she hides her face;
> Next time at distance eyes the lace:
> She now can all his terrors stand,
> Nor from his squeeze withdraws her hand.
> She plays familiar in his arms,
> And ev'ry soldier hath his charms;
> From tent to tent she spreads her flame;
> For custom conquers fear and shame.
>
> *Gay.*}
> John Gay, *Fables* (1727), 'The Tame Stag', 27–36.

reflection, and not the coyness of ignorance. The reserve of reason, which, like habitual cleanliness, is seldom seen in any great degree, unless the soul is active, may easily be distinguished from rustic shyness or wanton skittishness; and, so far from being incompatible with knowledge, it is its fairest fruit. What a gross idea of modesty had the writer of the following remark! 'The lady who asked the question whether women may be instructed in the modern system of botany, consistently with female delicacy? – was accused of ridiculous prudery: nevertheless, if she had proposed the question to me, I should certainly have answered – They cannot.'[46] Thus is the fair book of knowledge to be shut with an everlasting seal! On reading similar passages I have reverentially lifted up my eyes and heart to Him who liveth for ever and ever, and said, O my Father, hast Thou by the very constitution of her nature forbid Thy child to seek Thee in the fair forms of truth? And, can her soul be sullied by the knowledge that awfully calls her to Thee?

I have then philosophically pursued these reflections till I inferred that those women who have most improved their reason must have the most modesty – though a dignified sedateness of deportment may have succeeded the playful, bewitching bashfulness of youth.[47]

Chap. VIII   Morality Undermined by Sexual Notions of the Importance of a Good Reputation

[...] Weak minds are always fond of resting in the ceremonials of duty, but morality offers much simpler motives; and it were to be wished that superficial moralists had said less respecting behaviour, and outward observances, for unless virtue, of any kind, is built on knowledge, it will only produce a kind of insipid decency. Respect for the opinion of the world, has, however, been termed the principal duty of woman in the most express words, for Rousseau declares, 'that reputation is no less indispensable than chastity'. 'A man,' adds he,

> secure in his own good conduct, depends only on himself, and may brave the public opinion; but a woman, in behaving well, performs but half her duty; as what is thought of her, is as important to her as what she really is. It follows hence, that the system of a woman's education should, in this respect, be directly contrary to that of ours. Opinion is the grave of virtue among the men; but its throne among women.[48]

It is strictly logical to infer that the virtue that rests on opinion is merely worldly, and that it is the virtue of a being to whom reason has been denied. But, even

---

[46]   John Berkenhout, *A Volume of Letters to his Son at the University* (1790), Letter XXXII, p. 307.

[47]   {Modesty, is the graceful calm virtue of maturity; bashfulness, the charm of vivacious youth.}

[48]   *Emilius*, III, 173.

with respect to the opinion of the world, I am convinced that this class of reasoners are mistaken.

[If the honour of a woman ... is safe, she may neglect every social duty]

The leading principles which run through all my disquisitions, would render it
unnecessary to enlarge on this subject, if a constant attention to keep the varnish
of the character fresh, and in good condition, were not often inculcated as the sum
total of female duty; if rules to regulate the behaviour, and to preserve the reputation, did not too frequently supersede moral obligations. But, with respect to reputation, the attention is confined to a single virtue – chastity. If the honour of a
woman, as it is absurdly called, is safe, she may neglect every social duty; nay, ruin
her family by gaming and extravagance; yet still present a shameless front – for
truly she is an honourable woman!

Mrs. Macaulay has justly observed, that 'there is but one fault which a woman
of honour may not commit with impunity'. She then justly, and humanely adds –

> This has given rise to the trite and foolish observation, that the first fault against chas-
> tity in woman has a radical power to deprave the character. But no such frail beings
> come out of the hands of nature. The human mind is built of nobler materials than to
> be so easily corrupted; and with all their disadvantages of situation and education,
> women seldom become entirely abandoned till they are thrown into a state of despera-
> tion, by the venomous rancour of their own sex.[49]

But, in proportion as this regard for the reputation of chastity is prized by women,
it is despised by men: and the two extremes are equally destructive to morality.

[The two sexes mutually corrupt and improve each other]

The two sexes mutually corrupt and improve each other. This I believe to be an
indisputable truth, extending it to every virtue. Chastity, modesty, public spirit, and
all the noble train of virtues, on which social virtue and happiness are built, should
be understood and cultivated by all mankind, or they will be cultivated to little
effect. And, instead of furnishing the vicious or idle with a pretext for violating
some sacred duty, by terming it a sexual one, it would be wiser to shew that nature
has not made any difference, for that the unchaste man doubly defeats the purpose

---

[49]   Catherine Macaulay, *Letters on Education* (London: C. Dilly, 1790), pp. 210 and 212.

of nature, by rendering women barren, and destroying his own constitution, though he avoids the shame that pursues the crime in the other sex. These are the physical consequences, the moral are still more alarming; for virtue is only a nominal distinction when the duties of citizens, husbands, wives, fathers, mothers, and directors of families, become merely the selfish ties of convenience.

Chap. IX   Of the Pernicious Effects Which Arise from the Unnatural Distinctions Established in Society

[…] It is vain to expect virtue from women till they are, in some degree, independent of men; nay, it is vain to expect that strength of natural affection, which would make them good wives and mothers. Whilst they are absolutely dependent on their husbands they will be cunning, mean, and selfish, and the men who can be gratified by the fawning fondness of spaniel-like affection, have not much delicacy, for love is not to be bought, in any sense of the words, its silken wings are instantly shrivelled up when any thing beside a return in kind is sought. Yet whilst wealth enervates men; and women live, as it were, by their personal charms, how can we expect them to discharge those ennobling duties which equally require exertion and self-denial? Hereditary property sophisticates the mind, and the unfortunate victims to it, if I may so express myself, swathed from their birth, seldom exert the locomotive faculty of body or mind; and, thus viewing every thing through one medium, and that a false one, they are unable to discern in what true merit and happiness consist. False, indeed, must be the light when the drapery of situation hides the man, and makes him stalk in masquerade, dragging from one scene of dissipation to another the nerveless limbs that hang with stupid listlessness, and rolling round the vacant eye which plainly tells us that there is no mind at home.

I mean, therefore, to infer that the society is not properly organized which does not compel men and women to discharge their respective duties, by making it the only way to acquire that countenance from their fellow-creatures, which every human being wishes some way to attain. The respect, consequently, which is paid to wealth and mere personal charms, is a true north–east blast,[50] that blights the tender blossoms of affection and virtue. Nature has wisely attached affections to duties, to sweeten toil, and to give that vigour to the exertions of reason which only the heart can give. But, the affection which is put on merely because it is the appropriated insignia of a certain character, when its duties are not fulfilled, is one of the empty compliments which vice and folly are obliged to pay to virtue and the real nature of things.

---

[50]   The north–east wind; in Greek mythology the god Kaikias (Caecius), bearer of cold, hail and snow.

[How can a being be generous who has nothing of its own? or virtuous, who is not free?]

But, to render her really virtuous and useful, she must not, if she discharge her civil duties, want, individually, the protection of civil laws; she must not be dependent on her husband's bounty for her subsistence during his life, or support after his death – for how can a being be generous who has nothing of its own? or virtuous, who is not free? The wife, in the present state of things, who is faithful to her husband, and neither suckles nor educates her children, scarcely deserves the name of a wife, and has no right to that of a citizen. But take away natural rights, and there is of course an end of duties.

[I really think that women ought to have representatives]

Besides, when poverty is more disgraceful than even vice, is not morality cut to the quick? Still to avoid misconstruction, though I consider that women in the common walks of life are called to fulfil the duties of wives and mothers, by religion and reason, I cannot help lamenting that women of a superiour cast have not a road open by which they can pursue more extensive plans of usefulness and independence. I may excite laughter, by dropping an hint, which I mean to pursue, some future time, for I really think that women ought to have representatives, instead of being arbitrarily governed without having any direct share allowed them in the deliberations of government.

But, as the whole system of representation is now, in this country, only a convenient handle for despotism, they need not complain, for they are as well represented as a numerous class of hard working mechanics, who pay for the support of royalty when they can scarcely stop their children's mouths with bread. How are they represented whose very sweat supports the splendid stud of an heir apparent, or varnishes the chariot of some female favourite who looks down on shame? Taxes on the very necessaries of life, enable an endless tribe of idle princes and princesses to pass with stupid pomp before a gaping crowd, who almost worship the very parade which costs them so dear. This is mere gothic grandeur, something like the barbarous useless parade of having sentinels on horseback at Whitehall, which I could never view without a mixture of contempt and indignation.

How strangely must the mind be sophisticated when this sort of state impresses it! But, till these monuments of folly are levelled by virtue, similar follies will leaven the whole mass. For the same character, in some degree, will prevail in the aggregate of society: and the refinements of luxury, or the vicious repinings of envious poverty, will equally banish virtue from society, considered as the characteristic of that society, or only allow it to appear as one of the stripes of the harlequin coat, worn by the civilized man.

In the superior ranks of life, every duty is done by deputies, as if duties could ever be waved, and the vain pleasures which consequent idleness forces the rich to pursue, appear so enticing to the next rank, that the numerous scramblers for wealth sacrifice every thing to tread on their heels. The most sacred trusts are then considered as sinecures, because they were procured by interest, and only sought to enable a man to keep *good company*. Women, in particular, all want to be ladies. Which is simply to have nothing to do, but listlessly to go they scarcely care where, for they cannot tell what.

But what have women to do in society? I may be asked, but to loiter with easy grace; surely you would not condemn them all to suckle fools and chronicle small beer![51] No. Women might certainly study the art of healing, and be physicians as well as nurses. And midwifery, decency seems to allot to them, though I am afraid the word midwife, in our dictionaries, will soon give place to *accoucheur*,[52] and one proof of the former delicacy of the sex be effaced from the language.

They might, also, study politics, and settle their benevolence on the broadest basis; for the reading of history will scarcely be more useful than the perusal of romances, if read as mere biography; if the character of the times, the political improvements, arts, &c. be not observed. In short, if it be not considered as the history of man; and not of particular men, who filled a niche in the temple of fame, and dropped into the black rolling stream of time, that silently sweeps all before it, into the shapeless void called – eternity. – For shape, can it be called, 'that shape hath none?'[53]

Business of various kinds, they might likewise pursue, if they were educated in a more orderly manner, which might save many from common and legal prostitution. Women would not then marry for a support, as men accept of places under government, and neglect the implied duties; nor would an attempt to earn their own subsistence, a most laudable one! sink them almost to the level of those poor abandoned creatures who live by prostitution. For are not milliners and mantua-makers[54] reckoned the next class? The few employments open to women, so far from being liberal, are menial; and when a superiour education enables them to take charge of the education of children as governesses, they are not treated like the tutors of sons, though even clerical tutors are not always treated in a manner calculated to render them respectable in the eyes of their pupils, to say nothing of the private comfort of the individual. But as women educated like gentlewomen, are never designed for the humiliating situation which necessity sometimes forces them to fill; these situations are considered in

---

[51]   *Othello*, II.i.160.
[52]   A so-called 'man-midwife' or obstetrician.
[53]   *Paradise Lost*, II.667, referring to Death.
[54]   A mantua was a gown usually worn over stays, a stomacher, and a petticoat.

the light of a degradation; and they know little of the human heart, who need to be told, that nothing so painfully sharpens sensibility as such a fall in life.

Chap. X Parental Affection

[...] The formation of the mind must be begun very early, and the temper, in particular, requires the most judicious attention – an attention which women cannot pay who only love their children because they are their children, and seek no further for the foundation of their duty, than in the feelings of the moment. It is this want of reason in their affections which makes women so often run into extremes, and either be the most fond or most careless and unnatural mothers.

To be a good mother – a woman must have sense, and that independence of mind which few women possess who are taught to depend entirely on their husbands. Meek wives are, in general, foolish mothers; wanting their children to love them best, and take their part, in secret, against the father, who is held up as a scarecrow. If they are to be punished, though they have offended the mother, the father must inflict the punishment; he must be the judge in all disputes: but I shall more fully discuss this subject when I treat of private education, I now only mean to insist, that unless the understanding of woman be enlarged, and her character rendered more firm, by being allowed to govern her own conduct, she will never have sufficient sense or command of temper to manage her children properly. Her parental affection, indeed, scarcely deserves the name, when it does not lead her to suckle her children, because the discharge of this duty is equally calculated to inspire maternal and filial affection: and it is the indispensable duty of men and women to fulfil the duties which give birth to affections that are the surest preservatives against vice. Natural affection, as it is termed, I believe to be a very faint tie, affections must grow out of the habitual exercise of a mutual sympathy; and what sympathy does a mother exercise who sends her babe to a nurse, and only takes it from a nurse to send it to a school?

Chap. XI Duty to Parents

There seems to be an indolent propensity in man to make prescription always take place of reason, and to place every duty on an arbitrary foundation. The rights of kings are deduced in a direct line from the King of kings; and that of parents from our first parent.

Why do we thus go back for principles that should always rest on the same base, and have the same weight to-day that they had a thousand years ago – and not a jot more? If parents discharge their duty they have a strong hold and sacred claim on the gratitude of their children; but few parents are willing to receive the respectful affection of their offspring on such terms. They demand blind obedience, because they do not merit a reasonable service: and to render these demands of weakness and ignorance more binding, a mysterious sanctity is spread round the most arbitrary principle; for what other name can be given to the blind duty of obeying vicious or weak beings merely because they obeyed a powerful instinct?

The simple definition of the reciprocal duty, which naturally subsists between parent and child, may be given in a few words: The parent who pays proper attention to helpless infancy has a right to require the same attention when the feebleness of age comes upon him. But to subjugate a rational being to the mere will of another, after he is of age to answer to society for his own conduct, is a most cruel and undue stretch of power; and, perhaps, as injurious to morality as those religious systems which do not allow right and wrong to have any existence, but in the Divine will.

[They are prepared for the slavery of marriage]

Females, it is true, in all countries, are too much under the dominion of their parents; and few parents think of addressing their children in the following manner, though it is in this reasonable way that Heaven seems to command the whole human race. It is your interest to obey me till you can judge for yourself; and the Almighty Father of all has implanted an affection in me to serve as a guard to you whilst your reason is unfolding; but when your mind arrives at maturity, you must only obey me, or rather respect my opinions, so far as they coincide with the light that is breaking in on your own mind.

A slavish bondage to parents cramps every faculty of the mind; and Mr. Locke very judiciously observes, that 'if the mind be curbed and humbled too much in children; if their spirits be abased and broken much by too strict an hand over them; they lose all their vigour and industry.'[55] This strict hand may in some degree account for the weakness of women; for girls, from various causes, are more kept down by their parents, in every sense of the word, than boys. The duty expected from them is, like all the duties arbitrarily imposed on women, more from a sense of propriety, more out of respect for decorum, than reason; and thus taught slavishly to submit to their parents, they are prepared for the slavery of marriage. I may be told that a number of women are not slaves in the marriage state. True, but they then become tyrants; for it is not rational freedom, but a lawless kind of power resembling the authority exercised by the favourites of absolute monarchs, which they obtain by debasing means. I do not, likewise, dream of insinuating that either boys or girls are always slaves, I only insist that when they are obliged to submit to authority blindly, their faculties are weakened, and their tempers

---

[55]   John Locke, *Some Thoughts concerning Education* (London: A. and J. Churchill, 1693), pp. 46–7.

rendered imperious or abject. I also lament that parents, indolently availing themselves of a supposed privilege, damp the first faint glimmering of reason, rendering at the same time the duty, which they are so anxious to enforce, an empty name; because they will not let it rest on the only basis on which a duty can rest securely: for unless it be founded on knowledge, it cannot gain sufficient strength to resist the squalls of passion, or the silent sapping of self-love. But it is not the parents who have given the surest proof of their affection for their children, or, to speak more properly, who by fulfilling their duty, have allowed a natural parental affection to take root in their hearts, the child of exercised sympathy and reason, and not the over-weening offspring of selfish pride, who most vehemently insist on their children submitting to their will merely because it is their will. On the contrary, the parent, who sets a good example, patiently lets that example work; and it seldom fails to produce its natural effect – filial respect.

Chap. XII   On National Education

[...] I have already animadverted on the bad habits which females acquire when they are shut up together;[56] and, I think, that the observation may fairly be extended to the other sex, till the natural inference is drawn which I have had in view throughout – that to improve both sexes they ought, not only in private families, but in public schools, to be educated together. If marriage be the cement of society, mankind should all be educated after the same model, or the intercourse of the sexes will never deserve the name of fellowship, nor will women ever fulfil the peculiar duties of their sex, till they become enlightened citizens, till they become free by being enabled to earn their own subsistence, independent of men; in the same manner, I mean, to prevent misconstruction, as one man is independent of another. Nay, marriage will never be held sacred till women, by being brought up with men, are prepared to be their companions rather than their mistresses; for the mean doublings of cunning will ever render them contemptible, whilst oppression renders them timid. So convinced am I of this truth, that I will venture to predict that virtue will never prevail in society till the virtues of both sexes are founded on reason; and, till the affections common to both are allowed to gain their due strength by the discharge of mutual duties.

Were boys and girls permitted to pursue the same studies together, those graceful decencies might early be inculcated which produce modesty without those sexual distinctions that taint the mind. Lessons of politeness, and that formulary[57]

---

[56] Wollstonecraft speaks of the 'wearisome confinement' endured by girls, which 'contract[s] the faculties and spoil[s] the temper' by not allowing them to exercise freely.

[57] A prescriptive set of principles, according to which something is to be done (according to the *OED*, especially one that contains prescribed forms of religious belief or ritual).

of decorum, which treads on the heels of falsehood, would be rendered useless by habitual propriety of behaviour. Not indeed, put on for visitors like the courtly robe of politeness, but the sober effect of cleanliness of mind. Would not this simple elegance of sincerity be a chaste homage paid to domestic affections, far surpassing the meretricious compliments that shine with false lustre in the heartless intercourse of fashionable life? But, till more understanding preponderate in society, there will ever be a want of heart and taste, and the harlot's *rouge* will supply the place of that celestial suffusion which only virtuous affections can give to the face. Gallantry, and what is called love, may subsist without simplicity of character; but the main pillars of friendship, are respect and confidence – esteem is never founded on it cannot tell what!

[Morality, polluted in the national reservoir, sends off streams of vice]

In public schools women, to guard against the errors of ignorance, should be taught the elements of anatomy and medicine, not only to enable them to take proper care of their own health, but to make them rational nurses of their infants, parents, and husbands; for the bills of mortality are swelled by the blunders of self-willed old women, who give nostrums of their own without knowing any thing of the human frame.[58] It is likewise proper, only in a domestic view, to make women acquainted with the anatomy of the mind, by allowing the sexes to associate together in every pursuit; and by leading them to observe the progress of the human understanding in the improvement of the sciences and arts; never forgetting the science of morality, nor the study of the political history of mankind.

A man has been termed a microcosm; and every family might also be called a state. States, it is true, have mostly been governed by arts that disgrace the character of man; and the want of a just constitution, and equal laws, have so perplexed the notions of the worldly wise, that they more than question the reasonableness of contending for the rights of humanity. Thus morality, polluted in the national reservoir, sends off streams of vice to corrupt the constituent parts of the body politic; but should more noble, or rather, more just principles regulate the laws, which ought to be the government of society, and not those who execute them, duty might become the rule of private conduct.

Besides, by the exercise of their bodies and minds women would acquire that mental activity so necessary in the maternal character, united with the fortitude that distinguishes steadiness of conduct from the obstinate perverseness of weakness. For it is dangerous to advise the indolent to be steady, because they instantly

---

[58] 'Bills of mortality' were the records of deaths published by each parish, usually weekly. A nostrum is a home-made medicine, usually associated with quackery.

become rigorous, and to save themselves trouble, punish with severity faults that the patient fortitude of reason might have prevented.

Chap. XIII   Some Instances of the Folly Which the Ignorance of Women Generates; with Concluding Reflections on the Moral Improvement That a Revolution in Female Manners Might Naturally Be Expected to Produce[59] – Sect. ii   [Sentimental jargon]

Another instance of that feminine weakness of character, often produced by a confined education, is a romantic twist of the mind, which has been very properly termed *sentimental*.

Women subjected by ignorance to their sensations, and only taught to look for happiness in love, refine on sensual feelings, and adopt metaphysical notions respecting that passion, which lead them shamefully to neglect the duties of life, and frequently in the midst of these sublime refinements they plump into actual vice.

These are the women who are amused by the reveries of the stupid novelists, who, knowing little of human nature, work up stale tales, and describe meretricious scenes, all retailed in a sentimental jargon, which equally tend to corrupt the taste, and draw the heart aside from its daily duties. I do not mention the understanding, because never having been exercised, its slumbering energies rest inactive, like the lurking particles of fire which are supposed universally to pervade matter.[60]

Females, in fact, denied all political privileges, and not allowed, as married women, excepting in criminal cases, a civil existence, have their attention naturally drawn from the interest of the whole community to that of the minute parts, though the private duty of any member of society must be very imperfectly performed when not connected with the general good. The mighty business of female life is to please, and restrained from entering into more important concerns by political and civil oppression, sentiments become events, and reflection deepens what it should, and would have effaced, if the understanding had been allowed to take a wider range.

But, confined to trifling employments, they naturally imbibe opinions which the only kind of reading calculated to interest an innocent frivolous mind, inspires.

---

[59]   The sections of this chapter attack the following 'instances of folly': credulous superstition; sentimentality; fondness for dress and ornaments; selfish, clinging affection; ignorant upbringing of children and poor treatment of servants in their presence; failure to fix morals on rational, immutable principles.

[60]   A reference to the hypothetical inflammable element of air first postulated by Johann Joachim Becher, which the chemist Joseph Priestley discussed as 'phlogiston' (from the Greek verb *phlogizein*, 'to set fire to') and which had great circulation in explanatory theories of matter of the time. Priestley's main publisher was also Joseph Johnson.

Unable to grasp any thing great, is it surprising that they find the reading of history a very dry task, and disquisitions addressed to the understanding intolerably tedious, and almost unintelligible? Thus are they necessarily dependent on the novelist for amusement.[61] Yet, when I exclaim against novels, I mean when contrasted with those works which exercise the understanding and regulate the imagination. – For any kind of reading I think better than leaving a blank still a blank, because the mind must receive a degree of enlargement and obtain a little strength by a slight exertion of its thinking powers; besides, even the productions that are only addressed to the imagination, raise the reader a little above the gross gratification of appetites, to which the mind has not given a shade of delicacy.

Sect. vi   [Women at present are by ignorance rendered foolish or vicious]

[…] To render women truly useful members of society, I argue that they should be led, by having their understandings cultivated on a large scale, to acquire a rational affection for their country, founded on knowledge, because it is obvious that we are little interested about what we do not understand. And to render this general knowledge of due importance, I have endeavoured to shew that private duties are never properly fulfilled unless the understanding enlarges the heart; and that public virtue is only an aggregate of private. But, the distinctions established in society undermine both, by beating out the solid gold of virtue, till it becomes only the tinsel-covering of vice; for whilst wealth renders a man more respectable than virtue, wealth will be sought before virtue; and, whilst women's persons are caressed, when a childish simper shews an absence of mind – the mind will lie fallow. Yet, true voluptuousness must proceed from the mind – for what can equal the sensations produced by mutual affection, supported by mutual respect? What are the cold, or feverish caresses of appetite, but sin embracing death,[62] compared with the modest overflowings of a pure heart and exalted imagination? Yes, let me tell the libertine of fancy when he despises understanding in woman – that the mind, which he disregards, gives life to the enthusiastic affection from which rapture, short-lived as it is, alone can flow! And, that, without virtue, a sexual attachment must expire, like a tallow candle in the socket, creating intolerable disgust. To prove this, I need only observe, that men who have wasted great part of their lives with women, and with whom they have sought for pleasure with eager thirst, entertain the meanest opinion of the sex. – Virtue, true refiner of joy! – if foolish

---

[61]   Wollstonecraft reviewed novels regularly for the *Analytical Review* (see above, note 6). Compare Jane Austen's famous defence of the novel as capable of exercising the understanding and imagination in *Northanger Abbey*, a novel originally written in the 1790s.

[62]   See *Paradise Lost* II.793, where Sin subjects his mother Death to 'embraces forcible and foul'.

men were to fright thee from earth, in order to give loose to all their appetites without a check – some sensual wight[63] of taste would scale the heavens to invite thee back, to give a zest to pleasure!

That women at present are by ignorance rendered foolish or vicious, is, I think, not to be disputed; and, that the most salutary effects tending to improve mankind might be expected from a REVOLUTION in female manners, appears, at least, with a face of probability, to rise out of the observation.

[Let woman share the rights and she will emulate the virtues of man]

The affection of husbands and wives cannot be pure when they have so few sentiments in common, and when so little confidence is established at home, as must be the case when their pursuits are so different. That intimacy from which tenderness should flow, will not, cannot subsist between the vicious.

Contending, therefore, that the sexual distinction which men have so warmly insisted upon, is arbitrary, I have dwelt on an observation, that several sensible men, with whom I have conversed on the subject, allowed to be well founded; and it is simply this, that the little chastity to be found amongst men, and consequent disregard of modesty, tend to degrade both sexes; and further, that the modesty of women, characterized as such, will often be only the artful veil of wantonness instead of being the natural reflection of purity, till modesty be universally respected.

From the tyranny of man, I firmly believe, the greater number of female follies proceed; and the cunning, which I allow makes at present a part of their character, I likewise have repeatedly endeavoured to prove, is produced by oppression.

Were not dissenters, for instance, a class of people, with strict truth, characterized as cunning? And may I not lay some stress on this fact to prove, that when any power but reason curbs the free spirit of man, dissimulation is practised, and the various shifts of art are naturally called forth? Great attention to decorum, which was carried to a degree of scrupulosity, and all that puerile bustle about trifles and consequential solemnity, which Butler's caricature of a dissenter,[64] brings before the imagination, shaped their persons as well as their minds in the mould of prim littleness. I speak collectively, for I know how many ornaments to human nature have been enrolled amongst sectaries; yet, I assert, that the same narrow prejudice for their sect, which women have for their families, prevailed in the dissenting part of the community, however worthy in other respects; and also that the same timid prudence, or headstrong efforts, often disgraced the exertions of both. Oppression thus formed many of the features of their character perfectly to coincide with that

---

[63] A person.

[64] A reference to the eponymous protagonist of Samuel Butler's satire on Puritanism *Hudibras* (1662–3).

of the oppressed half of mankind; for is it not notorious that dissenters were, like women, fond of deliberating together, and asking advice of each other, till by a complication of little contrivances, some little end was brought about? A similar attention to preserve their reputation was conspicuous in the dissenting and female world, and was produced by a similar cause.

Asserting the rights which women in common with men ought to contend for, I have not attempted to extenuate their faults; but to prove them to be the natural consequence of their education and station in society. If so, it is reasonable to suppose that they will change their character, and correct their vices and follies, when they are allowed to be free in a physical, moral, and civil sense.[65]

Let woman share the rights and she will emulate the virtues of man; for she must grow more perfect when emancipated, or justify the authority that chains such a weak being to her duty. – If the latter, it will be expedient to open a fresh trade with Russia for whips;[66] a present which a father should always make to his son-in-law on his wedding day, that a husband may keep his whole family in order by the same means; and without any violation of justice reign, wielding this sceptre, sole master of his house, because he is the only being in it who has reason: – the divine, indefeasible earthly sovereignty breathed into man by the Master of the universe. Allowing this position, women have not any inherent rights to claim, and by the same rule, their duties vanish, for rights and duties are inseparable.

Be just then, O ye men of understanding! and mark not more severely what women do amiss, than the vicious tricks of the horse or the ass for whom ye provide provender – and allow her the privileges of ignorance, to whom ye deny the rights of reason, or ye will be worse than Egyptian task-masters, expecting virtue where nature has not given understanding!

---

[65] {I had further enlarged on the advantages which might reasonably be expected to result from an improvement in female manners, towards the general reformation of society; but it appeared to me that such reflections would more properly close the last volume.}

[66] Russians were notorious for wife-beating and flogging servants and serfs.

6

Thomas Paine

Rights of Man. Part the Second. Combining Principle and Practice

(London: J. S. Jordan, 1792)

Paine returned from Paris in summer 1791 and began the eagerly awaited Part II of *Rights of Man*. He attended dinners at the veteran radical John Horne Tooke's house in Wimbledon and also appeared at a meeting at the Thatched House Tavern in August, where he read a speech in favour of reform. During this period he extended contact with other authors associated with Joseph Johnson; and he dined with William Godwin and Mary Wollstonecraft on 13 November above the bookseller's shop – but his two companions didn't get on with each other on that occasion. Paine persuaded Jordan to publish Part II, which appeared on 16 February 1792. It is dedicated to General Lafayette, Paine's former colleague from the American War of Independence, despite growing differences in their political opinions. The introduction offers a sweeping view of the American Revolution as an event that will bring down the whole of the *ancien régime* across Europe. Paine's American experience dominates the opening chapters, on the practicality of representative democracy. The United States is brought forward as a genuinely constitutional government, in opposition to Britain's vaunted Glorious Revolution of 1688, which Paine represents as fudge in the interests of aristocracy. The most radical sections of Part II come in the final chapter, where Paine imagines a welfare system for Britain based on progressive taxation. It would include a national system of poor relief, child benefit, old-age pensions, and a system of maternity and death grants.

Parliamentary Whigs who had favoured some measure of political reform quickly distanced themselves from Paine's radicalism, but his writing spurred the formation of popular radical societies, first in Sheffield in 1791, then early in 1792 the London Corresponding Society (LCS). Paine himself attended

Romanticism and Revolution: A Reader.
Edited by Jon Mee and David Fallon.   © 2011 Blackwell Publishing Ltd.

meetings of the Society for Constitutional Information which were presided over by Horne Tooke, and put in train proposals for cheap editions of *Rights of Man* to be circulated in collaboration with the LCS, although neither organization went as far as to subscribe to Paine's republicanism in their official programmes. Government newspapers attempted to stir up feeling against Paine, and in mid-April he was briefly arrested for debt, which Johnson helped him to pay off. Meanwhile, in mid-May, Jordan was indicted for publishing *Rights of Man* and, against Paine's advice, agreed to plead guilty and to pay a fine. On 21 May Paine was charged with seditious libel; on the same day a royal proclamation was issued ordering magistrates to seek out and prosecute those involved in writing or printing wicked and seditious writings. On 8 June the government announced the postponement of Paine's trial until December. Paine embarked on a series of short daring polemics, including the *Letter Addressed to the Addressers of the Late Proclamation*, which challenged the legal basis of the prosecution and called for the British to set up a convention. By the time the *Letter Addressed to the Addressers* came out in October, Paine had left for France, to take up a seat in the National Convention in Paris. When the government finally began the prosecution in December, Thomas Erskine presented Paine as primarily responding to Burke and to part of a pantheon of political thinkers running from Milton to Hume. Such writing was not seditious but a contribution to political philosophy. The prosecution used the cheapness and popular style of Part II as evidence that Paine's real intention was to stir up the populace against the government. Forced to explain why he had not prosecuted Part I, the Attorney General insisted that the difference was in Part II's attempt to reach a new audience, which could not cope with the irreverent account of political and constitutional history found in Paine's pages.

Over in France by this time, Paine struggled to keep up with political developments. Like others involved in the British Club of radical expatriates in Paris, he fell foul of the Jacobins, who were rounding up Paine's erstwhile allies, including Brissot and Condorcet. Paine was eventually arrested in December 1793, but not before he handed over the manuscript of *The Age of Reason* to Joel Barlow. Barlow and other American citizens in Paris worked hard for Paine's release, but without support from their government. Paine was finally released only after the fall of Robespierre, nearly a year later. Recovering from illness, he wrote *Agrarian Justice* (1796) and the angry *Letter to Washington* (1796). Paine finally returned to America in 1802, but only Jefferson and a few republican allies welcomed him. *The Age of Reason*'s deist attack on Christianity had alienated many, even among his old political friends. His last few years were full of financial difficulties and drinking problems. He died in 1809. William Cobbett returned his bones to England in 1819, but their whereabouts are unknown.

Preface

[...] If Mr. Burke, or any person on his side the question, will produce an answer to the 'Rights of Man', that shall extend to an half, or even to a fourth part of the number of copies to which the Rights of Man extended, I will reply to his work. But until this be done, I shall so far take the sense of the public for my guide (and the world knows I am not a flatterer) that what they do not think worth while to read, is not worth mine to answer. I suppose the number of copies to which the first part of the *Rights of Man* extended, taking England, Scotland, and Ireland, is not less than between forty and fifty thousand.[1]

I now come to remark on the remaining part of the quotation I have made from Mr. Burke.[2]

'If,' says he, 'such writings shall be thought to deserve any other refutation than that of *criminal* justice.'

Pardoning the pun, it must be *criminal* justice indeed that should condemn a work as a substitute for not being able to refute it. The greatest condemnation that could be passed upon it would be a refutation. But in proceeding by the method Mr. Burke alludes to, the condemnation would, in the final event, pass upon the criminality of the process and not upon the work, and in this case, I had rather be the author, than be either the judge, or the jury that should condemn it.

But to come at once to the point. I have differed from some professional gentlemen on the subject of prosecutions, and I since find they are falling into my opinion, which I will here state as fully, but as concisely as I can.

I will first put a case with respect to any law, and then compare it with a government, or with what in England is, or has been, called a constitution.

It would be an act of despotism, or what in England is called arbitrary power, to make a law to prohibit investigating the principles, good or bad, on which such a law, or any other is founded.

If a law be bad, it is one thing to oppose the practice of it, but it is quite a different thing to expose its errors, to reason on its defects, and to shew cause why it should be repealed, or why another ought to be substituted in its place. I have always held it an opinion (making it also my practice) that it is better to obey a bad law, making use at the same time of every argument to shew its errors and procure its repeal, than forcibly to violate it; because the precedent of breaking a bad law might weaken the force, and lead to a discretionary violation, of those which are good.

---

[1] Argument has continued about the actual figures, which Paine seems certainly to have inflated here. For a recent discussion, see William St Clair, *The Reading Nation in the Romantic Period* (Cambridge: Cambridge University Press, 2004), pp. 256–7.

[2] Paine refers to Burke's *Appeal from the New to the Old Whigs* (London: J. Dodsley, 1791), which quotes copiously from Paine, but refuses to refute his arguments, preferring instead the suggestion about prosecution, pp. 95–6.

The case is the same with respect to principles and forms of government, or to what are called constitutions and the parts of which they are composed.

Introduction

What Archimedes said of the mechanical powers, may be applied to Reason and Liberty. *'Had we,'* said he, *'a place to stand upon, we might raise the world.'*[3]

The revolution of America presented in politics what was only theory in mechanics. So deeply rooted were all the governments of the old world, and so effectually had the tyranny and the antiquity of habit established itself over the mind, that no beginning could be made in Asia, Africa, or Europe, to reform the political condition of man. Freedom had been hunted round the globe; reason was considered as rebellion; and the slavery of fear had made men afraid to think.

But such is the irresistible nature of truth, that all it asks, and all it wants, is the liberty of appearing. The sun needs no inscription to distinguish him from darkness; and no sooner did the American governments display themselves to the world, than despotism felt a shock, and man began to contemplate redress.

The independence of America, considered merely as a separation from England, would have been a matter but of little importance, had it not been accompanied by a revolution in the principles and practice of governments. She made a stand, not for herself only, but for the world, and looked beyond the advantages herself could receive. Even the Hessian, though hired to fight against her,[4] may live to bless his defeat; and England, condemning the viciousness of its government, rejoice in its miscarriage.

As America was the only spot in the political world, where the principle of universal reformation could begin, so also was it the best in the natural world. An assemblage of circumstances conspired, not only to give birth, but to add gigantic maturity to its principles. The scene which that country presents to the eye of a spectator, has something in it which generates and encourages great ideas. Nature appears to him in magnitude. The mighty objects he beholds, act upon his mind by enlarging it, and he partakes of the greatness he contemplates. – Its first settlers were emigrants from different European nations, and of diversified professions of religion, retiring from the governmental persecutions of the old world, and meeting in the new, not as enemies, but as brothers. The wants which necessarily accompany the cultivation of a wilderness produced among them a state of society, which countries long harassed by the quarrels and intrigues of governments, had neglected to cherish. In such a situation man becomes what he ought. He sees his species, not

---

[3] Archimedes (c. 287–212 BC). The saying was attributed to him by Plutarch (*Marcellus* xiv.7) and related to his developing the theory of leverage in mechanics.

[4] Britain employed German mercenaries from the principality of Hesse during the American War of Independence.

with the inhuman idea of a natural enemy, but as kindred; and the example shews to the artificial world, that man must go back to Nature for information.

From the rapid progress which America makes in every species of improvement, it is rational to conclude, that if the governments of Asia, Africa, and Europe, had begun on a principle similar to that of America, or had not been very early corrupted therefrom, that those countries must by this time have been in a far superior condition to what they are. Age after age has passed away, for no other purpose than to behold their wretchedness. – Could we suppose a spectator who knew nothing of the world, and who was put into it merely to make his observations, he would take a great part of the old world to be new, just struggling with the difficulties and hardships of an infant settlement. He could not suppose that the hordes of miserable poor, with which old countries abound, could be any other than those who had not yet had time to provide for themselves. Little would he think they were the consequence of what in such countries is called government.

If, from the more wretched parts of the old world, we look at those which are in an advanced stage of improvement, we still find the greedy hand of government thrusting itself into every corner and crevice of industry, and grasping the spoil of the multitude. Invention is continually exercised, to furnish new pretences for revenue and taxation. It watches prosperity as its prey, and permits none to escape without a tribute.

As revolutions have begun, (and as the probability is always greater against a thing beginning, than of proceeding after it has begun), it is natural to expect that other revolutions will follow. The amazing and still increasing expences with which old governments are conducted, the numerous wars they engage in or provoke, the embarrassments they throw in the way of universal civilization and commerce, and the oppression and usurpation they act at home, have wearied out the patience, and exhausted the property of the world. In such a situation, and with the examples already existing, revolutions are to be looked for. They are become subjects of universal conversation, and may be considered as the *Order of the day.*[5]

If systems of government can be introduced, less expensive, and more productive of general happiness, than those which have existed, all attempts to oppose their progress will in the end be fruitless. Reason, like time, will make its own way, and prejudice will fall in a combat with interest. If universal peace, civilization, and commerce are ever to be the happy lot of man, it cannot be accomplished but by a revolution in the system of governments. All the monarchical governments are military. War is their trade, plunder and revenue their objects. While such governments continue, peace has not the absolute security of a day. What is the history of all monarchical governments, but a disgustful picture of human wretchedness, and the accidental respite of a few years' repose? Wearied with war, and tired with human butchery, they sat down to rest and called it peace. This certainly is not the condition that Heaven intended for man; and if *this be monarchy*, well might monarchy be reckoned among the sins of the Jews.[6]

---

[5]   Something necessary or usual at a certain time.
[6]   A reference to the decision taken by the Jews to appoint a King (I Samuel 8: 4–22). Paine had discussed the text in *Common Sense*.

The revolutions which formerly took place in the world, had nothing in them that interested the bulk of mankind. They extended only to a change of persons and measures but not of principles, and rose or fell among the common transactions of the moment. What we now behold, may not improperly be called a *'counter revolution'*. Conquest and tyranny, at some earlier period, dispossessed man of his rights, and he is now recovering them. And as the tide of all human affairs has its ebb and flow in directions contrary to each other, so also is it in this. Government founded on a *moral theory, on a system of universal peace, on the indefeasible hereditary Rights of Man*, is now revolving from west to east, by a stronger impulse than the government of the sword[7] revolved from east to west. It interests not particular individuals, but nations, in its progress, and promises a new æra to the human race.

Chap. I   Of Society and Civilization

Great part of that order which reigns among mankind is not the effect of government. It has its origin in the principles of society and the natural constitution of man. It existed prior to government, and would exist if the formality of government was abolished. The mutual dependence and reciprocal interest which man has upon man, and all the parts of a civilized community upon each other, create that great chain of connection which holds it together. The landholder, the farmer, the manufacturer, the merchant, the tradesman, and every occupation, prospers by the aid which each receives from the other, and from the whole. Common interest regulates their concerns, and forms their law; and the laws which common usage ordains, have a greater influence than the laws of government. In fine, society performs for itself almost everything which is ascribed to government.

To understand the nature and quantity of government proper for man, it is necessary to attend to his character. As Nature created him for social life, she fitted him for the station she intended. In all cases she made his natural wants greater than his individual powers. No one man is capable, without the aid of society, of supplying his own wants; and those wants, acting upon every individual, impel the whole of them into society, as naturally as gravitation acts to a center.

But she has gone further. She has not only forced man into society, by a diversity of wants, which the reciprocal aid of each other can supply, but she has implanted in him a system of social affections, which, though not necessary to his existence, are essential to his happiness. There is no period in life when this love for society ceases to act. It begins and ends with our being.

---

[7]   A reference to the spread of Islam.

Chap. II   Of the Origin of the Present Old Governments

It is impossible that such governments as have hitherto existed in the world, could have commenced by any other means than a total violation of every principle sacred and moral. The obscurity in which the origin of all the present old governments is buried, implies the iniquity and disgrace with which they began. The origin of the present government of America and France will ever be remembered, because it is honourable to record it; but with respect to the rest, even Flattery has consigned them to the tomb of time, without an inscription.

It could have been no difficult thing in the early and solitary ages of the world, while the chief employment of men was that of attending flocks and herds, for a banditti of ruffians[8] to overrun a country, and lay it under contributions. Their power being thus established, the chief of the band contrived to lose the name of Robber in that of Monarch; and hence the origin of Monarchy and Kings.

The origin of the government of England, so far as it relates to what is called its line of monarchy, being one of the latest, is perhaps the best recorded. The hatred which the Norman invasion and tyranny begat, must have been deeply rooted in the nation, to have outlived the contrivance to obliterate it. Though not a courtier will talk of the curfeu-bell,[9] not a village has forgotten it.

Those bands of robbers having parcelled out the world, and divided it into dominions, began, as is naturally the case, to quarrel with each other. What at first was obtained by violence, was considered by others as lawful to be taken, and a second plunderer succeeded the first. They alternately invaded the dominions which each had assigned to himself, and the brutality with which they treated each other explains the original character of monarchy. It was ruffian torturing ruffian. The conqueror considered the conquered, not as his prisoner, but his property. He led him in triumph rattling in chains, and doomed him, at pleasure, to slavery or death. As time obliterated the history of their beginning, their successors assumed new appearances, to cut off the entail of their disgrace, but their principles and objects remained the same. What at first was plunder, assumed the softer name of revenue; and the power originally usurped, they affected to inherit.

---

[8]   *Common Sense* described William the Conqueror as 'a French bastard landing with an [*sic*] armed banditti'. Paine expands his analysis of the Norman Conquest over the next few paragraphs.

[9]   Curfew, the custom of ringing a bell every evening to signal that fires and lights are to be extinguished, introduced by William the Conqueror in 1068. The idea of 'the Norman Yoke' extinguishing Anglo-Saxon liberties was common in Whig and radical circles, but Paine's reliance on natural rights does not seek a historical precedent for the representative republic he advocates.

Chap. III Of the Old and New Systems of Government

[…] The first general distinction between those two systems, is, that the one now called the old is *hereditary*, either in whole or in part; and the new is entirely *representative*. It rejects all hereditary government:

First, As being an imposition on mankind.
Secondly, As inadequate to the purposes for which government is necessary.

With respect to the first of these heads – It cannot be proved by what right hereditary government could begin: neither does there exist within the compass of mortal power, a right to establish it. Man has no authority over posterity in matters of personal right; and therefore, no man, or body of men, had, or can have, a right to set up hereditary government. Were even ourselves to come again into existence, instead of being succeeded by posterity, we have not now the right of taking from ourselves the rights which would then be ours. On what ground, then, do we pretend to take them from others?

All hereditary government is in its nature tyranny. An heritable crown, or an heritable throne, or by what other fanciful name such things may be called, have no other significant explanation than that mankind are heritable property. To inherit a government, is to inherit the people, as if they were flocks and herds.[10]

[Republicanism]

It appears to general observation, that revolutions create genius and talents; but those events do no more than bring them forward. There is existing in man, a mass of sense lying in a dormant state, and which, unless something excites it to action, will descend with him, in that condition, to the grave. As it is to the advantage of society that the whole of its faculties should be employed, the construction of government ought to be such as to bring forward, by a quiet and regular operation, all that extent of capacity which never fails to appear in revolutions.

This cannot take place in the insipid state of hereditary government, not only because it prevents, but because it operates to benumb. When the mind of a nation is bowed down by any political superstition in its government, such as hereditary succession is, it loses a considerable portion of its powers on all other subjects and objects. Hereditary succession requires the same obedience to

---

[10]   This paragraph was the first in the information laid against Paine in the prosecution against Part II of *Rights of Man*. See *The Trial of Thomas Paine* in John Barrell and Jon Mee (eds.), *Trials for Treason and Sedition, 1792–1794*, 8 vols (London: Pickering and Chatto, 2006–7), I.

ignorance, as to wisdom; and when once the mind can bring itself to pay this indiscriminate reverence, it descends below the stature of mental manhood. It is fit to be great only in little things. It acts a treachery upon itself, and suffocates the sensations that urge to detection.

Though the ancient governments present to us a miserable picture of the condition of man, there is one which above all others exempts itself from the general description. I mean the democracy of the Athenians. We see more to admire, and less to condemn, in that great, extraordinary people, than in anything which history affords.[11]

Mr. Burke is so little acquainted with constituent principles of government, that he confounds democracy and representation together. Representation was a thing unknown in the ancient democracies. In those the mass of the people met and enacted laws (grammatically speaking) in the first person. Simple democracy was no other than the common-hall of the ancients. It signifies the *form*, as well as the public principle of the government. As these democracies increased in population, and the territory extended, the simple democratical form became unwieldy and impracticable; and as the system of representation was not known, the consequence was, they either degenerated convulsively into monarchies, or became absorbed into such as then existed. Had the system of representation been then understood, as it now is, there is no reason to believe that those forms of government, now called monarchical or aristocratical, would ever have taken place. It was the want of some method to consolidate the parts of society, after it became too populous, and too extensive for the simple democratical form, and also the lax and solitary condition of shepherds and herdsmen in other parts of the world, that afforded opportunities to those unnatural modes of government to begin.

As it is necessary to clear away the rubbish of errors, into which the subject of government has been thrown, I will proceed to remark on some others.

It has always been the political craft of courtiers and court-governments, to abuse something which they called republicanism; but what republicanism was, or is, they never attempt to explain. Let us examine a little into this case.

The only forms of government are the democratical, the aristocratical, the monarchical, and what is now called the representative.

What is called a *republic* is not any *particular form* of government. It is wholly characteristical of the purport, matter, or object for which government ought to be instituted, and on which it is to be employed, RES-PUBLICA, the public affairs, or the public good; or, literally translated, the *public thing*. It is a word of a good original, referring to what ought to be the character and business of government; and in this sense it is naturally opposed to the word *monarchy*, which has a

---

[11]   Athenian democracy was widely admired in the eighteenth century, but also regarded by theorists such as Montesquieu and Rousseau as impossible to sustain in a modern populous nation of great geographical extent. Paine goes on to argue against this view, using the example of the United States and the principle of representation (which does not require everyone to assemble in person to debate).

base original signification. It means arbitrary power in an individual person; in the exercise of which, *himself*, and not the *res-publica*, is the object.

Every government that does not act on the principle of a *Republic*, or in other words, that does not make the *res-publica* its whole and sole object, is not a good government. Republican government is no other than government established and conducted for the interest of the public, as well individually as collectively. It is not necessarily connected with any particular form, but it most naturally associates with the representative form, as being best calculated to secure the end for which a nation is at the expence of supporting it.

[Monarchy ... is a scene of perpetual court cabal and intrigue]

A nation is not a body, the figure of which is to be represented by the human body; but is like a body contained within a circle, having a common center, in which every radius meets; and that center is formed by representation. To connect representation with what is called monarchy, is eccentric government. Representation is of itself the delegated monarchy of a nation, and cannot debase itself by dividing it with another.

Mr. Burke has two or three times, in his parliamentary speeches, and in his publications, made use of a jingle of words that convey no ideas. Speaking of government, he says, 'It is better to have monarchy for its basis, and republicanism for its corrective, than republicanism for its basis, and monarchy for its corrective.'[12] – If he means that it is better to correct folly with wisdom, than wisdom with folly, I will no otherwise contend with him, than that it would be much better to reject the folly entirely.

But what is this thing which Mr. Burke calls monarchy? Will he explain it? All men can understand what representation is; and that it must necessarily include a variety of knowledge and talents. But, what security is there for the same qualities on the part of monarchy? or, when this monarchy is a child, where then is the wisdom? What does it know about government? Who then is the monarch, or where is the monarchy? If it is to be performed by a regency, it proves to be a farce. A regency is a mock species of republic, and the whole of monarchy deserves no better description. It is a thing as various as imagination can paint. It has none of the stable character that government ought to possess. Every succession is a revolution, and every regency a counter-revolution. The whole of it is a scene of perpetual court cabal and intrigue, of which Mr. Burke is himself an instance. To render monarchy consistent with government, the next in

---

[12]   Paine actually paraphrases Burke, *Reflections on the Revolution in France* (London: J. Dodsley, 1790), p. 187. Burke – not in our excerpts – attributes the opinion to Bolingbroke.

succession should not be born a child, but a man at once, and that man a Solomon. It is ridiculous that nations are to wait, and government to be interrupted, till boys grow to be men.

Whether I have too little sense to see, or too much to be imposed upon; whether I have too much or too little pride, or of anything else, I leave out of the question; but certain it is, that what is called monarchy, always appears to me a silly, contemptible thing. I compare it to something kept behind a curtain, about which there is a great deal of bustle and fuss, and a wonderful air of seeming solemnity; but when, by any accident, the curtain happens to be open, and the company see what it is, they burst into laughter.

Chap. IV   Of Constitutions

That men mean distinct and separate things when they speak of constitutions and of governments, is evident; or why are those terms distinctly and separately used? A constitution is not the act of a government, but of a people constituting a government; and government without a constitution, is power without a right.

All power exercised over a nation, must have some beginning. It must either be delegated, or assumed. There are no other sources. All delegated power is trust, and all assumed power is usurpation. Time does not alter the nature and quality of either.

[Government ... has of itself no rights; they are altogether duties]

It may not be improper to observe, that in both those instances, (the one of Pennsylvania, and the other of the United States),[13] there is no such thing as the idea of a compact between the people on one side, and the government on the other. The compact was that of the people with each other, to produce and constitute a government. To suppose that any government can be a party in a compact with the whole people, is to suppose it to have existence before it can have a right to exist. The only instance in which a compact can take place between the people and those who exercise the government, is, that the people shall pay them, while they choose to employ them.

Government is not a trade which any man or body of men has a right to set up and exercise for his own emolument, but is altogether a trust, in right of those by

---

[13]   Paine has been discussing the consultative processes that produced the constitutions of the state of Pennsylvania and of the United States.

whom that trust is delegated, and by whom it is always resumeable. It has of itself no rights; they are altogether duties.

[The bill of rights is more properly a bill of wrongs]

If we begin with William of Normandy, we find that the government of England was originally a tyranny, founded on an invasion and conquest of the country. This being admitted, it will then appear, that the exertion of the nation, at different periods, to abate that tyranny, and render it less intolerable, has been credited for a constitution.

Magna Charta, as it was called (it is now like an almanack of the same date,) was no more than compelling the government to renounce a part of its assumptions.[14] It did not create and give powers to government in the manner a constitution does; but was, as far as it went, of the nature of a re-conquest, and not of a constitution; for could the nation have totally expelled the usurpation, as France has done its despotism, it would then have had a constitution to form.

The history of the Edwards and the Henries, and up to the commencement of the Stuarts, exhibits as many instances of tyranny as could be acted within the limits to which the nation had restricted it. The Stuarts endeavoured to pass those limits, and their fate is well known.[15] In all those instances we see nothing of a constitution, but only of restrictions on assumed power.

After this, another William, descended from the same stock, and claiming from the same origin, gained possession; and of the two evils, *James* and *William*, the nation preferred what it thought the least; since, from circumstances, it must take one. The act, called the Bill of Rights, comes here into view. What is it, but a bargain, which the parts of the government made with each other to divide powers, profits, and privileges? You shall have so much, and I will have the rest; and with respect to the nation, it said, for *your share*, YOU *shall have the right of petitioning*. This being the case, the bill of rights is more properly a bill of wrongs, and of insult. As to what is called the convention parliament,[16] it was a thing that made itself, and then made the authority by which it acted. A few persons got together, and called themselves by that name. Several of them had never been elected, and none of them for the purpose.

From the time of William, a species of government arose, issuing out of this coalition bill of rights; and more so, since the corruption introduced at the Hanover

---

[14] See note 13 to Chapter 2.

[15] The list of monarchs, from Edward I (1239–1307) onwards, culminates with the fateful Charles I (1600–49), executed by Parliament for high treason, and with James II (1633–1701), deposed in the 'Glorious Revolution' of 1688 in order to secure the Protestant succession.

[16] In 1689, a convention met and declared the throne vacant after the flight of James II. It offered the throne to Mary (eldest daughter of James) and her husband William of Orange. At Paine's trial, the prosecution described at great length the rights it took the settlement of 1689 to guarantee.

succession, by the agency of Walpole;[17] that can be described by no other name than a despotic legislation. Though the parts may embarrass each other, the whole has no bounds; and the only right it acknowledges out of itself, is the right of petitioning. Where then is the constitution either that gives or that restrains power?

It is not because a part of the government is elective, that makes it less a despotism, if the persons so elected, possess afterwards, as a parliament, unlimited powers. Election, in this case, becomes separated from representation, and the candidates are candidates for despotism.

I cannot believe that any nation, reasoning on its own rights, would have thought of calling these things *a constitution*, if the cry of constitution had not been set up by the government. It has got into circulation like the words *bore* and *quoz*, by being chalked up in the speeches of parliament, as those words were on window shutters and door posts;[18] but whatever the constitution may be in other respects, it has undoubtedly been *the most productive machine of taxation that was ever invented*. The taxes in France, under the new constitution, are not quite thirteen shillings per head,[19] and the taxes in England, under what is called its present constitution, are forty-eight shillings and sixpence per head, men, women, and children, amounting to nearly seventeen millions sterling, besides the expense of collection, which is upwards of a million more.

[The sepulchre of precedents]

Since the revolution of America, and more so since that of France, this preaching up the doctrines of precedents, drawn from times and circumstances antecedent to those events, has been the studied practice of the English government. The generality of those precedents are founded on principles and opinions, the reverse of what they ought; and the greater distance of time they are drawn from, the more they are to be suspected. But by associating those precedents with a superstitious reverence for ancient things, as monks shew relics and call them holy, the generality of mankind are deceived into the design. Governments now act as if they were afraid to awaken a single reflection in man. They are softly leading him to the sepulchre of

---

[17] Sir Robert Walpole (1676–1745) dominated Parliament via court appointments and other forms of corruption during the last years of the reign of the first Hanoverian king, George I (1714–27), and then during the first fifteen years of the reign of George II (1721–60). George I was the ruler of Hanover, and, as the nearest Protestant blood relative to Queen Anne, Parliament's chosen successor to her.

[18] 'Bore' in the sense of 'tedious' dates from the mid-eighteenth century. A 'quoz' was an absurd person or thing.

[19] {The whole amount of the assessed taxes of France, for the present year, is three hundred millions of livres, which is twelve millions and a half sterling; and the incidental taxes are estimated at three millions, making in the whole fifteen millions and a half; which, among twenty-four millions of people, is not quite thirteen shillings per head. France has lessened her taxes since the revolution, nearly nine millions sterling annually. Before the revolution, the city of Paris paid a duty of upwards of thirty per cent. on all articles brought into the city. This tax was collected at the city gates. It was taken off on the first of last May, and the gates taken down.}

precedents, to deaden his faculties and call his attention from the scene of revolutions. They feel that he is arriving at knowledge faster than they wish, and their policy of precedents is the barometer of their fears. This political popery, like the ecclesiastical popery of old, has had its day, and is hastening to its exit. The ragged relic and the antiquated precedent, the monk and the monarch, will moulder together.

Government by precedent, without any regard to the principle of the precedent, is one of the vilest systems that can be set up. In numerous instances, the precedent ought to operate as a warning, and not as an example, and requires to be shunned instead of imitated; but instead of this, precedents are taken in the lump, and put at once for constitution and for law.

[Europe may form but one great Republic]

The best constitution that could now be devised, consistent with the condition of the present moment, may be far short of that excellence which a few years may afford. There is a morning of reason rising upon man on the subject of government, that has not appeared before. As the barbarism of the present old governments expires, the moral condition of nations with respect to each other will be changed. Man will not be brought up with the savage idea of considering his species as his enemy, because the accident of birth gave the individuals existence in countries distinguished by different names; and as constitutions have always some relation to external as well as to domestic circumstances, the means of benefitting by every change, foreign or domestic, should be a part of every constitution.

We already see an alteration in the national disposition of England and France towards each other, which, when we look back to only a few years, is itself a revolution. Who could have foreseen, or who would have believed, that a French National Assembly would ever have been a popular toast in England, or that a friendly alliance of the two nations should become the wish of either?[20] It shews, that man, were he not corrupted by governments, is naturally the friend of man, and that human nature is not of itself vicious. That spirit of jealousy and ferocity, which the governments of the two countries inspired, and which they rendered subservient to the purpose of taxation, is now yielding to the dictates of reason, interest, and humanity. The trade of courts is beginning to be understood, and the affectation of mystery, with all the artificial sorcery by which they imposed upon mankind, is on the decline. It has received its death-wound; and though it may linger, it will expire.

Government ought to be as much open to improvement as any thing which appertains to man, instead of which it has been monopolised from age to age, by the most ignorant and vicious of the human race. Need we any other proof of

---

[20]   Paine refers to the various British societies, like the London Revolution Society and the Society of Constitutional Information, which had toasted the success of the National Assembly over the period 1789–91.

their wretched management, than the excess of debts and taxes with which every nation groans, and the quarrels into which they have precipitated the world?

Just emerging from such a barbarous condition, it is too soon to determine to what extent of improvement government may yet be carried. For what we can foresee, all Europe may form but one great Republic, and man be free of the whole.

Chap. V   Ways and Means of Improving the Condition of Europe, Interspersed with Miscellaneous Observations

In contemplating a subject that embraces with equatorial magnitude the whole region of humanity, it is impossible to confine the pursuit in one single direction. It takes ground on every character and condition that appertains to man, and blends the individual, the nation, and the world.

From a small spark, kindled in America, a flame has arisen, not to be extinguished. Without consuming, like the *Ultima Ratio Regum*,[21] it winds its progress from nation to nation, and conquers by a silent operation. Man finds himself changed, he scarcely perceives how. He acquires a knowledge of his rights by attending justly to his interest, and discovers in the event that the strength and powers of despotism consist wholly in the fear of resisting it, and that, in order '*to be free, it is sufficient that he wills it*'.

Having in all the preceding parts of this work endeavoured to establish a system of principles as a basis, on which governments ought to be erected, I shall proceed in this, to the ways and means of rendering them into practice. [...]

[I have been an advocate for commerce, because I am a friend to its effects]

All the European governments (France now excepted) are constructed not on the principle of universal civilization, but on the reverse of it. So far as those governments relate to each other, they are in the same condition as we conceive of savage uncivilized life; they put themselves beyond the law as well of GOD as of man, and are, with respect to principle and reciprocal conduct, like so many individuals in a state of nature.

The inhabitants of every country, under the civilization of laws, easily civilize together, but governments being yet in an uncivilized state, and almost continually at war, they pervert the abundance which civilized life produces to carry on the uncivilized part to a greater extent. By thus engrafting the barbarism of government

---

[21]   'The last argument of kings', the declaration of war.

upon the internal civilization of a country, it draws from the latter, and more especially from the poor, a great portion of those earnings, which should be applied to their own subsistence and comfort. – Apart from all reflections of morality and philosophy, it is a melancholy fact, that more than one-fourth of the labour of mankind is annually consumed by this barbarous system.

What has served to continue this evil, is the pecuniary advantage which all the governments of Europe have found in keeping up this state of uncivilization. It affords to them pretences for power, and revenue, for which there would be neither occasion nor apology, if the circle of civilization were rendered compleat. Civil government alone, or the government of laws, is not productive of pretences for many taxes; it operates at home, directly under the eye of the country, and precludes the possibility of much imposition. But when the scene is laid in the uncivilized contention of governments, the field of pretences is enlarged, and the country, being no longer a judge, is open to every imposition, which governments please to act.

Not a thirtieth, scarcely a fortieth, part of the taxes which are raised in England are either occasioned by, or applied to, the purposes of civil government. It is not difficult to see, that the whole which the actual government does in this respect, is to enact laws, and that the country administers and executes them, at its own expense, by means of magistrates, juries, sessions, and assize, over and above the taxes which it pays.

In this view of the case, we have two distinct characters of government; the one the civil government, or the government of laws, which operates at home, the other the court or cabinet government, which operates abroad, on the rude plan of uncivilized life; the one attended with little charge, the other with boundless extravagance; and so distinct are the two, that if the latter were to sink, as it were by a sudden opening of the earth, and totally disappear, the former would not be deranged. It would still proceed, because it is the common interest of the nation that it should, and all the means are in practice.

Revolutions, then, have for their object, a change in the moral condition of governments, and with this change the burthen of public taxes will lessen, and civilization will be left to the enjoyment of that abundance, of which it is now deprived.

In contemplating the whole of this subject, I extend my views into the department of commerce. In all my publications, where the matter would admit, I have been an advocate for commerce, because I am a friend to its effects.[22] It is a pacific system, operating to cordialize mankind, by rendering nations, as well as individuals, useful to each other. As to mere theoretical reformation, I have never preached it up. The most effectual process is that of improving the condition of man by means of his interest; and it is on this ground that I take my stand.

---

[22]   See, for instance, his *Letter to the Abbé Raynal* (Philadelphia: M. Steiner, 1782), p. 47, where he praises the influence of commerce in 'tempering the human mind'. Unlike many republican theorists, including Rousseau, who regarded commerce as the harbinger of luxury and corruption, Paine associates it with the spread of civilization and progress.

If commerce were permitted to act to the universal extent it is capable, it would extirpate the system of war, and produce a revolution in the uncivilized state of governments. The invention of commerce has arisen since those governments began, and is the greatest approach towards universal civilization, that has yet been made by any means not immediately flowing from moral principles.

Whatever has a tendency to promote the civil intercourse of nations, by an exchange of benefits, is a subject as worthy of philosophy as of politics. Commerce is no other than the traffic of two individuals, multiplied on a scale of numbers; and by the same rule that nature intended for the intercourse of two, she intended that of all. For this purpose she has distributed the materials of manufactures and commerce, in various and distant parts of a nation and of the world; and as they cannot be procured by war so cheaply or so commodiously as by commerce, she has rendered the latter the means of extirpating the former.

As the two are nearly the opposite of each other, consequently, the uncivilized state of European governments is injurious to commerce. Every kind of destruction or embarrassment serves to lessen the quantity, and it matters but little in what part of the commercial world the reduction begins. Like blood, it cannot be taken from any of the parts, without being taken from the whole mass in circulation, and all partake of the loss. When the ability in any nation to buy is destroyed, it equally involves the seller. Could the government of England destroy the commerce of all other nations, she would most effectually ruin her own.

It is possible that a nation may be the carrier for the world, but she cannot be the merchant. She cannot be the seller and buyer of her own merchandise. [...]

[When ... we see age going to the workhouse and youth to the gallows, something must be wrong in the system of government]

When, in countries that are called civilized, we see age going to the workhouse and youth to the gallows, something must be wrong in the system of government. It would seem, by the exterior appearance of such countries, that all was happiness; but there lies hidden from the eye of common observation, a mass of wretchedness that has scarcely any other chance, than to expire in poverty or infamy. Its entrance into life is marked with the presage of its fate; and until this is remedied, it is in vain to punish.

Civil government does not exist in executions; but in making that provision for the instruction of youth, and the support of age, as to exclude, as much as possible, profligacy from the one, and despair from the other. Instead of this, the resources of a country are lavished upon kings, upon courts, upon hirelings, imposters, and prostitutes; and even the poor themselves, with all their wants upon them, are compelled to support the fraud that oppresses them.

[The aristocracy are ... the drones, a seraglio of males]

Why then does Mr. Burke talk of his house of peers, as the pillar of the landed interest? Were that pillar to sink into the earth, the same landed property would continue, and the same ploughing, sowing, and reaping would go on. The aristocracy are not the farmers who work the land, and raise the produce, but are the mere consumers of the rent; and when compared with the active world, are the drones, a seraglio of males, who neither collect the honey nor form the hive, but exist only for lazy enjoyment.[23]

Mr. Burke, in his first essay, called aristocracy *the Corinthian capital of polished society*. Towards completing the figure, he has now added the *pillar*; but still the base is wanting; and whenever a nation chuses to act a Samson, not blind, but bold, down will go the temple of Dagon, the Lords and the Philistines.[24]

[The plan is easy in practice]

I shall now conclude this plan with enumerating the several particulars, and then proceed to other matters.

The enumeration is as follows:

First, Abolition of two million poor-rates.
Secondly, Provision for two hundred and fifty-two thousand poor families.
Thirdly, Education for one million and thirty thousand children.
Fourthly, Comfortable provision for one hundred and forty thousand aged persons.
Fifthly, Donation of twenty shillings each for fifty thousand births.
Sixthly, Donation of twenty shillings each for twenty thousand births.
Seventhly, Allowance of twenty thousand pounds for the funeral expences of persons travelling for work, and dying at a distance from their friends.
Eighthly, Employment, at all times, for the casual poor in the cities of London and Westminster.

By the operation of this plan, the poor laws,[25] those instruments of civil torture, will be superseded, and the wasteful expence of litigation prevented. The hearts

---

[23]   A harem. Paine, like Wollstonecraft, continuously associates aristocracy with Oriental despotism and an effeminate lack of independence. See note 8 to Chapter 3 above.
[24]   See above p. 45. Paine refers to Judges 16: 22–31, where the blinded Samson pulls down the temple of Dagon on the Philistines.
[25]   The laws governing the relief of the poor in England, funded by rates levied on parishes. The costs often led local authorities to eject those likely to become a burden.

of the humane will not be shocked by ragged and hungry children, and persons of seventy and eighty years of age begging for bread. The dying poor will not be dragged from place to place to breathe their last, as a reprisal of parish upon parish. Widows will have a maintenance for their children, and not be carted away, on the death of their husbands, like culprits and criminals; and children will no longer be considered as increasing the distresses of their parents. The haunts of the wretched will be known, because it will be to their advantage; and the number of petty crimes, the offspring of distress and poverty, will be lessened. The poor, as well as the rich, will then be interested in the support of government, and the cause and apprehension of riots and tumults will cease. – Ye who sit in ease, and solace yourselves in plenty, and such there are in Turkey and Russia, as well as in England, and who say to yourselves, 'Are we not well off,' have ye thought of these things? When ye do, ye will cease to speak and feel for yourselves alone.

The plan is easy in practice. It does not embarrass trade by a sudden interruption in the order of taxes, but effects the relief by changing the application of them; and the money necessary for the purpose can be drawn from the excise collections, which are made eight times a year in every market town in England.

[Active and passive revolutions]

When all the governments of Europe shall be established on the representative system, nations will become acquainted, and the animosities and prejudices fomented by the intrigue and artifice of courts, will cease. The oppressed soldier will become a freeman; and the tortured sailor, no longer dragged along the streets like a felon, will pursue his mercantile voyage in safety.[26] It would be better that nations should continue the pay of their soldiers during their lives, and give them their discharge and restore them to freedom and their friends, and cease recruiting, than retain such multitudes at the same expense, in a condition useless to society and to themselves. As soldiers have hitherto been treated in most countries, they might be said to be without a friend. Shunned by the citizen on an apprehension of being enemies to liberty, and too often insulted by those who commanded them, their condition was a double oppression. But where genuine principles of liberty pervade a people, every thing is restored to order; and the soldier civilly treated, returns the civility.

In contemplating revolutions, it is easy to perceive that they may arise from two distinct causes; the one, to avoid or get rid of some great calamity; the other, to

---

[26]   Paine refers to the system whereby merchant seamen were forced or 'pressed' into the navy against their wishes.

obtain some great and positive good; and the two may be distinguished by the names of active and passive revolutions. In those which proceed from the former cause, the temper becomes incensed and sowered; and the redress, obtained by danger, is too often sullied by revenge. But in those which proceed from the latter, the heart, rather animated than agitated, enters serenely upon the subject. Reason and discussion, persuasion and conviction, become the weapons in the contest, and it is only when those are attempted to be suppressed that recourse is had to violence. When men unite in agreeing that a *thing is good*, could it be obtained, such as relief from a burden of taxes and the extinction of corruption, the object is more than half accomplished. What they approve as the end, they will promote in the means.

[In what light religion appears to me]

Throughout this work, various and numerous as the subjects are, which I have taken up and investigated, there is only a single paragraph upon religion, viz. '*that every religion is good, that teaches man to be good*'.

I have carefully avoided to enlarge upon the subject, because I am inclined to believe, that what is called the present ministry wish to see contentions about religion kept up, to prevent the nation turning its attention to subjects of government. It is as if they were to say, '*Look that way, or any way, but this.*'

But as religion is very improperly made a political machine, and the reality of it is thereby destroyed, I will conclude this work with stating in what light religion appears to me.

If we suppose a large family of children, who, on any particular day, or particular circumstance, made it a custom to present to their parent some token of their affection and gratitude, each of them would make a different offering, and most probably in a different manner. Some would pay their congratulations in themes of verse or prose, by some little devices, as their genius dictated, or according to what they thought would please; and, perhaps, the least of all, not able to do any of those things, would ramble into the garden, or the field, and gather what it thought the prettiest flower it could find, though, perhaps, it might be but a simple weed. The parent would be more gratified by such a variety, than if the whole of them had acted on a concerted plan, and each had made exactly the same offering. This would have the cold appearance of contrivance, or the harsh one of controul. But of all unwelcome things, nothing could more afflict the parent than to know, that the whole of them had afterwards gotten together by the ears, boys and girls, fighting, scratching, reviling, and abusing each other about which was the best or the worst present.

[What pace the political summer may keep with the natural, no human foresight can determine]

Some gentlemen have affected to call the principles upon which this work and the former part of *Rights of Man* are founded, 'a new fangled doctrine'. The question is not whether those principles are new or old, but whether they are right or wrong. Suppose the former, I will show their effect by a figure easily understood.

It is now towards the middle of February. Were I to take a turn into the country, the trees would present a leafless, winterly appearance. As people are apt to pluck twigs as they walk along, I perhaps might do the same, and by chance might observe, that a *single bud* on that twig had begun to swell. I should reason very unnaturally, or rather not reason at all, to suppose *this* was the *only* bud in England which had this appearance. Instead of deciding thus, I should instantly conclude, that the same appearance was beginning, or about to begin, every where; and though the vegetable sleep will continue longer on some trees and plants than on others, and though some of them may not *blossom* for two or three years, all will be in leaf in the summer, except those which are *rotten*. What pace the political summer may keep with the natural, no human foresight can determine. It is, however, not difficult to perceive that the spring is begun. – Thus wishing, as I sincerely do, freedom and happiness to all nations, I close the SECOND PART.

7

William Godwin

An Enquiry concerning Political Justice, and Its Influence on General Virtue and Happiness

(London: G. G. J. and J. Robinson, 1793)

William Godwin (1756–1836) was born into a dissenting minister's family in Wisbech, Cambridgeshire. Owing to disagreements within the congregation, the family moved to Suffolk before settling near Norwich in 1760. William Godwin was a precocious child who aspired to become a minister. In 1767 he boarded with Samuel Newton, an independent clergyman in Norwich. Despite Godwin's great dislike of Newton, his Sandemanianism (a heterodox form of Calvinism) would be an important influence.

In 1770 Godwin applied to Homerton dissenting college, but was rejected on suspicion of Sandemanianism and instead attended Hoxton Academy, which was then run by Andrew Kippis and Abraham Rees. Afterwards Godwin attempted to practise as a minister, eventually securing a position in Suffolk which he held for two years. A parishioner's recommendation of texts by Rousseau and other French *philosophes* led Godwin to adopt deism and to leave the church, ultimately to pursue a career as a writer in London. He scraped a living, but managed to write his *Life of Lord Chatham* (1783) and to produce journalism and short novels. In 1784 Kippis recommended Godwin to the bookseller–publisher George Robinson, as a writer on 'British and Foreign History' for the *New Annual Register*. He left the post in 1791, when Robinson agreed to pay him to write a comprehensive work on political principles. In November of this year, Godwin met Mary Wollstonecraft for the first time, but they did not seem to get along; they would meet again later and fall in love, eventually marrying in 1797.

Romanticism and Revolution: A Reader.
Edited by Jon Mee and David Fallon.   © 2011 Blackwell Publishing Ltd.

An Enquiry concerning Political Justice was published in February 1793, in the period immediately following Louis XVI's execution, when Britain and France declared war on each other. Godwin would later attribute his escape from prosecution to the price of the book; at £1.16s, its reach was small and its readership elite. *Political Justice* found great support among radicals. The work promotes the primacy of individual judgement, the use of independent reason for the maximum benefit of fellow humans, and the progressive betterment of human existence through increased knowledge. Government and church institutions are considered to impose restraints on the individual mind and to be antithetical to human progress. The work is anchored in the philosophical doctrine of 'Necessity': that is, for Godwin, the notion that the material universe is comprised of a series of events, each originating inevitably from prior events, in a connected chain of causation. Influenced by David Hartley's associationist psychology, Godwin believed that the mind is likewise governed by laws of causation, but that, through enhanced perception and reasoning, an individual's thought and action can constitute events modifying the chain of causation and its outcomes.

Godwin followed *Political Justice* with the thrilling novel *Things as They Are; or, the Adventures of Caleb Williams* (1794), in which the eponymous servant discovers his aristocratic master Falkland's dark secret, and the latter pursues Caleb to prevent its communication. The novel dramatized many of the concerns of *Political Justice*, especially Godwin's notions of psychology and causation, his critique of aristocratic honour, and his sense of the corrupting effects of present government and institutions. Its great success further enhanced his reputation. In 1794, Godwin's friends Thomas Holcroft and John Thelwall were among a number of radicals arrested on trumped-up charges of treason. Godwin's *Cursory Strictures on the Charge Delivered by Lord Chief Justice Eyre to the Grand Jury* was credited by many with influencing the jury to acquit the accused. This was to prove the high water mark of Godwin's career; it ebbed in public significance over ensuing years.

In *The Spirit of the Age* (London: H. Colburn, 1825), Hazlitt later recalled the momentous impact of Godwin's opus: 'Tom Paine was considered for the time as a Tom Fool to him, [William] Paley an old woman; Edmund Burke a flashy sophist. Truth, moral truth, it was supposed, had here taken up its abode: and these were the oracles of thought.' The young Wordsworth and Coleridge were admirers; Hazlitt recalled Wordsworth advising a student to throw aside his chemistry books 'and read Godwin on Necessity' (p. 33). Both writers soon moderated their enthusiasm for *Political Justice*. Coleridge's Christianity made it difficult to stomach Godwin's atheism, whilst 'The Borderers' (1796–7), especially its villain Rivers, reflects Wordsworth's distrust of 'independent intellect' and abstract reasoning. In *The Prelude* (1805),

Wordsworth famously describes his short-lived and misguided enthusiasm for 'the philosophy / That promised to abstract the hopes of man / Out of his feelings' (X.806–7). Nevertheless, Godwin continued to exercise an influence on Wordsworth and Coleridge, with poems such as 'Anecdote for Fathers' and 'The Convict' in *Lyrical Ballads* (1798) showing their continuing interest in Godwinian theories of mind and of crime and punishment.

Although Hazlitt's portrait of Godwin reflects on the decline of his reputation, in part produced by merciless anti-Jacobin mockery, Godwin remained important to later writers. Most significantly, he was approached in 1812 by Percy Bysshe Shelley, an avid enthusiast for *Political Justice*. Godwinian ideas informed works such as *Queen Mab* (1813) and *Prometheus Unbound* (1820). As a result of this acquaintance, in 1814 the already married Shelley eloped to Europe with Godwin's daughter by Wollstonecraft, Mary. Mary's *Frankenstein* (1818) was dedicated to her father. Her other novels, especially *Valperga* (1823) and *The Last Man* (1824), reflect the influence of her upbringing, her father's writings and principles, but also her independent engagement with his ideas.

Preface

[...] The period in which the work makes its appearance is singular. The people of England have assiduously been excited to declare their loyalty, and to mark every man as obnoxious who is not ready to sign the Shibboleth[1] of the constitution. Money is raised by voluntary subscription to defray the expence of prosecuting men who shall dare to promulgate heretical opinions, and thus to oppress them at once with the enmity of government and of individuals. This was an accident wholly unforeseen when the work was undertaken; and it will scarcely be supposed that such an accident could produce any alteration in the writer's designs. Every man, if we may believe the voice of rumour, is to be prosecuted who shall appeal to the people by the publication of any unconstitutional paper or pamphlet; and it is added, that men are to be prosecuted for any unguarded words that may be dropped in the warmth of conversation and debate.[2] It is now to be tried whether, in addition to these alarming encroachments upon our liberty, a book is to fall under the arm of the civil power, which, beside the advantage of having for one of its express objects the dissuading from all tumult and violence, is by its very nature an appeal to men

---

[1]   A key tenet or word by which a group of people can be distinguished from non-members (for its biblical origins, see Judges 12: 4–6).

[2]   Godwin had attended Paine's trial. Other radicals were harassed by the loyalist Association movement at this time. Godwin may refer to the case of John Frost, indicted for seditious utterance over comments made in a London coffee house in November 1792.

of study and reflexion. It is to be tried whether a project is formed for suppressing the activity of mind, and putting an end to the disquisitions of science. Respecting the event in a personal view the author has formed this resolution. Whatever conduct his countrymen may pursue, they will not be able to shake his tranquillity. The duty he is most bound to discharge is the assisting the progress of truth; and if he suffer in any respect for such a proceeding, there is certainly no vicissitude that can befall him, that can ever bring along with it a more satisfactory consolation.

But, exclusively of this precarious and unimportant consideration, it is the fortune of the present work to appear before a public that is panic struck, and impressed with the most dreadful apprehensions of such doctrines as are here delivered. All the prejudices of the human mind are in arms against it. This circumstance may appear to be of greater advantage than the other. But it is the property of truth to be fearless, and to prove victorious over every adversary. It requires no great degree of fortitude, to look with indifference upon the false fire of the moment, and to foresee the calm period of reason which will succeed.

JANUARY 7, 1793.

Book I   Of the Importance of Political Institutions – Chap. i   Introduction

[…] It may fairly be questioned, whether government be not still more considerable in its incidental effects, than in those intended to be produced. Vice, for example, depends for its existence upon the existence of temptation. May not a good government strongly tend to extirpate, and a bad one to increase the mass of temptation? Again, vice depends for its existence upon the existence of error. May not a good government by taking away all restraints upon the enquiring mind hasten, and a bad one by its patronage of error procrastinate the discovery and establishment of truth? Let us consider the subject in this point of view. If it can be proved that the science of politics is thus unlimited in its importance, the advocates of liberty will have gained an additional recommendation, and its admirers will be incited with the greater eagerness to the investigation of its principles.

Chap. ii   History of Political Society

[…] If we turn from the foreign transactions of states with each other,[3] to the principles of their domestic policy, we shall not find much greater reason to be satisfied. A numerous class of mankind are held down in a state of abject penury,

---

[3]   Godwin begins with a historical view of war as 'the inseparable ally of political institution'.

and are continually prompted by disappointment and distress to commit violence upon their more fortunate neighbours. The only mode which is employed to repress this violence, and to maintain the order and peace of society, is punishment. Whips, axes and gibbets, dungeons, chains and racks are the most approved and established methods of persuading men to obedience, and impressing upon their minds the lessons of reason. Hundreds of victims are annually sacrificed at the shrine of positive law and political institution.

Add to this the species of government which prevails over nine tenths of the globe, which is despotism: a government, as Mr. Locke justly observes, altogether 'vile and miserable', and 'more to be deprecated than anarchy itself'.[4]

This account of the history and state of man is not a declamation, but an appeal to facts. He that considers it cannot possibly regard political disquisition as a trifle, and government as a neutral and unimportant concern. I by no means call upon the reader implicitly to admit that these evils are capable of remedy, and that wars, executions and despotism can be extirpated out of the world. But I call upon him to consider whether they may be remedied. I would have him feel that civil policy is a topic upon which the severest investigation may laudably be employed.

If government be a subject, which, like mathematics, natural philosophy and morals, admits of argument and demonstration, then may we reasonably hope that men shall some time or other agree respecting it. If it comprehend every thing that is most important and interesting to man, it is probable that, when the theory is greatly advanced, the practice will not be wholly neglected. Men may one day feel that they are partakers of a common nature, and that true freedom and perfect equity, like food and air, are pregnant with benefit to every constitution. If there be the faintest hope that this shall be the final result, then certainly no subject can inspire to a sound mind such generous enthusiasm, such enlightened ardour and such invincible perseverance.

The probability of this improvement will be sufficiently established, if we consider, FIRST, that the moral characters of men are the result of their perceptions: and, SECONDLY, that of all the modes of operating upon mind government is the most considerable. In addition to these arguments it will be found, THIRDLY, that the good and ill effects of political institution are not less conspicuous in detail than in principle; and, FOURTHLY, that perfectibility is one of the most unequivocal characteristics of the human species, so that the political, as well as the intellectual state of man, may be presumed to be in a course of progressive improvement.

---

[4]   {Locke on Government, Book I. Chap. i. §. 1; and Book II. Chap. vii. §. 91. The words in the last place are: 'Wherever any two men are, who have no standing rule and common judge to appeal to on earth for the determination of controversies of right betwixt them, there they are still in *the state of nature*, and under all the inconveniences of it, with only this woeful difference to the subject, &c.'

Most of the above arguments may be found much more at large in Burke's Vindication of Natural Society; a treatise, in which the evils of the existing political institutions are displayed with incomparable force of reasoning and lustre of eloquence, while the intention of the author was to show that these evils were to be considered as trivial.}

Chap. iv   Three Principal Causes of Moral Improvement Considered – I.   Literature

Few engines can be more powerful, and at the same time more salutary in their tendency, than literature. Without enquiring for the present into the cause of this phenomenon, it is sufficiently evident in fact, that the human mind is strongly infected with prejudice and mistake. The various opinions prevailing in different countries and among different classes of men upon the same subject, are almost innumerable; and yet of all these opinions only one can be true. Now the effectual way for extirpating these prejudices and mistakes seems to be literature.

Literature has reconciled the whole thinking world respecting the great principles of the system of the universe, and extirpated upon this subject the dreams of romance and the dogmas of superstition. Literature has unfolded the nature of the human mind, and Locke and others have established certain maxims respecting man, as Newton has done respecting matter, that are generally admitted for unquestionable.[5] Discussion has ascertained with tolerable perspicuity the preference of liberty over slavery; and the Mainwarings, the Sibthorpes, and the Filmers, the race of speculative reasoners in favour of despotism, are almost extinct.[6]

[Truth ... must infallibly be struck out by the collision of mind with mind]

Indeed, if there be such a thing as truth, it must infallibly be struck out by the collision of mind with mind. The restless activity of intellect will for a time be fertile in paradox and error; but these will be only diurnals, while the truths that occasionally spring up, like sturdy plants, will defy the rigour of season and climate. In proportion as one reasoner compares his deductions with those of another, the weak places of his argument will be detected, the principles he too hastily adopted will be overthrown, and the judgments, in which his mind was exposed to no sinister influence, will be confirmed. All that is requisite in these discussions is unlimited speculation, and a sufficient variety of systems and opinions. While we only dispute about the best way of doing a thing in itself wrong, we shall indeed make but a trifling progress; but, when we are once persuaded that

---

[5]   Godwin refers to Locke's *Essay concerning Human Understanding* (1688), which argues that human knowledge is built up through sensory experience and through reflection upon it. Isaac Newton (1643–1727) established a scientific understanding of the mechanical laws of the universe, and this understanding encompassed his theories of motion and gravity.

[6]   Roger Mainwaring (d. 1653): bishop who preached that Charles I was bound neither by Parliament nor by law. Robert Sibthorpe (d. 1662): Church of England clergyman and supporter of Charles I. Robert Filmer (c. 1588–1653): political theorist and defender of patriarchal kingship. All three supported the divine right of the monarch.

nothing is too sacred to be brought to the touchstone of examination, science will advance with rapid strides. Men, who turn their attention to the boundless field of enquiry, and still more who recollect the innumerable errors and caprices of mind, are apt to imagine that the labour is without benefit and endless. But this cannot be the case, if truth at last have any real existence. Errors will, during the whole period of their reign, combat each other; prejudices that have passed unsuspected for ages, will have their era of detection; but, if in any science we discover one solitary truth, it cannot be overthrown.

Such are the arguments that may be adduced in favour of literature. But, even should we admit them in their full force, and at the same time suppose that truth is the omnipotent artificer by which mind can infallibly be regulated, it would yet by no means sufficiently follow that literature is alone adequate to all the purposes of human improvement. Literature, and particularly that literature by which prejudice is superseded, and the mind is strung to a firmer tone, exists only as the portion of a few. The multitude, at least in the present state of human society, cannot partake of its illuminations. For that purpose it would be necessary, that the general system of policy should become favourable, that every individual should have leisure for reasoning and reflection, and that there should be no species of public institution, which, having falshood for its basis, should counteract their progress. This state of society, if it did not precede the general dissemination of truth, would at least be the immediate result of it.

But in representing this state of society as the ultimate result, we should incur an obvious fallacy. The discovery of truth is a pursuit of such vast extent, that it is scarcely possible to prescribe bounds to it. Those great lines, which seem at present to mark the limits of human understanding, will, like the mists that rise from a lake, retire farther and farther the more closely we approach them. A certain quantity of truth will be sufficient for the subversion of tyranny and usurpation; and this subversion, by a reflected force, will assist our understandings in the discovery of truth. In the mean time, it is not easy to define the exact portion of discovery that must necessarily precede political melioration. The period of partiality and injustice will be shortened, in proportion as political rectitude occupies a principal share in our disquisition. When the most considerable part of a nation, either for numbers or influence, becomes convinced of the flagrant absurdity of its institutions, the whole will soon be prepared tranquilly and by a sort of common consent to supersede them.

II.   Education

But, if it appears that literature, unaided by the regularity of institution and disci-pline, is inadequate to the reformation of the species, it may perhaps be imagined, that education, commonly so called, is the best of all subsidiaries for making up its defects. Education may have the advantage of taking mind in its original state, a soil prepared for culture, and as yet uninfested with weeds; and it is a common and a reasonable opinion, that the task is much easier to plant right and virtuous dispositions in an unprejudiced understanding, than to root up the errors that have already become as it were a part of ourselves. If an erroneous and vicious education be, as it has been shown to be, the source of all our depravity, an education, deprived of these errors, seems to present itself as the most natural exchange, and must necessarily render its subject virtuous and pure.

I will imagine the pupil never to have been made the victim of tyranny or the slave of caprice. He has never been permitted to triumph in the success of importunity, and cannot therefore well have become restless, inconstant, fantastical or unjust. He has been inured to ideas of equality and independence, and therefore is not passionate, haughty and overbearing. The perpetual witness of a temperate conduct and reasonable sentiments, he is not blinded with prejudice, is not liable to make a false estimate of things, and of consequence has no immoderate desires after wealth, and splendour, and the gratifications of luxury. Virtue has always been presented to him under the most attractive form, as the surest medium of success in every honourable pursuit, the never-failing consolation of disappointment, and infinitely superior in value to every other acquisition.

It cannot be doubted that such an education is calculated to produce very considerable effects. In the world indeed the pupil will become the spectator of scenes very different from what his preconceived ideas of virtue might have taught him to expect. Let us however admit it to be possible so to temper the mind, as to render it proof against the influence of example and the allurements of luxury. Still it may be reasonable to doubt of the sufficiency of education. How many instances may we expect to find, in which a plan has been carried into execution, so enlightened, unremitted and ardent, as to produce these extraordinary effects? Where must the preceptor himself have been educated, who shall thus elevate his pupil above all the errors of mankind? If the world teach an implicit deference to birth and riches and accidental distinctions, he will scarcely be exempt from this deference. If the world be full of intrigue and rivalship and selfishness, he will not be wholly disinterested.

III.   Political Justice[7]

The benefits of political justice will best be understood, if we consider society in the most comprehensive view, taking into our estimate the erroneous institutions by which the human mind has been too often checked in its career, as well as those well founded opinions of public and individual interest, which perhaps need only to be clearly explained, in order to their being generally received.

---

[7]   In the introduction to this chapter, Godwin defines political justice as 'the adoption of any principle of morality and truth into the practice of a community'.

Now in whatever light it be considered, we cannot avoid perceiving, first, that political institution is peculiarly strong in that very point in which the efficacy of education was deficient, the extent of its operation. That it in some way influences our conduct will hardly be disputed. It is sufficiently obvious that a despotic government is calculated to render men pliant, and a free one resolute and independent. All the effects that any principle adopted into the practice of a community may produce, it produces upon a comprehensive scale. It creates a similar bias in the whole, or a considerable part of the society. The motive it exhibits, the stimulus it begets, are operative, because they are fitted to produce effect upon mind. They will therefore inevitably influence all to whom they are equally addressed. Virtue, where virtue is the result, will cease to be a task of perpetual watchfulness and contention. It will neither be, nor appear to be, a sacrifice of our personal advantage to disinterested considerations. It will render those the confederates, support and security of our rectitude, who were before its most formidable enemies.

Again, an additional argument in favour of the efficacy of political institutions, arises from the extensive influence which certain false principles, engendered by an imperfect system of society, have been found to exert. Superstition, an immoderate fear of shame, a false calculation of interest, are errors that have been always attended with the most extensive consequences. How incredible at the present day do the effects of superstition exhibited in the middle ages, the horrors of excommunication and interdict, and the humiliation of the greatest monarchs at the feet of the pope, appear? What can be more contrary to European modes than the dread of disgrace, which induces the Brahmin widows of Indostan to destroy themselves upon the funeral pile of their husbands?[8] What more horribly immoral than the mistaken idea which leads multitudes in commercial countries to regard fraud, falshood and circumvention as the truest policy? But, however powerful these errors may be, the empire of truth, if once established, would be incomparably greater. The man, who is enslaved by shame, superstition or deceit, will be perpetually exposed to an internal war of opinions, disapproving by an involuntary censure the conduct he has been most persuaded to adopt. No mind can be so far alienated from truth, as not in the midst of its degeneracy to have incessant returns of a better principle. No system of society can be so thoroughly pervaded with mistake, as not frequently to suggest to us sentiments of virtue, liberty and justice. But truth is in all its branches harmonious and consistent.

The recollection of this circumstance induces me to add as a concluding observation, that it may reasonably be doubted whether error could ever be formidable or long-lived, if government did not lend it support. The nature of mind is adapted to the perception of ideas, their correspondence and difference. In the right discernment of these is its true element and most congenial

---

[8]   Godwin refers to the Hindu rite of sati or suttee. Late eighteenth-century campaigners, including prominent Evangelicals, called upon the East India Company and the government to ban the practice.

pursuit. Error would indeed for a time have been the result of our partial perceptions; but, as our perceptions are continually changing, and continually
becoming more definite and correct, our errors would have been momentary,
and our judgments have hourly approached nearer to the truth. The doctrine
of transubstantiation, the belief that men were really eating flesh when they
seemed to be eating bread, and drinking human blood when they seemed to be
drinking wine, could never have maintained its empire so long, if it had not
been reinforced by civil authority. Men would not have so long persuaded
themselves that an old man elected by the intrigues of a conclave of cardinals,
from the moment of that election became immaculate and infallible, if the
persuasion had not been maintained by revenues, endowments and palaces.[9]
A system of government, that should lend no sanction to ideas of fanaticism
and hypocrisy, would presently accustom its subject to think justly upon topics
of moral worth and importance. A state, that should abstain from imposing
contradictory and impracticable oaths, and thus perpetually stimulating its
members to concealment and perjury, would soon become distinguished for
plain dealing and veracity.[10] A country, in which places of dignity and confidence should cease to be at the disposal of faction, favour and interest, would
not long be the residence of servility and deceit.

These remarks suggest to us the true answer to an obvious objection, that might
otherwise present itself, to the conclusion to which these principles appear to lead.
It might be said, that an erroneous government can never afford an adequate solution for the existence of moral evil, since government was itself the production of
human intelligence, and therefore, if ill, must have been indebted for its ill qualities
to some wrong which had previous existence.

The proposition asserted in this objection is undoubtedly true. All vice is nothing
more than error and mistake reduced into practice, and adopted as the principle
of our conduct. But error is perpetually hastening to its own detection. Vicious
conduct is soon discovered to involve injurious consequences. Injustice therefore
by its own nature is little fitted for a durable existence. But government 'lays its
hand upon the spring there is in society, and puts a stop to its motion'.[11] It gives
substance and permanence to our errors. It reverses the genuine propensities of
mind, and, instead of suffering us to look forward, teaches us to look backward
for perfection. It prompts us to seek the public welfare, not in innovation and
improvement, but in a timid reverence for the decisions of our ancestors, as if it
were the nature of mind always to degenerate, and never to advance.

---

[9]   Like many Protestants and Dissenters, Godwin abhorred the Catholic doctrines of transubstantiation and
papal infallibility, regarding them as institutionalized superstition.
[10]   Some Dissenters outwardly conformed to the articles of the Church of England whilst privately maintaining
noncomformist beliefs in order to hold public offices.
[11]   {Logan, Philosophy of History, p. 69.} John Logan (1748–88), Edinburgh writer, minister, and associate of
leading Scottish Enlightenment figures; the book referred to here, published in 1781, collected his lectures in
history.

Chap. vi   Human Inventions Capable of Perpetual Improvement

If we would form to ourselves a solid estimate of political, or indeed of any other science, we ought not to confine our survey to that narrow portion of things which passes under our immediate inspection, and rashly pronounce every thing that we have not ourselves seen, to be impossible. There is no characteristic of man, which seems at present at least so eminently to distinguish him, or to be of so much importance in every branch of moral science, as his perfectibility. Let us carry back our minds to man in his original state, a being capable of impressions and knowledge to an unbounded extent, but not having as yet received the one or cultivated the other; and let us contrast this being with all that science and genius have effected: and from hence we may form some idea what it is of which human nature is capable. It is to be remembered, that this being did not as now derive assistance from the communications of his fellows, nor had his feeble and crude conceptions assisted by the experience of successive centuries; but that in the state we are figuring all men were equally ignorant. The field of improvement was before them, but for every step in advance they were to be indebted to their untutored efforts.

[Let us not look back]

Such was man in his original state, and such is man as we at present behold him. Is it possible for us to contemplate what he has already done, without being impressed with a strong presentiment of the improvements he has yet to accomplish? There is no science that is not capable of additions; there is no art that may not be carried to a still higher perfection. If this be true of all other sciences, why not of morals? If this be true of all other arts, why not of social institution? The very conception of this as possible, is in the highest degree encouraging. If we can still farther demonstrate it to be a part of the natural and regular progress of mind, our confidence and our hopes will then be complete. This is the temper with which we ought to engage in the study of political truth. Let us look back, that we may profit by the experience of mankind; but let us not look back, as if the wisdom of our ancestors was such as to leave no room for future improvement.

Book II   Principles of Society – Chap. i   Introduction

[…] It is farther necessary before we enter upon the subject carefully to distinguish between society and government. Men associated at first for the sake of mutual assistance. They did not foresee that any restraint would be necessary, to regulate the conduct of individual members of the society, towards each other, or towards the whole. The necessity of restraint grew out of the errors and perverseness of a few. An acute writer has expressed this idea with peculiar felicity. 'Society and government', says he, 'are different in themselves, and have different origins. Society is produced by our wants, and government by our wickedness. Society is in every state a blessing; government even in its best state but a necessary evil.'[12]

Chap. ii   Of Justice

[...] Considerable light will probably be thrown upon our investigation, if, quitting for the present the political view, we examine justice merely as it exists among individuals. Justice is a rule of conduct originating in the connection of one percipient being with another. A comprehensive maxim which has been laid down upon the subject is, 'that we should love our neighbour as ourselves'.[13] But this maxim, though possessing considerable merit as a popular principle, is not modelled with the strictness of philosophical accuracy.

In a loose and general view I and my neighbour are both of us men; and of consequence entitled to equal attention. But in reality it is probable that one of us is a being of more worth and importance than the other. A man is of more worth than a beast; because, being possessed of higher faculties, he is capable of a more refined and genuine happiness. In the same manner the illustrious archbishop of Cambray[14] was of more worth than his chambermaid, and there are few of us that would hesitate to pronounce, if his palace were in flames, and the life of only one of them could be preserved, which of the two ought to be preferred.

But there is another ground of preference, beside the private consideration of one of them being farther removed from the state of a mere animal. We are not connected with one or two percipient beings, but with a society, a nation, and in some sense with the whole family of mankind. Of consequence that life ought to be preferred which will be most conducive to the general good. In saving the life of Fenelon, suppose at the moment when he was conceiving the project of his immortal Telemachus,[15] I should be promoting the benefit of thousands, who have been cured by the perusal of it of some error, vice and consequent unhappiness. Nay, my benefit would extend farther than this, for every individual thus cured has

---

12   {*Common Sense*, p. 1.} In *Common Sense* (1776), Paine first stated his distinction between society and government, also made in *Rights of Men*. See above, p. 128.
13   Leviticus 19: 18 and Matthew 22: 39.
14   François Fénelon (1651–1715), Catholic theologian, writer, and Bishop of Cambrai (1696–1715).
15   *Les Aventures de Télémaque* (1699) describes the education of Ulysses' son, Telemachus, from the perspective of his tutor, Mentor, and implicitly satirizes Louis XIV and his rule. It opposes imperialism and advocates altruism, constitutional monarchy, and reduced tax burdens on the labouring poor.

become a better member of society, and has contributed in his turn to the happiness, the information and improvement of others.

Supposing I had been myself the chambermaid, I ought to have chosen to die, rather than that Fenelon should have died. The life of Fenelon was really preferable to that of the chambermaid. But understanding is the faculty that perceives the truth of this and similar propositions; and justice is the principle that regulates my conduct accordingly. It would have been just in the chambermaid to have preferred the archbishop to herself. To have done otherwise would have been a breach of justice.

Supposing the chambermaid had been my wife, my mother or my benefactor.[16] This would not alter the truth of the proposition. The life of Fenelon would still be more valuable than that of the chambermaid; and justice, pure, unadulterated justice, would still have preferred that which was most valuable. Justice would have taught me to save the life of Fenelon at the expence of the other. What magic is there in the pronoun 'my', to overturn the decisions of everlasting truth? My wife or my mother may be a fool or a prostitute, malicious, lying or dishonest. If they be, of what consequence is it that they are mine?

'But my mother endured for me the pains of child bearing, and nourished me in the helplessness of infancy.' When she first subjected herself to the necessity of these cares, she was probably influenced by no particular motives of benevolence to her future offspring. Every voluntary benefit however entitles the bestower to some kindness and retribution. But why so? Because a voluntary benefit is an evidence of benevolent intention, that is, of virtue. It is the disposition of the mind, not the external action, that entitles to respect. But the merit of this disposition is equal, whether the benefit was conferred upon me or upon another. I and another man cannot both be right in preferring our own individual benefactor, for no man can be at the same time both better and worse than his neighbour. My benefactor ought to be esteemed, not because he bestowed a benefit upon me, but because he bestowed it upon a human being. His desert will be in exact proportion to the degree, in which that human being was worthy of the distinction conferred. Thus every view of the subject brings us back to the consideration of my neighbour's moral worth and his importance to the general weal, as the only standard to determine the treatment to which he is entitled. Gratitude therefore, a principle which has so often been the theme of the moralist and the poet, is no part either of justice or virtue. By gratitude I understand a sentiment, which would lead me to prefer one man to another, from some other consideration than that of his superior usefulness or worth: that is, which would make something true to me (for example this preferableness), which cannot be true to another man, and is not true in itself.[17]

---

[16]   Godwin revised the notorious 'fire case' in the second edition (1796): the chambermaid became a 'valet' who might be 'my brother, my father or my benefactor'.

[17]   {This argument respecting gratitude is stated with great clearness in an Essay on the Nature of True Virtue, by the Rev. Jonathan Edwards. 12mo. Dilly.} Jonathan Edwards (1703–58), American theologian, published this dissertation in 1765, distinguishing between true ('saving') virtue, associated with divine love, and common morality, associated with gratitude for benevolence shown to oneself.

It may be objected, 'that my relation, my companion, or my benefactor will of course in many instances obtain an uncommon portion of my regard: for, not being universally capable of discriminating the comparative worth of different men, I shall inevitably judge most favourably of him, of whose virtues I have received the most unquestionable proofs; and thus shall be compelled to prefer the man of moral worth whom I know, to another who may possess unknown to me, an essential superiority.'

This compulsion however is founded only in the present imperfection of human nature. It may serve as an apology for my error, but can never turn error into truth. It will always remain contrary to the strict and inflexible decisions of justice. The difficulty of conceiving this is owing merely to our confounding the disposition from which an action is chosen, with the action itself. The disposition, that would prefer virtue to vice and a greater degree of virtue to a less, is undoubtedly a subject of approbation; the erroneous exercise of this disposition by which a wrong object is selected, if unavoidable, is to be deplored, but can by no colouring and under no denomination be converted into right.

It may in the second place be objected, 'that a mutual commerce of benefits tends to increase the mass of benevolent action, and that to increase the mass of benevolent action is to contribute to the general good'. Indeed! Is general good promoted by falshood, by treating a man of one degree of worth, as if he had ten times that worth? or as if he were in any degree different from what he really is? Would not the most beneficial consequences result from a different plan; from my constantly and carefully enquiring into the deserts of all those with whom I am connected, and from their being sure, after a certain allowance for the fallibility of human judgment, of being treated by me exactly as they deserved? Who can tell what would be the effects of such a plan of conduct universally adopted?

Chap. iv   Of the Equality of Mankind

[...] In the uncultivated state of man diseases, effeminacy and luxury were little known, and of consequence the strength of every one much more nearly approached to the strength of his neighbour. In the uncultivated state of man the understandings of all were limited, their wants, their ideas and their views nearly upon a level. It was to be expected that in their first departure from this state great irregularities would introduce themselves; and it is the object of subsequent wisdom and improvement to mitigate these irregularities.

Secondly, notwithstanding the incroachments that have been made upon the equality of mankind, a great and substantial equality remains. There is no such disparity among the human race as to enable one man to hold several other men in subjection, except so far as they are willing to be subject. All government is founded in opinion.[18] Men at present live under any particular form, because they conceive it their interest to do so. One part indeed of a community or empire may be held in subjection by force; but this cannot be the personal force of their despot; it must be the force of another part of the community, who are of opinion that it is their interest to support his authority. Destroy this opinion, and the fabric which is built upon it falls to the ground. It follows therefore that all men are essentially independent. – So much for the physical equality.

The moral equality is still less open to reasonable exception. By moral equality I understand the propriety of applying one unalterable rule of justice to every case that may arise. This cannot be questioned but upon arguments that would subvert the very nature of virtue. 'Equality', it has been affirmed, 'will always be an unintelligible fiction, so long as the capacities of men shall be unequal, and their pretended claims have neither guarantee nor sanction by which they can be inforced.'[19] But surely justice is sufficiently intelligible in its own nature, abstracted from the consideration whether it be or be not reduced into practice. Justice has relation to beings endowed with perception, and capable of pleasure and pain. Now it immediately results from the nature of such beings, independently of any arbitrary constitution, that pleasure is agreeable and pain odious, pleasure to be desired and pain to be obviated. It is therefore just and reasonable that such beings should contribute, so far as it lies in their power, to the pleasure and benefit of each other. Among pleasures some are more exquisite, more unalloyed and less precarious than others. It is just that these should be preferred.

From these simple principles we may deduce the moral equality of mankind. We are partakers of a common nature, and the same causes that contribute to the benefit of one contribute to the benefit of another. Our senses and faculties are of the same denomination. Our pleasures and pains will therefore be the same. We are all of us endowed with reason, able to compare, to judge and to infer. The improvement therefore which is to be desired for the one is to be desired for the other. We shall be provident for ourselves and useful to each other, in proportion as we rise above the atmosphere of prejudice. The same independence, the same freedom from any such restraint, as should prevent us from giving the reins to our own understanding, or from uttering upon all occasions whatever we think to be true, will conduce to the improvement of all. There are certain opportunities and a certain situation most advantageous to every human being, and it is just that these should be communicated to all, as nearly at least as the general economy will permit.

There is indeed one species of moral inequality parallel to the physical inequality that has been already described. The treatment to which men are entitled is to be measured by their merits and their virtues. That country would not be the seat of wisdom and reason, where the benefactor of his species was considered in the

---

[18]   In this Godwin follows David Hume (1711–76), and especially 'On the First Principles of Government', published in his *Essays Moral and Political* (1741).
[19]   In a footnote, Godwin quotes the original French from Abbé Raynal's *Révolution d'Amérique* (1781), p. 34.

same point of view as their enemy. But in reality this distinction, so far from being adverse to equality in any tenable sense, is friendly to it, and is accordingly known by the appellation of equity, a term derived from the same origin.[20] Though in some sense an exception, it tends to the same purpose to which the principle itself is indebted for its value. It is calculated to infuse into every bosom an emulation of excellence. The thing really to be desired is the removing as much as possible arbitrary distinctions, and leaving to talents and virtue the field of exertion unimpaired. We should endeavour to afford to all the same opportunities and the same encouragement, and to render justice the common interest and choice.

Chap. v   Rights of Man

[...] Whatever is meant by the term right, for it will presently appear that the sense of the term itself has never been clearly understood, there can neither be opposite rights, nor rights and duties hostile to each other. The rights of one man cannot clash with or be destructive of the rights of another; for this, instead of rendering the subject an important branch of truth and morality, as the advocates of the rights of man certainly understand it to be, would be to reduce it to a heap of unintelligible jargon and inconsistency. If one man have a right to be free, another man cannot have a right to make him a slave; if one man have a right to inflict chastisement upon me, I cannot have a right to withdraw myself from chastisement; if my neighbour have a right to a sum of money in my possession, I cannot have a right to retain it in my pocket. – It cannot be less incontrovertible, that I have no right to omit what my duty prescribes.

From hence it inevitably follows that men have no rights. By right, as the word is employed in this subject, has always been understood discretion, that is, a full and complete power of either doing a thing or omitting it, without the person's becoming liable to animadversion or censure from another, that is, in other words, without his incurring any degree of turpitude or guilt. Now in this sense I affirm that man has no rights, no discretionary power whatever.

It is commonly said, 'that a man has a right to the disposal of his fortune, a right to the employment of his time, a right to the uncontrolled choice of his profession or pursuits'. But this can never be consistently affirmed till it can be shewn that he has no duties, prescribing and limiting his mode of proceeding in all these respects. My neighbour has just as much right to put an end to my existence with dagger or poison, as to deny me that pecuniary assistance without which I must starve, or as to deny me that assistance without which my intellectual attainments or my moral exertions will be materially injured. He has just as much right to amuse himself

---

[20]   A separate legal system operating alongside common and statute law, which was given priority when standard procedures would prove inadequate or result in injustice.

with burning my house or torturing my children upon the rack, as to shut himself up in a cell careless about his fellow men, and to hide 'his talent in a napkin'.[21]

If men have any rights, any discretionary powers, they must be in things of total indifference, as whether I sit on the right or on the left side of my fire, or dine on beef today or tomorrow. Even these rights are much fewer than we are apt to imagine, since before they can be completely established, it must be proved that my choice on one side or the other can in no possible way contribute to the benefit or injury of myself or of any other person in the world. Those must indeed be rights well worth the contending for, the very essence of which consists in their absolute nugatoriness and inutility.

[The impossibility by any compulsatory method of bringing men to uniformity of opinion]

One obvious reason against this assumption on the part of the society[22] is the impossibility by any compulsatory method of bringing men to uniformity of opinion. The judgment we form upon topics of general truth, is or is imagined to be founded upon evidence: and, however it may be soothed by gentle applications to the betraying its impartiality, it is apt to repel with no little pertinacity whatever comes under the form of compulsion. Persecution cannot persuade the understanding, even when it subdues our resolution. It may make us hypocrites; but cannot make us converts. The government therefore, which is anxious above all things to imbue its subjects with integrity and virtue, will be the farthest in the world from discouraging them in the explicit avowal of their sentiments.

But there is another reason of a higher order. Man is not, as has been already shewn, a perfect being, but perfectible. No government, that has yet existed, or is likely presently to exist upon the face of the earth, is faultless. No government ought therefore pertinaciously to resist the change of its own institutions; and still less ought it to set up a standard upon the various topics of human speculation, to restrain the excursions of an inventive mind. It is only by giving a free scope to these excursions, that science, philosophy and morals have arrived at their present degree of perfection, or are capable of going on to that still greater perfection, in comparison of which all that has been already done will perhaps appear childish. But a proceeding, absolutely necessary for the purpose of exciting the mind to these salutary excursions, and still more necessary in order to give them their proper operation, consists in the unrestrained communication of men's thoughts and discoveries to each other. If every man have to begin again at the point from

---

[21]   The parable of the talents: Luke 19: 20.
[22]   Godwin has been asserting that society has no right to prescribe limits to conscience in 'matters of pure speculation'.

which his neighbour set out, the labour will be endless, and the progress in an unvarying circle. There is nothing that more eminently contributes to intellectual energy, than for every man to be habituated to follow without alarm the train of his speculations, and to utter without fear the conclusions that have suggested themselves to him. – But does all this imply that men have a right to act any thing but virtue, and to utter any thing but truth? Certainly not. It implies indeed that there are points with which society has no right to interfere, not that discretion and caprice are more free, or duty less strict upon these points, than upon any others with which human action is conversant.

Chap. vi   Of the Exercise of Private Judgment

[...] If there be any truth more unquestionable than the rest, it is, that every man is bound by the exertion of his faculties in the discovery of right, and to the carrying into effect all the right with which he is acquainted. It may be granted that an infallible standard, if it could be discovered, would be considerably beneficial. But this infallible standard itself would be of little use in human affairs, unless it had the property of reasoning as well as deciding, of enlightening the mind as well as constraining the body. If a man be in some cases obliged to prefer his own judgment, he is in all cases obliged to consult that judgment before he can determine whether the matter in question be of the sort provided for or no. So that from this reasoning it ultimately appears, that no man is obliged to conform to any rule of conduct, farther than the rule is consistent with justice.

Such are the genuine principles of human society. Such would be the unconstrained concord of its members, in a state where every individual within the society, and every neighbour without, was capable of listening with sobriety to the dictates of reason. We shall not fail to be impressed with considerable regret, if, when we descend to the present mixed characters of mankind, we find ourselves obliged in any degree to depart from so simple and grand a principle. The universal exercise of private judgment is a doctrine so unspeakably beautiful, that the true politician will certainly resolve to interfere with it as sparingly and in as few instances as possible. [...]

[Punishment inevitably excites in the sufferer ... a sense of injustice]

Punishment inevitably excites in the sufferer, and ought to excite, a sense of injustice. Let its purpose be to convince me of the truth of a proposition, which I at present believe to be false. It is not abstractedly considered of the nature of an argument, and therefore it cannot begin with producing conviction. Punishment is a specious name, but is in reality nothing more than force put upon one being by another who happens to be stronger. Now strength does not constitute justice, nor ought 'might', according to a trite proverb, to 'overcome right'. The case of punishment, which we are now considering, is the case of you and I differing in opinion, and your telling me that you must be right, since you have a more brawny arm, or have applied your mind more to the acquiring skill in your weapons than I have.

Book III – Chap. vii   Of Forms of Government

[…] Man is in a state of perpetual progress. He must grow either better or worse, either correct his habits or confirm them. The government proposed must either increase our passions and prejudices by fanning the flame, or by gradually discouraging tend to extirpate them. In reality, it is sufficiently difficult to imagine a government that shall have the latter tendency. By its very nature political institution has a tendency to suspend the elasticity, and put an end to the advancement of mind. Every scheme for embodying imperfection must be injurious. That which is to-day a considerable melioration, will at some future period, if preserved unaltered, appear a defect and disease in the body politic. It were earnestly to be desired that each man was wise enough to govern himself without the intervention of any compulsory restraint; and, since government even in its best state is an evil, the object principally to be aimed at is, that we should have as little of it as the general peace of human society will permit.

But the grand instrument for forwarding the improvement of mind is the publication of truth. Not the publication on the part of the government; for it is infinitely difficult to discover infallibly what the truth is, especially upon controverted points, and government is as liable as individuals to be mistaken in this respect. In reality it is more liable; for the depositaries of government have a very obvious temptation to desire, by means of ignorance and implicit faith, to perpetuate the existing state of things. The only substantial method for the propagation of truth is discussion, so that the errors of one man may be detected by the acuteness and severe disquisition of his neighbours. All we have to demand from the officers of government, at least in their public character, is neutrality. The intervention of authority in a field proper to reasoning and demonstration is always injurious. If on the right side, it can only discredit truth, and call off the attention of men to a foreign consideration. If on the wrong, though it may not be able to suppress the spirit of enquiry, it will have a tendency to convert the calm pursuit of knowledge into passion and tumult.

'But in what manner shall the principles of truth be communicated so as best to lead to the practice? By shewing to mankind truth in all its evidence, or concealing one half of it? Shall they be initiated by a partial discovery, and thus led on by regular degrees to conclusions that would at first have wholly alienated their minds?'

This question will come to be more fully discussed in a following chapter. In the mean time let us only consider for the present the quantity of effect that may be expected from these two opposite plans.

An inhabitant of Turkey or Morocco may perhaps be of opinion, that the vesting power in the arbitrary will or caprice of an individual has in it more advantages than disadvantages. If I be desirous to change his opinion, should I undertake to recommend to him in animated language some modification of this caprice? I should attack it in its principle. If I do otherwise, I shall betray the strength of my cause. The principle opposite to his own, will not possess half the irresistible force which I could have given to it. His objections will assume vigour. The principle I am maintaining being half truth and half falshood, he will in every step of the contest possess an advantage in the offensive, of which, if he be sufficiently acute, I can never deprive him.

Now the principle I should have to explain of equal law and equal justice to the inhabitant of Morocco, would be as new to him, as any principle of the boldest political description that I could propagate in this country. Whatever apparent difference may exist between the two cases, may fairly be suspected to owe its existence to the imagination of the observer. The rule therefore which suggests itself in this case is fitted for universal application.

As to the improvements which are to be introduced into the political system, their quantity and their period must be determined by the degree of knowledge existing in any country, and the state of preparation of the public mind for the changes that are to be desired. Political renovation may strictly be considered as one of the stages in intellectual improvement. Literature and disquisition cannot of themselves be rendered sufficiently general; it will be only the cruder and grosser parts that can be expected to descend in their genuine form to the multitude; while those abstract and bold speculations, in which the value of literature principally consists, must necessarily continue the portion of the favoured few. It is here that social institution offers itself in aid of the abstruser powers of argumentative communication. As soon as any important truth has become established to a sufficient extent in the minds of the enterprising and the wise, it may tranquilly and with ease be rendered a part of the general system; since the uninstructed and the poor are never the strenuous supporters of those complicated systems by which oppression is maintained; and since they have an obvious interest in the practical introduction of simplicity and truth. One valuable principle being thus realised, prepares the way for the realising of more. It serves as a resting-place to the human mind in its great business of exploring the regions of truth, and gives it new alacrity and encouragement for farther exertions.

Book IV   Miscellaneous Principles – Chap. ii   Of Revolutions – Section I.   Duties of a Citizen

No question can be more important than that which respects the best mode of effecting revolutions. Before we enter upon it however, it may be proper to remove a difficulty which has suggested itself to the minds of some men, how far we ought generally speaking to be the friends of revolution; or, in other words, whether it be justifiable in a man to be the enemy of the constitution of his country.

'We live', it will be said, 'under the protection of this constitution; and protection, being a benefit conferred, obliges us to a reciprocation of support in return.'

To this it may he answered, first, that this protection is a very equivocal thing; and, till it can be shown that the vices, from the effects of which it protects us, are not for the most part the produce of that constitution, we shall never sufficiently understand the quantity of benefit it includes.

Secondly, gratitude, as has already been proved,[23] is a vice and not a virtue. Every man and every collection of men ought to be treated by us in a manner founded upon their intrinsic qualities and capacities, and not according to a rule which has existence only in relation to ourselves.

Add to this, thirdly, that no motive can be more equivocal than the gratitude here recommended. Gratitude to the constitution, an abstract idea, an imaginary existence, is altogether unintelligible. Affection to my countrymen will be much better proved, by my exertions to procure them a substantial benefit, than by my supporting a system which I believe to be fraught with injurious consequences.

Section II.   Mode of Effecting Revolutions

To return to the enquiry respecting the mode of effecting revolutions. If no question can be more important, there is fortunately no question perhaps that admits of a more complete and satisfactory general answer. The revolutions of states, which a philanthropist would desire to witness, or in which he would willingly co-operate, consist principally in a change of sentiments and dispositions in the members of those states.[24] The true instruments for changing the opinions of men are argument and persuasion. The best security for an advantageous issue is free and unrestricted discussion. In that field truth must always prove the successful champion. If then we would improve the social institutions of mankind, we must write, we

---

[23]   {Book II. chap ii. p. 83.}
[24]   See Wollstonecraft's 'revolution in female manners', p. 100 above.

must argue, we must converse.[25] To this business there is no close; in this pursuit there should be no pause. Every method should be employed, – not so much positively to allure the attention of mankind, or persuasively to invite them to the adoption of our opinions, – as to remove every restraint upon thought, and to throw open the temple of science and the field of enquiry to all the world.

Those instruments will always be regarded by the discerning mind as suspicious, which may be employed with equal prospect of success on both sides of every question. This consideration should make us look with aversion upon all resources of violence. When we descend into the listed field, we of course desert the vantage ground of truth, and commit the decision to uncertainty and caprice. The phalanx of reason is invulnerable; it advances with deliberate and determined pace; and nothing is able to resist it. But when we lay down our arguments, and take up our swords, the case is altered. Amidst the barbarous pomp of war and the clamorous din of civil brawls, who can tell whether the event shall be prosperous or miserable?

We must therefore carefully distinguish between informing the people and inflaming them. Indignation, resentment and fury are to be deprecated; and all we should ask is sober thought, clear discernment and intrepid discussion. Why were the revolutions of America and France a general concert of all orders and descriptions of men, without so much (if we bear in mind the multitudes concerned) as almost a dissentient voice; while the resistance against our Charles the first divided the nation into two equal parts? Because the latter was the affair of the seventeenth century, and the former happened in the close of the eighteenth. Because in the case of America and France philosophy had already developed some of the great principles of political truth, and Sydney and Locke and Montesquieu and Rousseau[26] had convinced a majority of reflecting and powerful minds of the evils of usurpation. If these revolutions had happened still later, not one drop of the blood of one citizen would have been shed by the hands of another, nor would the event have been marked so much perhaps as with one solitary instance of violence and confiscation.

There are two principles therefore which the man who desires the regeneration of his species ought ever to bear in mind, to regard the improvement of every hour as essential in the discovery and dissemination of truth, and willingly to suffer the lapse of years before he urges the reducing his theory into actual execution. With all his caution it is possible that the impetuous multitude will run before the still and quiet progress of reason; nor will he sternly pass sentence upon every revolution that shall by a few years have anticipated the term that wisdom would have prescribed. But, if his caution be firmly exerted, there is no doubt that he will supersede many abortive attempts, and considerably prolong the general tranquillity.

---

[25] Godwin alludes to Milton's *Areopagitica* (1644): 'Where there is much desire to learn, there of necessity will be much arguing, much writing, many opinions; for opinion in good men is but knowledge in the making' (*The Riverside Milton*, ed. by Roy Flanagan (Boston: Houghton Mifflin, 1998), p. 1019).

[26] For Sydney, Locke, and Montesquieu, see Chapter 1, note 4; for Rousseau, see Chapter 2, note 42.

Section III.   Of Political Associations

[…] In the first place revolutions less originate in the energies of the people at large, than in the conceptions of persons of some degree of study and reflection. I say, originate, for it must be admitted, that they ought ultimately to be determined on by the choice of the whole nation. It is the property of truth to diffuse itself. The difficulty is to distinguish it in the first instance, and in the next to present it in that unequivocal form which shall enable it to command universal assent. This must necessarily be the task of a few. Society, as it at present exists in the world, will long be divided into two classes, those who have leisure for study, and those whose importunate necessities perpetually urge them to temporary industry. It is no doubt to be desired, that the latter class should be made as much as possible to partake of the privileges of the former. But we should be careful, while we listen to the undistinguishing demands of benevolence, that we do not occasion a greater mischief than that we undertake to cure. We should be upon our guard against an event the consequences of which are always to be feared, the propagating blind zeal, where we meant to propagate reason.

The studious and reflecting only can be expected to see deeply into future events. To conceive an order of society totally different from that which is now before our eyes, and to judge of the advantages that would accrue from its institution, are the prerogatives only of a few favoured minds. When these advantages have been unfolded by superior penetration, they cannot yet for some time be expected to be understood by the multitude. Time, reading and conversation are necessary to render them familiar. They must descend in regular gradation from the most thoughtful to the most unobservant. He, that begins with an appeal to the people, may be suspected to understand little of the true character of mind. A sinister design may gain by precipitation; but true wisdom is best adapted to a slow, unvarying, incessant progress.

Human affairs, through every link of the great chain of necessity, are admirably harmonised and adapted to each other. As the people form the last step in the progress of truth, they need least preparation to induce them to assert it. Their prejudices are few and upon the surface. They are the higher orders of society, that find, or imagine they find, their advantage in injustice, and are eager to invent arguments for its defence. In sophistry they first seek an excuse for their conduct, and then become the redoubted champions of those errors which they have been assiduous to cultivate. The vulgar have no such interest, and submit to the reign of injustice from habit only and the want of reflection. They do not want preparation to receive the truth, so much as examples to embody it. A very short catalogue of reasons is sufficient for them, when they see the generous and the wise resolved to assert the cause of justice. A very short period is long enough for them to imbibe the sentiments of patriotism and liberty.

Secondly, associations must be formed with great caution not to be allied to tumult. The conviviality of a feast may lead to the depredations of a riot. While the sympathy of opinion catches from man to man, especially in numerous meetings, and among persons whose passions have not been used to the curb of judgment, actions may be determined on, which solitary reflection would have rejected. There is nothing more barbarous, cruel and blood-thirsty, than the triumph of a mob. Sober thought should always prepare the way to the public assertion of truth. He, that would be the founder of a republic, should, like the first Brutus,[27] be insensible to the energies of the most imperious passions of our nature.

[There is at present in the world a cold reserve that keeps man at a distance from man]

But, though association, in the received sense of that term, must be granted to be an instrument of a very dangerous nature, it should be remembered that unreserved communication in a smaller circle, and especially among persons who are already awakened to the pursuit of truth, is of unquestionable advantage. There is at present in the world a cold reserve that keeps man at a distance from man. There is an art in the practice of which individuals communicate for ever, without any one telling his neighbour what estimate he should form of his attainments and character, how they ought to be employed, and how to be improved. There is a sort of domestic tactics, the object of which is to instruct us to elude curiosity, and to keep up the tenour of conversation, without the disclosure either of our feelings or our opinions. The philanthropist has no object more deeply at heart than the annihilation of this duplicity and reserve.[28] No man can have much kindness for his species, who does not habituate himself to consider upon each successive occasion of social intercourse how that occasion may be most beneficently improved. Among the topics to which he will be anxious to awaken attention, politics will occupy a principal share.

Books have by their very nature but a limited operation; though, on account of their permanence, their methodical disquisition, and their easiness of access, they are entitled to the foremost place. But their efficacy ought not to engross our confidence. The number of those by whom reading is neglected is exceedingly great. Books to those by whom they are read have a sort of constitutional coldness. We review the arguments of an 'insolent innovator' with sullenness, and are unwilling

---

[27]   Lucius Junius Brutus, founder of the Roman Republic and one of its two first consuls. He was elected to this typically republican magistrature in 509 BC, having led the revolt against the last Roman king, Tarquinius Superbus. Legend has it that, as consul, he persuaded the people to swear never to allow another man to be king of Rome.

[28]   Values of 'transparency' and fundamental sincerity were identified with primitive virtue by Rousseau, especially in the *Letter to D'Alembert on the Theatre* (1758) and in *The Social Contract* II.ix–x.

to stretch our minds to take in all their force. It is with difficulty that we obtain the courage of striking into untrodden paths, and questioning tenets that have been generally received. But conversation accustoms us to hear a variety of sentiments, obliges us to exercise patience and attention, and gives freedom and elasticity to our mental disquisitions. A thinking man, if he will recollect his intellectual history, will find that he has derived inestimable advantage from the stimulus and surprise of colloquial suggestions; and, if he review the history of literature, will perceive that minds of great acuteness and ability have commonly existed in a cluster.

It follows that the promoting of the best interests of mankind eminently depends upon the freedom of social communication. [...]

Section IV.   Of the Species of Reform to Be Desired

[...] To recapitulate the principal object of this chapter, I would once again repeat, that violence may suit the plan of any political partisan, rather than of him that pleads the cause of simple justice. There is even a sense in which the reform aimed at by the true politician may be affirmed to be less a gradual than an entire one, without contradicting the former position. The complete reformation that is wanted, is not instant but future reformation. It can in reality scarcely be considered as of the nature of action. It consists in an universal illumination. Men feel their situation, and the restraints, that shackled them before, vanish like a mere deception. When the true crisis shall come, not a sword will need to be drawn, not a finger to be lifted up. The adversaries will be too few and too feeble to dare to make a stand against the universal sense of mankind.

Chap. iv   Of the Cultivation of Truth –
Section II.   Of Sincerity

It is evident in the last place, that a strict adherence to truth will have the best effect upon our minds in the ordinary commerce of life. This is the virtue which has commonly been known by the denomination of sincerity; and, whatever certain accommodating moralists may teach us, the value of sincerity will be in the highest degree obscured, when it is not complete. Real sincerity deposes me from all authority over the statement of facts. Similar to the duty which Tully imposes upon the historian, it compels me not to dare 'to utter what is false, or conceal what is true'.[29] It annihilates the bastard prudence, which would instruct me to

---

[29]   Cicero, *De oratore* II.xv.

give language to no sentiment that may be prejudicial to my interests. It extirpates the low and selfish principle, which would induce me to utter nothing 'to the disadvantage of him from whom I have received no injury'. It compels me to regard the concerns of my species as my own concerns. What I know of truth, of morals, of religion, of government, it compels me to communicate. All the praise which a virtuous man and an honest action can merit, I am obliged to pay to the uttermost mite. I am obliged to give language to all the blame to which profligacy, venality, hypocrisy and circumvention are so justly entitled. I am not empowered to conceal any thing I know of myself, whether it tend to my honour or to my disgrace. I am obliged to treat every other man with equal frankness, without dreading the imputation of flattery on the one hand, without dreading his resentment and enmity on the other.

Did every man impose this law upon himself, he would be obliged to consider before he decided upon the commission of an equivocal action, whether he chose to be his own historian, to be the future narrator of the scene in which he was engaging. It has been justly observed that the popish practice of auricular confession[30] has been attended with some salutary effects. How much better would it be, if, instead of a practice thus ambiguous, and which may be converted into so dangerous an engine of ecclesiastical despotism, every man would make the world his confessional, and the human species the keeper of his conscience?

How extensive an effect would be produced, if every man were sure of meeting in his neighbour the ingenuous censor, who would tell to himself, and publish to the world, his virtues, his good deeds, his meannesses and his follies? I have no right to reject any duty, because it is equally incumbent upon my neighbours, and they do not practise it. When I have discharged the whole of my duty, it is weakness and vice to make myself unhappy about the omissions of others. Nor is it possible to say how much good one man sufficiently rigid in his adherence to truth would effect. One such man, with genius, information and energy, might redeem a nation from vice.

[A gradation in discovery and a progress in the improvement, which do not need to be assisted by the stratagems of their votaries]

As truth has nothing to fear from her enemies, she needs not have any thing to fear from her friends. The man, who publishes the sublimest discoveries, is not of all others the most likely to inflame the vulgar, and hurry the great question of human happiness to a premature crisis. The object to be pursued undoubtedly is, the

---

[30]   The private confession of sins to a priest.

gradual improvement of mind. But this end will be better answered by exhibiting as much truth as possible, enlightening a few, and suffering knowledge to expand in the proportion which the laws of nature and necessity prescribe, than by any artificial plan of piecemeal communication that we can invent. There is in the nature of things a gradation in discovery and a progress in improvement, which do not need to be assisted by the stratagems of their votaries. In a word, there cannot be a more unworthy idea, than that truth and virtue should be under the necessity of seeking alliance with concealment. The man, who would artfully draw me into a little, that by so doing he may unawares surprise me into much, I infallibly regard as an impostor. Will truth, contracted into some petty sphere and shorn of its beams, acquire additional evidence? Rather let me trust to its omnipotence, to its congeniality with the nature of intellect, to its direct and irresistible tendency to produce liberty, and happiness, and virtue. Let me fear that I have not enough of it, that my views are too narrow to produce impression, and anxiously endeavour to add to my stock; not apprehend that, exhibited in its noon-day brightness, its lustre and genial nature should not be universally confessed.

Chap. v   Of Free Will and Necessity[31]

[...] To the right understanding of any arguments that may be adduced under this head, it is requisite that we should have a clear idea of the meaning of the term necessity. He who affirms that all actions are necessary, means, that, if we form a just and complete view of all the circumstances in which a living or intelligent being is placed, we shall find that he could not in any moment of his existence have acted otherwise than he has acted. According to this assertion there is in the transactions of mind nothing loose, precarious and uncertain. Upon this question the advocate of liberty in the philosophical sense must join issue. He must, if he mean any thing, deny this certainty of conjunction between moral antecedents and consequents. Where all is constant and invariable, and the events that arise uniformly flow from the circumstances in which they originate, there can be no liberty.

It is acknowledged that in the events of the material universe every thing is subjected to this necessity. The tendency of investigation and enquiry relatively to this topic of human knowledge has been, more effectually to exclude chance, as our improvements extended. Let us consider what is the species of evidence that has satisfied philosophers upon this point. Their only solid ground of reasoning has been from experience. The argument which has induced mankind to conceive of the universe as governed by certain laws, and to entertain the idea of necessary connexion between successive events, has been an observed similarity in the order

---

[31]   Godwin's discussion of necessity was especially influential upon the young Wordsworth (see Godwin headnote, above), and informed his tragedy 'The Borderers' (originally written 1797–9).

of succession. If, when we had once remarked two events succeeding each other, we had never had occasion to see that individual succession repeated; if we saw innumerable events in perpetual progression without any apparent order, so that all our observation would not enable us, when we beheld one, to pronounce that another of such a particular class might be expected to follow; we should never have conceived of the existence of necessary connexion, or have had an idea corresponding to the term cause.

Hence it follows that all that strictly speaking we know of the material universe is this succession of events. Uniform succession irresistibly forces upon the mind the idea of abstract connexion. When we see the sun constantly rise in the morning and set at night, and have had occasion to observe this phenomenon invariably taking place through the whole period of our existence, we cannot avoid believing that there is some cause producing this uniformity of event. But the principle or virtue by which one event is conjoined to another we never see.

[Mind is a topic of science]

Let us proceed to apply these reasonings concerning matter to the illustration of the theory of mind. Is it possible in this latter theory, as in the former subject, to discover any general principles? Can intellect be made a topic of science? Are we able to reduce the multiplied phenomena of mind to any certain standard of reasoning? If the affirmative of these questions be conceded, the inevitable consequence appears to be, that mind, as well as matter, exhibits a constant conjunction of events, and affords a reasonable presumption to the necessary connexion of those events. It is of no importance that we cannot see the ground of that connexion, or imagine how propositions and reasoning, when presented to the mind of a percipient being, are able by necessary consequence to generate volition and animal motion; for, if there be any truth in the above reasonings, we are equally incapable of perceiving the ground of connexion between any two events in the material universe, the common and received opinion that we do perceive such ground of connexion being in reality nothing more than a vulgar prejudice.

That mind is a topic of science may be argued from all those branches of literature and enquiry which have mind for their subject. What species of amusement or instruction would history afford us, if there were no ground of inference from moral causes to effects, if certain temptations and inducements did not in all ages and climates produce a certain series of actions, if we were unable to trace connexion and a principle of unity in men's tempers, propensities and transactions? The amusement would be inferior to that which we derive from the perusal of a chronological table, where events have no order but that of time; since, however the chronologist may neglect to mark the internal connexion between successive transactions, the mind of the reader is busied in supplying that connexion from memory or imagination: but the very idea of such connexion would never have suggested itself, if we had never found the source of that idea in experience. The instruction arising from the perusal of history would be absolutely none; since instruction implies in its very nature the classing and generalising of objects. But, upon the supposition on which we are arguing, all objects would be unconnected and disjunct, without the possibility of affording any grounds of reasoning or principles of science.

The idea correspondent to the term character inevitably includes in it the assumption of necessary connexion. The character of any man is the result of a long series of impressions communicated to his mind, and modifying it in a certain manner, so as to enable us, from a number of these modifications and impressions being given, to predict his conduct. Hence arise his temper and habits, respecting which we reasonably conclude, that they will not be abruptly superseded and reversed; and that, if they ever be reversed, it will not be accidentally, but in consequence of some strong reason persuading, or some extraordinary event modifying his mind. If there were not this original and essential connexion between motives and actions, and, which forms one particular branch of this principle, between men's past and future actions, there could be no such thing as character, or as a ground of inference enabling us to predict what men would be from what they have been.

From the same idea of necessary connexion arise all the schemes of policy, in consequence of which men propose to themselves by a certain plan of conduct to prevail upon others to become the tools and instruments of their purposes. All the arts of courtship and flattery, of playing upon men's hopes and fears, proceed upon the supposition that mind is subject to certain laws, and that, provided we be skilful and assiduous enough in applying the cause, the effect will inevitably follow.

Lastly, the idea of moral discipline proceeds entirely upon this principle. If I carefully persuade, exhort, and exhibit motives to another, it is because I believe that motives have a tendency to influence his conduct. If I reward or punish him, either with a view to his own improvement or as an example to others, it is because I have been led to believe that rewards and punishments are calculated in their own nature to affect the sentiments and practices of mankind.

There is but one conceivable objection against the inference from these premises to the necessity of human actions. It may be alledged, that 'though there is a real connexion between motives and actions, yet that this connexion may not amount to a certainty, and that of consequence the mind still retains an inherent activity by which it can at pleasure dissolve this connexion. Thus for example, when I address argument and persuasion to my neighbour to induce him to adopt a certain species of conduct, I do it not with a certain expectation of success, and am not utterly disappointed if all my efforts fail of their effect. I make a reserve for a certain faculty of liberty he is supposed to possess, which may at last counteract the best digested projects.'

But in this objection there is nothing peculiar to the case of mind. It is just so to matter. I see a part only of the premises, and therefore can pronounce only with uncertainty upon the conclusion. A philosophical experiment, which has succeeded a hundred times, may altogether fail upon the next trial. But what does the philosopher conclude from this? Not that there is a liberty of choice in his retort and his materials, by which they baffle the best formed expectations. Not that the connexion between effects and causes is imperfect, and that part of the effect happens from no cause at all. But that there was some other cause concerned whose operation he did not perceive, but which a fresh investigation will probably lay open to him. When the science of the material universe was in its infancy, men were sufficiently prompt to refer events to accident and chance; but the farther they have extended their enquiries and observation, the more reason they have found to conclude that every thing takes place according to necessary and universal laws.

The case is exactly parallel with respect to mind. The politician and the philosopher, however they may speculatively entertain the opinion of free will, never think of introducing it into their scheme of accounting for events. If an incident turn out otherwise than they expected, they take it for granted, that there was some unobserved bias, some habit of thinking, some prejudice of education, some singular association of ideas, that disappointed their prediction; and, if they be of an active and enterprising temper, they return, like the natural philosopher, to search out the secret spring of this unlooked for event.

[That in which the mind exercises its freedom, must be an act of the mind]

Another argument in favour of the doctrine of necessity, not less clear and irresistible than that from the consideration of cause and effect, will arise from any consistent explication that can be given of the nature of voluntary motion. The motions of the animal system distribute themselves into two great classes, voluntary and involuntary. Involuntary motion, whether it be conceived to take place independently of the mind, or to be the result of thought and perception, is so called, because the consequences of that motion, either in whole or in part, did not enter into the view of the mind when the motion commenced. Thus the cries of a new-born infant are not less involuntary than the circulation of the blood; it being impossible that the sounds first resulting from a certain agitation of the animal frame should be foreseen, since foresight is the fruit of experience.

From these observations we may deduce a rational and consistent account of the nature of volition. Voluntary motion is that which is accompanied with foresight, and flows from intention and design. Volition is that state of an intellectual being, in which, the mind being affected in a certain manner by the apprehension of an end to be accomplished, a certain motion of the organs and members of the animal frame is found to be produced.

Here then the advocates of intellectual liberty have a clear dilemma proposed to their choice. They must ascribe this freedom, this imperfect connexion of effects and causes, either to our voluntary or our involuntary motions. They have already made their determination. They are aware that to ascribe freedom to that which is involuntary, even if the assumption could be maintained, would be altogether foreign to the great subjects of moral, theological or political enquiry. Man would not be in any degree more of an agent or an accountable being, though it could be proved that all his involuntary motions sprung up in a fortuitous and capricious manner.

But on the other hand to ascribe freedom to our voluntary actions is an express contradiction in terms. No motion is voluntary any farther than it is accompanied with intention and design, and flows from the apprehension of an end to be accomplished. So far as it flows in any degree from another source, so far it is involuntary. The new-born infant foresees nothing, therefore all his motions are involuntary. A person arrived at maturity takes an extensive survey of the consequences of his actions, therefore he is eminently a voluntary and rational being. If any part of my conduct be destitute of all foresight of the effects to result, who is there that ascribes to it depravity and vice? Xerxes acted just as soberly as such a reasoner, when he caused his attendants to inflict a thousand lashes on the waves of the Hellespont.[32]

The truth of the doctrine of necessity will be still more evident, if we consider the absurdity of the opposite hypothesis. One of its principal ingredients is self determination. Liberty in an imperfect and popular sense, is ascribed to the motions of the animal system, when they result from the foresight and deliberation of the intellect, and not from external compulsion. It is in this sense that the word is commonly used in moral and political reasoning. Philosophical reasoners therefore, who have desired to vindicate the property of freedom, not only to our external motions, but to the acts of mind, have been obliged to repeat this process. Our external actions are then said to be free, when they truly result from the determination of the mind. If our volitions, or internal acts be also free, they must in like manner result from the determination of the mind, or in other words, 'the mind in adopting them' must be 'self determined'. Now nothing can be more evident than that that in which the mind exercises its freedom, must be an act of the mind. Liberty therefore according to this hypothesis consists in this, that every choice we make has been chosen by us, and every act of the mind been preceded and produced by an act of the mind. This is so true, that in reality the ultimate act is not styled free from any quality of its own, but because the mind in adopting it was self determined, that is, because it was preceded by another act. The ultimate act

---

[32]   Herodotus, *Histories*, VII.xxxv. After a storm destroyed Xerxes' bridge of boats, he ordered his men to lash the Hellespont three hundred times and to drop a set of fetters into it as punishment.

resulted completely from the determination which was its precursor. It was itself necessary; and, if we would look for freedom, it must be in the preceding act. But in that preceding act also, if the mind were free, it was self determined, that is, this volition was chosen by a preceding volition, and by the same reasoning this also by another antecedent to itself. All the acts except the first were necessary, and followed each other as inevitably as the links in a chain do, when the first link is drawn forward. But then neither was the first act free, unless the mind in adopting it were self determined, that is, unless this act were chosen by a preceding act. Trace back the chain as far as you please, every act at which you arrive is necessary. That act, which gives the character of freedom to the whole, can never be discovered; and, if it could, in its own nature includes a contradiction.

[So far as we act with liberty ... our conduct is as independent of morality as it is of reason]

Lastly, it may be observed upon the hypothesis of free will, that the whole system is built upon a distinction where there is no difference, to wit, a distinction between the intellectual and active powers of the mind. A mysterious philosophy taught men to suppose, that, when the understanding had perceived any object to be desirable, there was need of some distinct power to put the body in motion. But reason finds no ground for this supposition; nor is it possible to conceive, that, in the case of an intellectual faculty placed in an aptly organised body, preference can exist, together with a consciousness, gained from experience, of our power to obtain the object preferred, without a certain motion of the animal frame being the necessary result. We need only attend to the obvious meaning of the terms in order to perceive that the will is merely, as it has been happily termed, the last act of the understanding, one of the different cases of the association of ideas. What indeed is preference, but a perception of something that really inheres or is supposed to inhere in the objects themselves? It is the judgement, true or erroneous, which the mind makes respecting such things as are brought into comparison with each other. If this had been sufficiently attended to, the freedom of the will would never have been gravely maintained by philosophical writers, since no man ever imagined that we were free to feel or not to feel an impression made upon our organs, and to believe or not to believe a proposition demonstrated to our understanding.

It must be unnecessary to add any thing farther on this head, unless it be a momentary recollection of the sort of benefit that freedom of the will would confer upon us, supposing it to be possible. Man being, as we have now found him to be, a simple substance, governed by the apprehensions of his understanding, nothing farther is requisite but the improvement of his reasoning faculty, to make him virtuous and happy. But, did he possess a faculty independent of the understanding, and capable of resisting from mere caprice the most powerful arguments, the best education and the most sedulous instruction might be of no use to him. This freedom we shall easily perceive to be his bane and his curse; and the only hope of lasting benefit to the species would be, by drawing closer the connexion between the external motions and the understanding, wholly to extirpate it. The virtuous man, in proportion to his improvement, will be under the constant influence of fixed and invariable principles; and such a being as we conceive God to be, can never in any one instance have exercised this liberty, that is, can never have acted in a foolish and tyrannical manner. Freedom of the will is absurdly represented as necessary to render the mind susceptible of moral principles; but in reality, so far as we act with liberty, so far as we are independent of motives, our conduct is as independent of morality as it is of reason, nor is it possible that we should deserve either praise or blame for a proceeding thus capricious and indisciplinable.

Book V   Of Legislative and Executive Power – Chap. xiii   Of the Aristocratical Character

Aristocracy in its proper signification implies neither less nor more than a scheme for rendering more permanent and visible by the interference of political institution the inequality of mankind. Aristocracy, like monarchy, is founded in falshood, the offspring of art foreign to the real nature of things, and must therefore, like monarchy, be supported by artifice and false pretences. Its empire however is founded in principles more gloomy and unsocial than those of monarchy. The monarch often thinks it advisable to employ blandishments and courtship with his barons and officers; but the lord deems it sufficient to rule with a rod of iron.

Both depend for their perpetuity upon ignorance. Could they, like Omar, destroy the productions of profane reasoning, and persuade mankind that the Alcoran contained every thing which it became them to study, they might then renew their lease of empire.[33] But here again aristocracy displays its superior harshness. Monarchy admits of a certain degree of monkish learning among its followers. But aristocracy holds a stricter hand. Should the lower ranks of society once come to be generally taught to write and read, its power would be at an end. To make men serfs and villains[34] it is indispensibly necessary to make them brutes. This is a question which has long been canvassed with great eagerness and avidity. The resolute advocates of the old system have with no contemptible foresight opposed this alarming innovation. In their well known observation, 'that a servant who has

---

[33]   Omar or Umar the Great (c. 586–644), companion of Muhammad and Caliph, alleged to have ordered the burning of the great library at Alexandria.
[34]   In the original sense of a poor rustic.

been taught to write and read ceases to be any longer a passive machine',[35] is contained the embryo from which it would be easy to explain the whole philosophy of human society.

[The principle of aristocracy is founded in the extreme inequality of conditions]

The principle of aristocracy is founded in the extreme inequality of conditions. No man can be an useful member of society, except so far as his talents are employed in a manner conducive to the general advantage. In every society the produce, the means of contributing to the necessities and conveniences of its members, is of a certain amount. In every society the bulk at least of its members contribute by their personal exertions to the creation of this produce. What can be more reasonable and just, than that the produce itself should with some degree of equality be shared among them? What more injurious than the accumulating upon a few every means of superfluity and luxury, to the total destruction of the ease, and plain, but plentiful, subsistence of the many? It may be calculated that the king even of a limited monarchy, receives as the salary of his office, an income equivalent to the labour of fifty thousand men.[36] Let us set out in our estimate from this point, and figure to ourselves the shares of his counsellors, his nobles, the wealthy commoners by whom the nobility will be emulated, their kindred and dependents. Is it any wonder that in such countries the lower orders of the community are exhausted by all the hardships of penury and immoderate fatigue? When we see the wealth of a province spread upon the great man's table, can we be surprised that his neighbours have not bread to satiate the cravings of hunger?

[Is it sedition to enquire whether this state of things may not be exchanged for a better?]

There is no mistake more thoroughly to be deplored on this subject, than that of persons, sitting at their ease and surrounded with all the conveniences of life, who are apt to exclaim, 'We find things very well as they are'; and to inveigh bitterly against all projects of reform, as 'the romances of visionary men, and the declamations of those who are never to be satisfied'. Is it well, that so large a part of the community should be kept in abject penury, rendered stupid with ignorance and

---

[35] Here, Godwin may allude to Bernard Mandeville's 'An Essay on Charity and Charity Schools', included in *The Fable of the Bees: Or, Private Vices, Publick Benefits*, 2nd edn (1723), pp. 294–379.

[36] {Taking the average price of labour at one shilling per diem.}

disgustful with vice, perpetuated in nakedness and hunger, goaded to the commission of crimes, and made victims to the merciless laws which the rich have instituted to oppress them? Is it sedition to enquire whether this state of things may not
be exchanged for a better? Or can there be any thing more disgraceful to ourselves
than to exclaim that 'All is well,' merely because we are at our ease, regardless of
the misery, degradation and vice that may be occasioned in others?

Book VI   Of Opinion Considered as a Subject of Political Institution – Chap. i   General Effects of the Political Superintendence of Opinion

[…] The mistake which had been made in this case, is similar to the mistake which
is now universally exploded upon the subject of commerce. It was long supposed
that, if any nation desired to extend its trade, the thing most immediately necessary was for government to interfere, and institute protecting duties, bounties and
monopolies. It is now well known that commerce never flourishes so much, as
when it is delivered from the guardianship of legislators and ministers, and is built
upon the principle, not of forcing other people to buy our commodities dear when
they might purchase them elsewhere cheaper and better, but of ourselves feeling
the necessity of recommending them by their intrinsic advantages. Nothing can be
at once so unreasonable and hopeless, as to attempt by positive regulations to dis-
arm the unalterable laws of the universe.

The same truth which has been felt under the article of commerce, has also
made a considerable progress as to the subjects of speculative enquiry. Formerly it
was thought that the true religion was to be defended by acts of uniformity,[37] and
that one of the principal duties of the magistrate was to watch the progress of
heresy. It was truly judged that the connexion between error and vice is of the
most intimate nature, and it was concluded that no means could be more effectual
to prevent men from deviating into error, than to check their wanderings by the
scourge of authority. Thus writers, whose political views in other respects have
been uncommonly enlarged, have told us 'that men ought indeed to be permitted
to think as they please, but not to propagate their pernicious opinions; as they may
be permitted to keep poisons in their closet, but not to offer them to sale under the
denomination of cordials'.[38] Or, if humanity have forbidden them to recommend
the extirpation of a sect which has already got footing in a country, they have however earnestly advised the magistrate to give no quarter to any new extravagance

---

[37]   Parliament passed a number of Acts of Uniformity (1549, 1552, 1559, and 1662) to enforce the Book of
Common Prayer as the only source of orthodox and legal forms of worship.
[38]   {Gulliver's Travels, Part II, Chap. VI.}

that might be attempted to be introduced.[39] – The reign of these two errors respecting commerce and theoretical speculation is nearly at an end, and it is reasonable to believe that the idea of teaching virtue through the instrumentality of government will not long survive them.

All that is to be asked on the part of government in behalf of morality and virtue is a clear stage upon which for them to exert their own energies, and perhaps some restraint for the present upon the violent disturbers of the peace of society, that the efforts of these principles may be allowed to go on uninterrupted to their natural conclusion. Who ever saw an instance in which error unaided by power was victorious over truth?[40] Who is there so absurd as to believe, that with equal arms truth can be ultimately defeated? Hitherto every instrument of menace or influence has been employed to counteract her. Has she made no progress? – Has the mind of man the capacity to chuse falshood and reject truth, when her evidence is fairly presented? When it has been once thus presented and has gained a few converts, does she ever fail to go on perpetually increasing the number of her votaries? Exclusively of the fatal interference of government, and the violent irruptions of barbarism threatening to sweep her from the face of the earth, has not this been in all instances the history of science?

Book VII   Of Crimes and Punishments –
Chap. i   Limitations of the Doctrine of
Punishment Which Result from the Principles of Morality

[...] Punishment is generally used to signify the voluntary infliction of evil upon a vicious being, not merely because the public advantage demands it, but because there is apprehended to be a certain fitness and propriety in the nature of things, that render suffering, abstractedly from the benefit to result, the suitable concomitant of vice.

The justice of punishment therefore, in the strict import of the word, can only be a deduction from the hypothesis of free-will, and must be false, if human actions be necessary. Mind, as was sufficiently apparent when we treated of that subject,[41] is an agent, in no other sense than matter is an agent. It operates and is operated upon, and the nature, the force and line of direction of the first, is exactly in proportion to the nature, force and line of direction of the second. Morality in a rational and designing mind is not essentially different

---

[39]   {Mably, *de la Législation, Liv. IV, Chap. III: des Etats Unis d'Amerique, Lettre III.*} A text from 1776, by Gabriel Bonnot de Mably (1709–85), French republican philosopher and politician.

[40]   See Milton's *Areopagitica* (1644): 'Let her and Falshood grapple; who ever knew Truth put to the worse, in a free and open encounter' (*Riverside Milton*, p. 1021).

[41]   {Book IV, Chap. VI.}

from morality in an inanimate substance. A man of certain intellectual habits is
fitted to be an assassin, a dagger of a certain form is fitted to be his instrument.
The one or the other excites a greater degree of disapprobation, in proportion
as its fitness for mischievous purposes appears to be more inherent and direct.
I view a dagger on this account with more disapprobation than a knife, which
is perhaps equally adapted for the purposes of the assassin; because the dagger
has few or no beneficial uses to weigh against those that are hurtful, and because
it has a tendency by means of association to the exciting of evil thoughts. I view
the assassin with more disapprobation than the dagger, because he is more to
be feared, and it is more difficult to change his vicious structure or take from
him his capacity to injure. The man is propelled to act by necessary causes and
irresistible motives, which, having once occurred, are likely to occur again. The
dagger has no quality adapted to the contraction of habits, and, though it have
committed a thousand murders, is not at all more likely (unless so far as those
murders, being known, may operate as a slight associated motive with the pos-
sessor) to commit murder again. Except in the articles here specified, the two
cases are exactly parallel. The assassin cannot help the murder he commits any
more than the dagger.

These arguments are merely calculated to set in a more perspicuous light a principle, which is admitted by many by whom the doctrine of necessity has never
been examined; that the only measure of equity is utility, and whatever is not
attended with any beneficial purpose, is not just. This is so evident a proposition
that few reasonable and reflecting minds will be found inclined to reject it. Why
do I inflict suffering on another? If neither for his own benefit nor the benefit of
others, can that be right? Will resentment, the mere indignation and horror I have
conceived against vice, justify me in putting a being to useless torture? 'But suppose I only put an end to his existence.' What, with no prospect of benefit either
to himself or others? The reason the mind easily reconciles itself to this supposition is, that we conceive existence to be less a blessing than a curse to a being incor-
rigibly vicious. But in that case the supposition does not fall within the terms of
the question: I am in reality conferring a benefit. It has been asked, 'If we conceive
ourselves two beings, each of them solitary, but the first virtuous and the second
vicious, the first inclined to the highest acts of benevolence, if his situation were
changed for the social, the second to malignity, tyranny and injustice, do we not
feel that the first is entitled to felicity in preference to the second?' If there be any
difficulty in the question, it is wholly caused by the extravagance of the supposition. No being can be either virtuous or vicious who has no opportunity of influencing the happiness of others. He may indeed, though now solitary, recollect or
imagine a social state; but this sentiment and the propensities it generates can
scarcely be vigorous, unless he have hopes of being at some future time restored
to that state. The true solitaire cannot be considered as a moral being, unless the
morality we contemplate be that which has relation to his own permanent advantage. But, if that be our meaning, punishment, unless for reform, is peculiarly

absurd. His conduct is vicious, because it has a tendency to render him miserable: shall we inflict calamity upon him, for this reason only because he has already inflicted calamity upon himself? It is difficult for us to imagine to ourselves a solitary intellectual being, whom no future accident shall ever render social. It is difficult for us to separate even in idea virtue and vice from happiness and misery; and of consequence not to imagine that, when we bestow a benefit upon virtue, we bestow it where it will turn to account; and, when we bestow a benefit upon vice, we bestow it where it will be unproductive. For these reasons the question of a solitary being will always be extravagant and unintelligible, but will never convince.

[The abstract congruity of crime and punishment]

It is of the utmost importance that we should bear these ideas constantly in mind during our whole examination of the theory of punishment. This theory would in the past transactions of mankind have been totally different, if they had divested themselves of all emotions of anger and resentment; if they had considered the man who torments another for what he has done, as upon par with the child who beats the table; if they had figured to their imagination, and then properly estimated, the man, who should shut up in prison some atrocious criminal, and afterwards torture him at stated periods, merely in consideration of the abstract congruity of crime and punishment, without any possible benefit to others or to himself; if they had regarded infliction as that which was to be regulated solely by the dispassionate calculation of the future, without suffering the past, in itself considered, for a moment to enter into the account.

Book VIII　　Of Property[42] – Chap. vii　　Of the Objection to This System from the Principle of Population

An author who has speculated widely upon subjects of government,[43] has recommended equal, or, which was rather his idea, common property, as a complete remedy, to the usurpation and distress which are at present the most powerful enemies of human kind, to the vices which infect education in some instances, and

---

[42]　This book is devoted to Godwin's proposal of the equalization of property and defends it against a number of anticipated criticisms.

[43]　{Wallace: Various Prospects of Mankind, Nature and Providence, 1761.} In this work, Robert Wallace (1697–1771), a Church of Scotland minister, argued that the perfection of society brought with it population growth, and thus the means of its own decay.

the neglect it encounters in more, to all the turbulence of passion, and all the injustice of selfishness. But, after having exhibited this picture, not less true than delightful, he finds an argument that demolishes the whole, and restores him to indifference and despair, in the excessive population that would ensue.

One of the most obvious answers to this objection is, that to reason thus is to foresee difficulties at a great distance. Three fourths of the habitable globe is now uncultivated. The parts already cultivated are capable of immeasurable improvement. Myriads of centuries of still increasing population may probably pass away, and the earth still be found sufficient for the subsistence of its inhabitants.[44] Who can say how long the earth itself will survive the casualties of the planetary system? Who can say what remedies shall suggest themselves for so distant an inconvenience, time enough for practical application, and of which we may yet at this time have not the smallest idea? It would be truly absurd for us to shrink from a scheme of essential benefit to mankind, lest they should be too happy, and by necessary consequence at some distant period too populous.

But, though these remarks may be deemed a sufficient answer to the objection, it may not be amiss to indulge in some speculations to which such an objection obviously leads. The earth may, to speak in the style of one of the writers of the Christian Scriptures, 'abide for ever'.[45] It may be in danger of becoming too populous. A remedy may then be necessary. If it may, why should we sit down in supine indifference and conclude that we can discover no simple glimpse of it? The discovery, if made, would add to the firmness and consistency of our prospects; nor is it improbable to conjecture that that which would form the regulating spring of our conduct then, might be the medium of a salutary modification now. What follows must be considered in some degree as a deviation into the land of conjecture. If it be false, it leaves the great system to which it is appended in all sound reason as impregnable as ever. If this do not lead us to the true remedy, it does not follow that there is no remedy. The great object of enquiry will still remain open, however defective may be the suggestions that are now to be offered.

Let us here return to the sublime conjecture of Franklin, that 'mind will one day become omnipotent over matter'.[46] If over all other matter, why not over the matter of our own bodies? If over matter at ever so great a distance, why not over matter which, however ignorant we may be of the tie that connects it with the thinking principle, we always carry about with us, and which is in all cases the

---

[44]   These assertions drew Godwin into a fierce debate about population with Thomas Robert Malthus, whose *An Essay on the Principle of Population* (1798) challenged Godwin and Condorcet's confidence in the future improvement of human society.

[45]   {Ecclesiastes, Chap. I, ver. 4.}

[46]   {I have no other authority to quote for this expression than the conversation of Dr. Price. Upon enquiry I am happy to find it confirmed to me by Mr. William Morgan, the nephew of Dr Price, who recollects to have heard it repeatedly mentioned by his uncle.} Godwin's speculations on immortality were a common source of derision.

medium of communication between that principle and the external universe? In a word, why may not man one day be immortal?

The different cases in which thought modifies the external universe are obvious to all. It is modified by our voluntary thoughts or design. We desire to stretch out our hand, and it is stretched out. We perform a thousand operations of the same species every day, and their familiarity annihilates the wonder. They are not in themselves less wonderful than any of those modifications which we are least accustomed to conceive. – Mind modifies body involuntarily. Emotion excited by some unexpected word, by a letter that is delivered to us, occasions the most extraordinary revolutions in our frame, accelerates the circulation, causes the heart to palpitate, the tongue to refuse its office, and has been known to occasion death by extreme anguish or extreme joy. These symptoms we may either encourage or check. By encouraging them habits are produced of fainting or of rage. To discourage them is one of the principal offices of fortitude. The effort of mind in resisting pain in the stories of Cranmer and Mucius Scævola is of the same kind.[47] It is reasonable to believe that that effort with a different direction might have cured certain diseases of the system. There is nothing indeed of which physicians themselves are more frequently aware, than of the power of the mind in assisting or retarding convalescence.

---

[47] Thomas Cranmer (1489–1556): Archbishop of Canterbury, tried for treason and heresy by the Catholic Mary I and burned at the stake, first fearlessly thrusting his hand into the fire. Gaius Mucius Scævola: legendary Roman youth. Captured by the Etruscan King Porsenna during an attempt to assassinate him, he accepted his punishment of burning and unflinchingly thrust his hand into the fire, gaining Porsenna's admiration and as a result his reprieve.

William Godwin

Enquiry concerning Political Justice, and Its Influence on Morals and Happiness

2nd edn (London: G. G. and J. Robinson, 1796)
and 3rd edn (1798)

After the zenith of the mid-1790s, Godwin's star declined. He continued to produce varied writings, moving his philosophical speculations into essay form in *The Enquirer* (1797) and composing five more novels, *St Leon* (1799), *Fleetwood, or the New Man of Feeling* (1805), *Mandeville* (1817), *Cloudesley* (1830) and *Deloraine* (1833). He wrote a number of ill-fated plays, including the tragedy *Antonio* (1800), as well as several well-received biographies and histories, most notably his *Life of Geoffrey Chaucer* (1803) and his *History of the Commonwealth of England* (1824–8).

Godwin revised *Political Justice* in two further editions, in 1796 and then again in 1798. Although he insisted that the core of the work remained consistent, these editions include important changes. The influence of reading David Hume and Adam Smith is evident in Godwin's less confident conception of 'truth' and in his sense of man as a being led by his passions and feelings, although Mary Hays and others had been urging him to take these last more into consideration, in letters and conversation from late 1794.

Some of the changes in Godwin's philosophy, particularly his revised positions on feelings, sympathy, and marriage, have often been attributed to the influence of his romance with Mary Wollstonecraft. In early 1796, Hays reintroduced Godwin and Wollstonecraft, and a relationship developed over the summer. In December, Wollstonecraft realized she was pregnant, and, despite their antipathy towards marriage, they decided to wed in March 1797. They moved in together, although Godwin maintained a separate address for his study, and they lived happily until September, when Wollstonecraft died whilst giving birth to their daughter Mary (later Mary Shelley). Godwin's

Romanticism and Revolution: A Reader.
Edited by Jon Mee and David Fallon.   © 2011 Blackwell Publishing Ltd.

Memoirs of the Author of A Vindication of the Rights of Woman (1798) scandalized the public with details of Wollstonecraft's life, relationships, and suicide attempts.

Godwin married a neighbour, Mary Jane Clairmont, in 1801. Together, from 1805, they ran a children's bookshop. Their most famous production was Charles and Mary Lamb's *Tales from Shakespeare* (1807). Godwin perpetually struggled financially and, despite regular bequests of money from Percy Shelley, his large household and responsibilities led to threats of eviction and finally bankruptcy in 1825.

As Godwin's prefatory remarks to the second and third editions of *Political Justice* indicate, his revisions are not simply a recantation of the more extreme positions of the first edition, but also an attempt to practise the candour and rigorous self-reflection advocated in the first edition. These revisions also indicate that, despite Wordsworth's suggestion in Book X of *The Prelude* that Godwin's thought was arid, he was already asking some of the same questions and moving in a similar direction to that of many other writers.

Preface to the Second Edition

[…] After repeated revisals the jealous eye of a man habituated to the detection of errors, still discovers things that might be better. Some are obscure; some are doubtful. As to the last, the author did not conceive himself at liberty to retract anything without a conviction, or something near a conviction, that he was wrong. He deemed it by no means justifiable to suppress any opinion because it was inconsistent with the prejudice or persuasion of others. A circumstance by which it was originally intended that this book should be characterised, was a perfect explicitness and unreserve; and even if this intention should at last be an improper one, it was apparently too late to reverse it. It would have been an act incompatible with every pretension to integrity, to have rescinded sentiments originally advanced as true, so long as they stood forward to the author's mind accompanied with their original evidence.

It will perhaps be asked by some persons in perusing the present edition, how it has happened that the author has varied in so many points from the propositions advanced in the former? and this variation may even be treated as a topic of censure. To this he has only to answer, in the first place, that the spirit and great outlines of the work, he believes, remain untouched, and that it is reasoned in various particulars with more accuracy from the premises and fundamental positions, than it was before. Secondly, he presumes to ascribe the variations to an industrious and conscientious endeavour to keep his mind awake to correction and improvement.

He has in several instances detected error; and so far is he from feeling mortified at the discovery, that he hopes yet, by such activity and impartiality as he shall be able to exert, to arrive at many truths, of which he has scarcely at present perhaps the slightest presentiment.

[No man can more fervently deprecate scenes of commotion and tumult, than the author of this book]

The Enquiry concerning Political Justice has been treated by some persons as of a seditious and inflammatory nature. This is probably an aspersion. If the political principles in favour of which it is written have no solid foundation, they have little chance to obtain more than a temporary fashion; and the present work is ill calculated to answer a temporary purpose. If on the contrary they be founded in immutable truth, it is highly probably, to say the least, that they will one day gain a decisive ascendancy. In that case, the tendency of such a disquisition will be to smooth the gradation, and to prepare the enlightened to sympathise with the just claims of the oppressed and the humble. No man can more fervently deprecate scenes of commotion and tumult, than the author of this book; no man would more anxiously avoid the lending his assistance in the most distant manner to animosity and bloodshed; but he persuades himself that, whatever may be the events with which the present crisis of human history shall be distinguished, the effect of his writings, as far as they are in any degree remembered, will be found favourable to the increase and preservation of general kindness and benevolence.

OCTOBER 29, 1795.

Book VIII   Of Property – Chap. viii   Appendix. Of Cooperation, Cohabitation and Marriage[1]

[...] The objectors of a former chapter[2] were partly in the right, when they spoke of the endless variety of the mind. It would be absurd to say that we are not capable of truth, of evidence and agreement. In these respects, so far as mind is in a state of progressive improvement, we are perpetually coming nearer to each other. But there are subjects about which we shall continually differ, and ought to differ. The ideas, associations and circumstances of each man, are properly his own; and it is a pernicious system that would lead us to require all men, however different

---

[1]   Text taken from third edition.
[2]   {Chap. V.}

their circumstances, to act by a precise general rule. Add to this, that, by the doctrine of progressive improvement, we shall always be erroneous, though we shall
every day become less erroneous. The proper method for hastening the decline of
error, and producing uniformity of judgment, is not, by brute force, by laws, or by
imitation; but, on the contrary, by exciting every man to think for himself.

From these principles it appears, that every thing that is usually understood by
the term cooperation, is, in some degree, an evil. A man in solitude, is obliged to
sacrifice or postpone the execution of his best thoughts, in compliance with his
necessities, or his frailties. How many admirable designs have perished in the conception, by means of this circumstance? It is still worse, when a man is also obliged
to consult the convenience of others. If I be expected to eat or to work in conjunction with my neighbour, it must either be at a time most convenient to me, or to
him, or to neither of us. We cannot be reduced to a clock-work uniformity.

Hence it follows that all supererogatory cooperation is carefully to be avoided,
common labour and common meals. 'But what shall we say to a cooperation, that
seems dictated by the nature of the work to be performed?' It ought to be diminished. There is probably considerably more of injury in the concert of industry,
than of sympathies. At present, it is unreasonable to doubt, that the consideration
of the evil of cooperation, is, in certain urgent cases, to be postponed to that
urgency. Whether, by the nature of things, cooperation of some sort will always
be necessary, is a question we are scarcely competent to decide. At present, to pull
down a tree, to cut a canal, to navigate a vessel, require the labour of many. Will
they always require the labour of many? When we recollect the complicated
machines of human contrivance, various sorts of mills, of weaving engines, steam
engines, are we not astonished at the compendium of labour they produce? Who
shall say where this species of improvement must stop? At present, such inventions
alarm the labouring part of the community; and they may be productive of temporary distress, though they conduce, in the sequel, to the most important interests of the multitude. But, in a state of equal labour, their utility will be liable to no
dispute. Hereafter it is by no means clear, that the most extensive operations will
not be within the reach of one man; or, to make use of a familiar instance, that a
plough may not be turned into a field, and perform its office without the need of
superintendence. It was in this sense that the celebrated Franklin conjectured, that
'mind would one day become omnipotent over matter'.[3]

The conclusion of the progress which has here been sketched, is something like
a final close to the necessity of manual labour. It may be instructive in such cases,
to observe, how the sublime geniuses of former times, anticipated what seems
likely to be the future improvement of mankind. It was one of the laws of Lycurgus,
that no Spartan should be employed in manual labour. For this purpose, under his
system, it was necessary, that they should be plentifully supplied with slaves devoted
to drudgery. Matter, or, to speak more accurately, the certain and unremitting laws

---

[3]   Godwin repeats here the footnote given above (see Chapter 7, n. 46).

of the universe, will be the Helots of the period we are contemplating.[4] We shall end in this respect, oh immortal legislator! at the point from which you began.

To return to the subject of cooperation. It may be a curious speculation to attend to the progressive steps, by which this feature of human society may be expected to decline. For example: shall we have concerts of music? The miserable state of mechanism of the majority of the performers, is so conspicuous, as to be, even at this day, a topic of mortification and ridicule. Will it not be practicable hereafter for one man to perform the whole? Shall we have theatrical exhibitions? This seems to include an absurd and vicious cooperation. It may be doubted, whether men will hereafter come forward in any mode, formally to repeat words and ideas that are not their own? It may be doubted, whether any musical performer will habitually execute the compositions of others? We yield supinely to the superior merit of our predecessors, because we are accustomed to indulge the inactivity of our faculties. All formal repetition of other men's ideas, seems to be a scheme for imprisoning, for so long a time, the operations of our own mind. It borders perhaps, in this respect, upon a breach of sincerity, which requires that we should give immediate utterance to every useful and valuable idea that occurs.[5]

[Our judgement in favour of marriage]

Another article which belongs to the subject of cooperation, is cohabitation. The evils attendant on this practice, are obvious. In order to the human understanding's being successfully cultivated, it is necessary, that the intellectual operations of men should be independent of each other.[6] We should avoid such practices as are calculated to melt our opinions into a common mould. Cohabitation is also hostile to that fortitude, which should accustom a man, in his actions, as well as in his opinions, to judge for himself, and feel competent to the discharge of his own duties. Add to this, that it is absurd to expect the inclinations and wishes of two human beings to coincide, through any long period of time. To oblige them to act and to live together, is to subject them to some inevitable portion of thwarting, bickering and unhappiness. This cannot be otherwise, so long as men shall continue to vary in their habits, their preferences and their views. No man is always chearful and kind; and it is better that his fits of irritation should subside of themselves, since the mischief in that case is more limited, and since the jarring of opposite tempers, and the suggestions of a wounded pride, tend inexpressibly to increase the irritation. When I seek to correct the defects of a stranger, it is with

---

4   Lycurgus (c. 800–730 BC), lawgiver to the Spartan republic. In ancient Sparta, helots were a servant or slave social class, whose agricultural and other labour supported the free citizens.
5   Despite this antipathy towards performance, Godwin's writings and his diary reveal a great interest in theatrical and musical entertainments. See David O'Shaughnessy, *William Godwin and the Theatre* (Pickering & Chatto, 2010).
6   {Vol. I, Book IV, Chap. III, p. 288.}

urbanity and good humour. I have no idea of convincing him through the medium of surliness and invective. But something of this kind inevitably obtains, where the intercourse is too unremitted.

The subject of cohabitation is particularly interesting, as it includes in it the subject of marriage. It will therefore be proper to pursue the enquiry in greater detail. The evil of marriage, as it is practiced in European countries, extends further than we have yet described. The method is, for a thoughtless and romantic youth of each sex, to come together, to see each other, for a few times, and under circumstances full of delusion, and then to vow to eternal attachment. What is the consequence of this? In almost every instance they find themselves deceived. They are reduced to make the best of an irretrievable mistake. They are led to conceive it their wisest policy, to shut their eyes upon realities, happy, if, by any perversion of intellect, they can persuade themselves that they were right in their first crude opinion of each other. Thus the institution of marriage is made a system of fraud; and men who carefully mislead their judgments in the daily affair of their life, must be expected to have a crippled judgment in every other concern.

Add to this, that marriage, as now understood, is a monopoly, and the worst of monopolies. So long as two human beings are forbidden, by positive institution, to follow the dictates of their own mind, prejudice will be alive and vigorous. So long as I seek, by despotic and artificial means, to maintain my possession of a woman, I am guilty of the most odious selfishness. Over this imaginary prize, men watch with perpetual jealousy; and one man finds his desire, and his capacity to circumvent, as much excited, as the other is excited, to traverse his projects, and frustrate his hopes. As long as this state of society continues, philanthropy will be crossed and checked in a thousand ways, and the still augmenting stream of abuse will continue to flow.

The abolition of the present system of marriage, appears to involve no evils. We are apt to represent that abolition to ourselves, as the harbinger of brutal lust and depravity. But it really happens, in this, as in other cases, that the positive laws which are made to restrain our vices, irritate and multiply them. Not to say, that the same sentiments of justice and happiness, which, in a state of equality, would destroy our relish for expensive gratifications, might be expected to decrease our inordinate appetites of every kind, and to lead us universally to prefer the pleasures of intellect to the pleasures of sense.

It is a question of some moment, whether the intercourse of the sexes, in a reasonable state of society, would be promiscuous, or whether each man would select for himself a partner, to whom he will adhere, as long as that adherence shall continue to be the choice of both parties. Probability seems to be greatly in favour of the latter. Perhaps this side of the alternative is most favourable to population. Perhaps it would suggest itself in preference, to the man who would wish to maintain the several propensities of his frame, in the order due to their relative importance, and to prevent a merely sensual appetite from engrossing excessive attention. It is scarcely to be imagined, that this commerce, in any state of society, will be stripped of its adjuncts, and that men will as willingly hold it, with a woman whose personal and mental qualities they disapprove, as with one of a different description. But it is the nature of the human mind, to persist, for a certain length of time, in its opinion or choice. The parties therefore, having acted upon selection, are not likely to forget this selection when the interview is over. Friendship, if by friendship we understand that affection for an individual which is measured singly by what we know of his worth, is one of the most exquisite gratifications, perhaps one of the most improving exercises, of a rational mind. Friendship therefore may be expected to come in aid of the sexual intercourse, to refine its grossness, and increase its delight. All these arguments are calculated to determine our judgement in favour of marriage as a salutary and respectable institution, but not of that species of marriage in which there is no room for repentance, and to which liberty and hope are equally strangers.

Admitting these principles therefore as the basis of the sexual commerce, what opinion ought we to form respecting infidelity to this attachment? Certainly no ties ought to be imposed upon either party, preventing them from quitting the attachment, whenever their judgement directs them to quit it. With respect to such infidelities as are compatible with an intention to adhere to it, the point of principal importance is a determination to have recourse to no species of disguise. In ordinary cases, and where the periods of absence are of no long duration, it would seem, that any inconstancy would reflect some portion of discredit on the person that practised it. It would argue that the person's propensities were not under that kind of subordination, which virtue and self-government appear to prescribe. But inconstancy, like any other temporary dereliction, would not be found incompatible with a character of uncommon excellence. What, at present, renders it, in many instances, peculiarly loathsome, is its being practised in a clandestine manner. It leads to a train of falsehood and a concerted hypocrisy, than which there is scarcely any thing that more eminently depraves and degrades the human mind.

The mutual kindness of persons of an opposite sex will, in such a state, fall under the same system as any other species of friendship. Exclusively of groundless and obstinate attachments, it will be impossible for me to live in the world, without finding in one man a worth superior to that of another. To this man I shall feel kindness, in exact proportion to my apprehension of his worth. The case will be the same with respect to the other sex. I shall assiduously cultivate the intercourse of that woman, whose moral and intellectual accomplishments strike me in the most powerful manner. But 'it may happen, that other men will feel for her the same preference that I do'. This will create no difficulty. We may all enjoy her conversation; and, her choice being declared, we shall all be wise enough to consider the sexual commerce as unessential to our regard. It is a mark of the extreme depravity of our present habits, that we are inclined to suppose the sexual commerce necessary to the advantages arising from the purest friendship. It is by no means indispensible, that the female to whom each man attaches himself in that matter, should appear to each the most deserving and excellent of her sex.

Further Reading

Anthologies of the Revolution Controversy

Butler, Marilyn (ed.), *Burke, Paine, Godwin, and the Revolution Controversy* (Cambridge: Cambridge University Press, 1984)

Claeys, Gregory (ed.), *Political Writings of the 1790s*, 8 vols (London: Pickering & Chatto, 1995)

Hampsher-Monk, Iain (ed.), *The Impact of the French Revolution: Texts from Britain in the 1790s* (Cambridge: Cambridge University Press, 2005)

Historical Context

Bradley, J. E., *Religion, Revolution and English Radicalism: Non-Conformity in Eighteenth-Century Politics and Society* (Cambridge: Cambridge University Press, 1990)

Christie, Ian R., *Stress and Stability in Late Eighteenth-Century Britain: Reflections on the British Avoidance of Revolution* (Oxford: Clarendon Press, 1984)

Claeys, Gregory, 'The French Revolution Debate and British Political Thought', *History and Political Thought*, 11 (1990), 59–80.

Colley, Linda, *Britons: Forging the Nation, 1707–1837* (New Haven: Yale University Press, 1992)

Dickinson, H. T., *British Radicalism and the French Revolution, 1785–1815* (Oxford: Oxford University Press, 1985)

Goodwin, Albert, *The Friends of Liberty: The English Democratic Movement in the Age of the French Revolution* (Cambridge, MA: Harvard University Press, 1979)

Mori, Jennifer, *William Pitt and the French Revolution, 1785–1795* (Edinburgh: Keele University Press, 1997)

Philp, Mark (ed.), *The French Revolution and British Popular Politics* (Cambridge: Cambridge University Press, 1991)

Romanticism and Revolution: A Reader.
Edited by Jon Mee and David Fallon.   © 2011 Blackwell Publishing Ltd.

Schofield, Thomas Philip, 'Conservative Political Thought in Britain in Response to the French Revolution', *Historical Journal*, 29 (1986), 601–22

Thompson, E. P., *The Making of the English Working Class* (London: Pelican, 1968)

General Works on the Revolution Controversy

Claeys, Gregory, *The French Revolution Debate in Britain: The Origins of Modern Politics* (Basingstoke: Palgrave, rev. edn, 2007)

Cobban, Alfred, *The Debate on the French Revolution, 1789–1800*, 2nd edn (London: A. & C. Black, 1960)

Cracuin, Adriana and Lokke, Kari E. (eds), *Rebellious Hearts: British Women Writers and the French Revolution* (New York: State University of New York Press, 2001)

O'Neill, Daniel I., *The Burke-Wollstonecraft Debate: Savagery, Civilization, and Democracy* (University Park: University of Pennsylvania Press, 2007)

Richardson, R. C., 'The French Revolution and English History', in idem, *The Debate on the English Revolution*, 2nd edn (London: Methuen, 1988), 63–73

Richard Price

Further texts

Price, Richard, *Observations on the Importance of the American Revolution and the Means of Making It a Benefit to the World* (London: T. Cadell, 1785)

Price, Richard, *Political Writings*, ed. by D. O. Thomas (Cambridge: Cambridge University Press, 1992)

Secondary material and criticism

Fitzpatrick, Martin, 'Reflections on a Footnote: Richard Price and Love of Country', *Enlightenment and Dissent*, 6 (1987), 41–58

Fitzpatrick, Martin, 'Richard Price and the London Revolutionary Society', *Enlightenment and Dissent*, 10 (1991), 35–50

Fruchtman, J., Jr, 'The Apocalyptic Politics of Richard Price and Joseph Priestley: A Study in Late-Eighteenth Century English Republican Millennialism', *Transactions of the American Philosophical Society*, 73 (1983), 1–125

Robbins, Caroline, 'Price, Priestley, and Some Other Dissenters', in eadem, *The Eighteenth-Century Commonwealthman* [1959] (Indianapolis: Liberty Fund, 1987), 327–48

Thomas, D. O., *The Honest Mind: The Thought and Work of Richard Price* (Oxford: Oxford University Press, 1977)

Edmund Burke

Further texts

Burke, Edmund, *A Philosophical Enquiry into the Origin of our Ideas of the Sublime and Beautiful* (London: R. and J. Dodsley, 1757; expanded edn 1759)

Burke, Edmund, *A Letter from Mr. Burke to a Member of the National Assembly; in Answer to Some Objections to his Book on French Affairs* (London: J. Dodsley, 1791)

Burke, Edmund, *An Appeal from the New to the Old Whigs* (London: J. Dodsley, 1791)

Burke, Edmund, *A Letter to a Noble Lord* (London: J. Owen and F. and C. Rivington, 1796)

Burke, Edmund, *Two Letters on Peace with the Regicide Directory of France* (London: F. and C. Rivington, 1796)

Burke, Edmund, *The Writings and Speeches of Edmund Burke*, gen. ed. Paul Langford, 12 vols (Oxford: Clarendon Press, 1981–)

Secondary material and criticism

Blakemore, Steven (ed.), *Burke and the French Revolution: Bicentennial Essays* (Athens, GA: University of Georgia Press, 1992)

Bourke, Richard, 'Edmund Burke and Enlightenment Sociability: Justice, Honour and the Principles Of Government', *History of Political Thought*, 21 (2000), 632–56

Bromwich, David, *Edmund Burke: An Intellectual Biography* (London: Penguin, 2010)

de Bruyn, Frans, *The Literary Genres of Edmund Burke* (Oxford: Oxford University Press, 1996)

Byrne, William F., 'Burke's Higher Romanticism: Politics and the Sublime', *Humanitas*, 19 (2006), 14–34

Carlson, Julie, 'Command Performances: Burke and Coleridge's Dramatic Reflections on the Revolution in France', *Nineteenth-Century Contexts*, 15 (1991), 153–60

Deane, Seamus, *Foreign Affections: Essays on Edmund Burke* (Cork: Cork University Press, 2004)

Furniss, Tom, *Edmund Burke's Aesthetic Ideology: Language, Gender and Political Economy in Revolution* (Cambridge: Cambridge University Press, 1993)

Hazlitt, William, 'Character of Mr. Burke', in idem, *Political Essays* (1819), 264–9

Lock, F. P., *Edmund Burke*, 2 vols (Oxford: Oxford University Press, 1998, 2006)

O'Brien, Conor Cruise, *The Great Melody: A Thematic Biography and Commented Anthology of Edmund Burke* (London: Sinclair-Stevenson, 1992)

Pocock, J. G. A., 'Burke and the Ancient Constitution', *Historical Journal,* 3 (1960), 125–43

Reid, Christopher, *Edmund Burke and the Practice of Political Writing* (Basingstoke: Macmillan, 1986)

Whale, John (ed.), *Edmund Burke's* Reflections on the Revolution in France: *New Interdisciplinary Essays* (Manchester: Manchester University Press, 2000)

Mary Wollstonecraft

Further texts

Wollstonecraft, Mary, *An Historical and Moral View of the Origin and Progress of the French Revolution; and the Effect It Has Produced in Europe* (London: J. Johnson, 1794)

Wollstonecraft, Mary, *The Works of Mary Wollstonecraft*, 7 vols, ed. by Marilyn Butler and Janet Todd (London: Pickering and Chatto, 1989)

Secondary material and criticism

Bahar, Saba, 'Richard Price and the Moral Foundations of Mary Wollstonecraft's Feminism', *Enlightenment and Dissent*, 18 (1999), 1–15

Barker-Benfield, G. J., 'Mary Wollstonecraft: Eighteenth-Century Commonwealthwoman', *Journal of the History of Ideas*, 50 (1989), 95–115

Bromwich, David, 'Wollstonecraft as a Critic of Burke', *Political Theory*, 23 (1995), 617–32

Conniff, J., 'Edmund Burke and His Critics: The Case of Mary Wollstonecraft', *Journal of the History of Ideas*, 60 (1999), 299–318

Gordon, Lyndall, *Mary Wollstonecraft: A New Genus* (London: Little, Brown, 2005)

Guest, Harriet, *Small Change: Women, Learning, Patriotism, 1750–1810* (Chicago: University of Chicago Press, 2000)

Hays, Mary, 'Memoirs of Mary Wollstonecraft', *Annual Necrology, 1797–8* (London, 1800), 411–60

Janes, R. M., 'On the Reception of Mary Wollstonecraft's *A Vindication of the Rights of Women*', *Journal of the History of Ideas*, 39 (1978), 293–302

Johnson, Claudia L. (ed.), *The Cambridge Companion to Mary Wollstonecraft* (Cambridge: Cambridge University Press, 2002)

Kelly, Gary, *Revolutionary Feminism: The Mind and Career of Mary Wollstonecraft* (New York: St Martin's, 1992)

Mellor, Ann K., *Romanticism and Gender* (London: Routledge, 1993), Part II: 'Feminine Romanticisms'

O'Brien, Karen, *Women and Enlightenment in Eighteenth-Century Britain* (Cambridge: Cambridge University Press, 2009), Chapter 5

Philp, Mark, 'Mary Wollstonecraft and *Political Justice*', in idem, *Godwin's Political Justice* (London, 1986), 175–92

Poovey, Mary, *The Proper Lady and the Woman Writer: Ideology as Style in the Works of Mary Wollstonecraft, Mary Shelley, and Jane Austen* (Chicago: University of Chicago Press, 1984), Chapter 2

Sapiro, V., *A Vindication of Political Virtue: The Political Theory of Mary Wollstonecraft* (Chicago, 1992)

Taylor, Barbara, *Mary Wollstonecraft and the Feminist Imagination* (Cambridge: Cambridge University Press, 2003)

Todd, Janet, *Mary Wollstonecraft: A Revolutionary Life* (London: Weidenfeld & Nicolson, 2000)

Tomaselli, Sylvana, 'The Enlightenment Debate on Women', *History Workshop Journal*, 20 (1985), 101–24

Thomas Paine

Further texts

Paine, Thomas, *Common Sense* (Philadelphia: R. Bell, 1776)

Paine, Thomas, *The Age of Reason* (London: H. D. Symonds, 1794–95)

Paine, Thomas, *Agrarian Justice* (Paris: W. Adlard, 1795)

Paine, Thomas, *The Complete Writings of Thomas Paine*, 2 vols, ed. by Philip S. Foner (New York: Citadel Press, 1945)

Secondary material and criticism

Boulton, James, 'Tom Paine and the Vulgar Style', *Essays in Criticism*, 12 (1962), 18–33

Claeys, Gregory, *Thomas Paine: Social and Political Thought* (London: Routledge, 1989)

Dyck, Ian (ed.), *Citizen of the World: Essays on Thomas Paine* (London: Croom Helm, 1987)

Kates, Gary, 'From Liberalism to Radicalism: Tom Paine's *Rights of Man*', *Journal of the History of Ideas*, 50 (1989), 569–87

Keane, John, *Thomas Paine: A Political Life* (London: Bloomsbury, 1995)

Larkin, Edward, *Thomas Paine and the Literature of Revolution* (Cambridge: Cambridge University Press, 2005)

McLamore, Richard V., ' "To Forge a New Language": Burke and Paine', *Prose Studies*, 16 (1993), 179–92

Mee, Jon, 'Thomas Paine's Tendency', *Romantic Praxis* (forthcoming)

Nelson, Craig, *Thomas Paine: His Life, His Time and the Birth of Modern Nations* (London: Profile, 2006)

Philp, Mark, *Thomas Paine* (Oxford: Oxford University Press, 2007)

Turner, John, 'Burke, Paine and the Nature of Language', *Yearbook of English Studies*, 19 (1989), 36–53

William Godwin

Further texts

Godwin, William, *Things as They Are; or, The Adventures of Caleb Williams* (London: B. Crosby, 1794)

Godwin, William, *The Political and Philosophical Writings of William Godwin*, gen. ed. Mark Philp (London: Pickering & Chatto, 1993)

Secondary material and criticism

Balfour, Ian, 'Promises, Promises: Social and Other Contracts in the English Jacobins (Godwin/Inchbald)', in David Clark and Donald Goellnicht (eds), *New Romanticisms: Theory and Critical Practice* (Toronto: University of Toronto Press, 1994), 225–50

Boulton, James T., 'William Godwin: Philosopher and Novelist', in idem, *The Language of Politics in the Age of Wilkes and Burke* (London: RKP, 1963), 207–49

Butler, Marilyn, 'Godwin, Burke, and *Caleb Williams*', *Essays in Criticism*, 32 (1982), 237–57

Claeys, Gregory, 'The Concept of Political Justice in Godwin's *Political Justice*: A Reconsideration', *Political Theory*, 11 (1983), 565–84 (and erratum in volume 12)

Clemit, Pamela, *The Godwinian Novel: The Rational Fictions of Godwin, Brockden Brown, Mary Shelley* (Oxford: Clarendon Press, 1993)

Collings, David, 'The Romance of the Impossible: William Godwin in the Empty Place of Reason', *English Literary History*, 70 (2003), 847–74

Manaquis, Robert and Myers, Victoria (eds), *The Godwinian Moment* (Toronto: University of Toronto Press, 2010/11)

Locke, Don, *A Fantasy of Reason: The Life and Thought of William Godwin* (London: Routledge, 1980)

McCracken, David, 'Godwin and *Caleb Williams*: A Fictional Rebuttal of Burke', *Studies in Burke and His Time*, 11–12 (1969–71), 1442–52

McCracken, David, 'Godwin's Reading in Burke', *English Language Notes*, 7 (1970), 264–70

O'Shaughnessy, David, *William Godwin and the Theatre* (London: Pickering & Chatto, 2010)

Philp, Mark, *Godwin's Political Justice* (London: Duckworth, 1989)

Philp, Mark, 'Thompson, Godwin, and the French Revolution', *History Workshop Journal*, 39 (1995), 89–101

Scrivener, Michael, 'William Godwin's Political Philosophy: A Revaluation', *Journal of the History of Ideas*, 39 (1978), 615–26

St Clair, William, *The Godwins and the Shelleys: The Biography of a Family* (London: Faber and Faber, 1989)

Romanticism and the Revolution Controversy

Barker-Benfield, G. J., *The Culture of Sensibility: Sex and Society in Eighteenth-Century Britain* (Chicago: University of Chicago Press, 1992)

Bindman, David, *The Shadow of the Guillotine: Britain and the French Revolution* (London: British Museum, 1989)

Bromwich, David, *Disowned by Memory: Wordsworth's Poetry of the 1790s* (Chicago: Chicago University Press, 1998)

Butler, Marilyn, *Jane Austen and the War of Ideas* (Oxford: Clarendon Press, 1975)

Butler, Marilyn, *Romantics, Rebels and Reactionaries* (Oxford: Oxford University Press, 1981)

Chandler, James, *Wordsworth's Second Nature: A Study of the Poetry and the Politics* (Chicago: University of Chicago Press, 1984)

Connell, Philip, *Romanticism, Economics and the Question of 'Culture'* (Oxford: Oxford University Press, 2001)

Cronin, Richard, *The Politics of Romantic Poetry: In Search of the Pure Commonwealth* (Basingstoke: Macmillan, 2000)

Dart, Gregory, *Rousseau, Robespierre and English Romanticism* (Cambridge: Cambridge University Press, 1999)

Ellis, Markman, *The Politics of Sensibility: Race, Gender and Commerce in the Sentimental Novel* (Cambridge: Cambridge University Press, 1996)

Erdman, David V., *Blake: Prophet against Empire*, 3rd edn (Princeton: Princeton University Press, 1977)

Favret, Mary, *Romantic Correspondence: Women, Politics and the Fiction of Letters* (Cambridge: Cambridge University Press, 1993)

Gilmartin, Kevin, *Writing against Revolution: Literary Conservatism in Britain, 1790–1832* (Cambridge: Cambridge University Press, 2007)

Goode, Mike, *Sentimental Masculinity and the Rise of History, 1790–1890* (Cambridge: Cambridge University Press, 2009)

Haywood, Ian, *The Revolution in Popular Literature: Print, Politics, and the People, 1790–1860* (Cambridge: Cambridge University Press, 2004)

Haywood, Ian, *Bloody Romanticism: Spectacular Violence and the Politics of Representation 1776–1832* (Basingstoke: Palgrave, 2006)

Hodson, Jane, *Language and Revolution in Burke, Wollstonecraft, Paine, and Godwin* (Aldershot: Ashgate, 2007)

Jones, Chris, *Radical Sensibility: Literature and Ideas in the 1790s* (London: Routledge, 1993)

Keen, Paul, *The Crisis of Literature: Print Culture and the Public Sphere* (Cambridge: Cambridge University Press, 1999)

Kelly, Gary, *The English Jacobin Novel, 1780–1805* (Oxford: Oxford University Press, 1975)

Makdisi, Saree, *William Blake and the Impossible History of the 1790s* (Chicago: Chicago University Press, 2003)

McCalman, Iain, *An Oxford Companion to the Romantic Age: British Culture 1776–1832* (Oxford: Oxford University Press, 1999)

Mee, Jon, *Dangerous Enthusiasm: William Blake and the Culture of Radicalism in the 1790s* (Oxford: Clarendon Press, 1992)

Mee, Jon, *Romanticism, Enthusiasm and Regulation: Poetics and the Policing of Culture in the Romantic Period* (Oxford: Oxford University Press, 2003)

Paley, Morton D., *Apocalypse and Millennium in English Romantic Poetry* (Oxford: Clarendon Press, 1999)

Paulson, Ronald, *Representations of Revolution, 1789–1820* (New Haven: Yale University Press, 1983)

Plummer Crafton, Lisa (ed.), *The French Revolution Debate in English Politics and Culture* (Westport: Greenwood Press, 1997)

Priestman, Martin, *Romantic Atheism: Poetry and Freethought, 1780–1830* (Cambridge: Cambridge University Press, 2000)

Roe, Nicholas, *Wordsworth and Coleridge: The Radical Years* (Oxford: Clarendon Press, 1988)

Simpson, David, *Romanticism, Nationalism, and the Revolt against Theory* (Chicago: University of Chicago Press, 1993)

Smith, Olivia, *The Politics of Language, 1791–1819* (Oxford: Oxford University Press, 1984)

Stabler, Jane, *Burke to Byron, Barbauld to Baillie, 1790–1830* (Basingstoke: Palgrave, 2002)

Stauffer, Andrew, *Anger, Revolution, and Romanticism* (Cambridge: Cambridge University Press, 2005)

Todd, Janet, *Sensibility: An Introduction* (London: Methuen, 1986)

Whale, John, *Imagination under Pressure, 1789–1832: Aesthetics, Politics and Utility* (Cambridge: Cambridge University Press, 2000)

White, R. S., *Natural Rights and the Birth of English Romanticism* (Basingstoke: Palgrave, 2005)

Wood, Marcus, *Radical Satire* (Oxford: Clarendon Press, 1994)

Index of Authors and Works

Romanticism and Revolution: A Reader.
Edited by Jon Mee and David Fallon.   © 2011 Blackwell Publishing Ltd.